W9-BUG-327

Florida's Fragile Wildlife

Florida A&M University, Tallahassee
Florida Atlantic University, Boca Raton
Florida Gulf Coast University, Ft. Myers
Florida International University, Miami
Florida State University, Tallahassee
University of Central Florida, Orlando
University of Florida, Gainesville
University of North Florida, Jacksonville
University of South Florida, Tampa
University of West Florida, Pensacola

Florida's Fragile Wildlife

Conservation and Management

ຈ ໑

Don A. Wood

University Press of Florida

Gainesville · Tallahassee · Tampa · Boca Raton

Pensacola · Orlando · Miami · Jacksonville · Ft. Myers

Copyright 2001 by the Board of Regents of the State of Florida
Printed in the United States of America on acid-free paper
All rights reserved

06 05 04 03 02 01   6 5 4 3 2 1

Library of Congress Cataloging-in-Publication Data
Wood, Don A.
Florida's fragile wildlife: conservation and management / Don A. Wood.
p. cm.
Includes bibliographical references (p.) and index.
ISBN 0-8130-1888-9 (cloth: alk. paper)
1. Endangered species—Florida. 2. Wildlife conservation—Florida.
I. Title.
QL84.22.F6 W657 2001
333.95'42'x 09759—dc21   00-048837

The University Press of Florida is the scholarly publishing agency for
the State University System of Florida, comprising Florida A&M
University, Florida Atlantic University, Florida Gulf Coast University,
Florida International University, Florida State University, University of
Central Florida, University of Florida, University of North Florida,
University of South Florida, and University of West Florida.

University Press of Florida
15 Northwest 15th Street
Gainesville, FL 32611–2079
http://www.upf.com

In memoriam

Claud H. Wood and Erma A. Wood

Contents

Tables and Figures

Tables

Figures

Contributors

This publication would not have been possible had it not been for the selfless contributions of many biologists and others with particular expertise relative to the targeted species, and their incisive input is gratefully acknowledged.

Co-authorship

Certain sections in the preliminary drafts of four of the chapters in this volume were prepared interactively with four experts eminently knowledgeable about the respective species concerned. Accordingly, these contributors in effect co-authored those chapters, and anyone wishing to cite or otherwise refer to them in future publications is therefore requested to make such acknowledgments.

Joan E. Berish (Florida Fish and Wildlife Conservation Commission): Chapter 3, Gopher Tortoise.
Michael F. Delany (Florida Fish and Wildlife Conservation Commission): Chapter 5, Florida Grasshopper Sparrow.
Joan L. Morrison (Colorado State University): Chapter 10, Crested Caracara.
Stephen A. Nesbitt (Florida Fish and Wildlife Conservation Commission): Chapter 9, Sandhill Crane.

Manuscript Overview

While most contributors reviewed drafts of chapters involving species for which they are particularly authoritative, Tom H. Logan (Endangered Species Coordinator, Florida Fish and Wildlife Conservation Commission), Clay Henderson (President, Florida Audubon Society), and naturalist/author Vic McLeran reviewed early drafts of the manuscript in its entirety and provided many salient and helpful suggestions not only as regards content but also style and format.

Chapter Review

Chapter 1: Red-cockaded Woodpecker
Ralph Costa (U.S. Fish and Wildlife Service)
Roy S. DeLotelle (DeLotelle and Guthrie, Inc.)
Stephen A. Nesbitt (Florida Fish and Wildlife Conservation Commission)
Chapter 2: Bald Eagle
Brian A. Millsap (Florida Fish and Wildlife Conservation Commission)
Tom Murphy (South Carolina Department of Natural Resources)
Stephen A. Nesbitt (Florida Fish and Wildlife Conservation Commission)
Petra B. Wood (West Virginia Cooperative Fish and Wildlife Research Unit)
Chapter 3: Gopher Tortoise
David R. Breininger (The Bionetics Corporation)
Paul Moler (Florida Fish and Wildlife Conservation Commission)
Chapter 4: Florida Scrub-jay
David R. Breininger (The Bionetics Corporation)
Ronald L. Mumme (Allegheny College)
Chapter 5: Florida Grasshopper Sparrow
Tylan F. Dean (Massachusetts Cooperative Fish and Wildlife Research Unit)
Patrick B. Walsh (Avon Park Air Force Range)
Chapter 6: Fox Squirrel
John W. Edwards (Clemson University)
Patrick Jodice (Oregon State University)
Joshua Laerm (University of Georgia)
James N. Layne (Archbold Biological Station)
John Wooding (University of Florida)
Chapter 7: Beach Mice
Philip A. Frank (Florida Fish and Wildlife Conservation Commission)
Jeffrey A. Gore (Florida Fish and Wildlife Conservation Commission)
I. Jack Stout (University of Central Florida)
Chapter 8: Southeastern American Kestrel
Michael F. Collopy (U.S. Biological Service)
Brian A. Millsap (Florida Fish and Wildlife Conservation Commission)

Petra B. Wood (West Virginia Cooperative Fish and Wildlife Research Unit)

Chapter 9: Sandhill Crane

Rod Drewien (U.S. Fish and Wildlife Service)

James C. Lewis (U.S. Fish and Wildlife Service)

Lovett E. Williams, Jr. (Real Turkeys)

Chapter 10: Crested Caracara

Nancy Douglass (Florida Fish and Wildlife Conservation Commission)

James N. Layne (Archbold Biological Station)

Chapter 11: Florida Burrowing Owl

Eugene S. Botelho (New Mexico State University)

Pamela J. Bowen (University of Central Florida)

Brian Mealey (Miami Museum of Science and Space Transit Planetarium)

Matthew Rowe (Appalachian State University)

Ricardo Zambrano (Florida Fish and Wildlife Conservation Commission)

Chapter 12: Bats

Philip A. Frank (Florida Fish and Wildlife Conservation Commission)

Barbara French (Bat Conservation International)

Jeffrey A. Gore (Florida Fish and Wildlife Conservation Commission)

Stephen R. Humphrey (University of Florida)

Chapter 13: Saltmarsh Songbirds

John L. Cornutt (University of Tennessee)

Don Kroodsma (University of Massachusetts)

Michael F. Delany (Florida Fish and Wildlife Conservation Commission)

M. Victoria McDonald (University of Central Arkansas)

William Post (The Charlotte Museum)

Chapter 14: Wood Stork

John C. Ogden (South Florida Water Management District)

James A. Rodgers, Jr. (Florida Fish and Wildlife Conservation Commission)

Photos and Graphics

Joan E. Berish, Michael F. Delany, Todd Engstrom, Jeffrey A. Gore, Barry Mansell, Joan L. Morrison, and Stephen A. Nesbitt graciously allowed publication of their photographs. Stephen A. Nesbitt prepared the bald eagle nest distribution map, and the remainder of the range/distribution maps were prepared by Keith Singleton.

Preface

All species of wildlife are sensitive to ecological perturbations, either benefiting or suffering, depending on the nature of the perturbation. When a
given array of ecological variables is manipulated, either naturally or artificially, the wildlife populations subjected to that manipulation are inde-
pendently affected, sometimes profoundly, in terms of total numbers,
densities, distributions, etc. And the result is not necessarily merely an
unbalanced or otherwise reconfigured system. The result is often a system
dominated by a single species or a small group of species and the outright
extirpation of others. In most such instances, species inherently dependent
on a narrowly specific range of ecological factors, "specialists," are particularly susceptible to adverse impacts when those factors are compromised. Conversely, those ecologically tolerant of a wide range of factors,
or "generalists," have inherently higher adaptability potentials and are
therefore less likely to be adversely affected by change.

In Florida, the fragility of the more vulnerable native species in that
respect is heightened by the marooning effect of the state being a peninsula. Such isolation renders wildlife populations much more discrete and
thereby more vulnerable to being adversely affected by ecological changes
than they would be in non-isolated geographic areas. Moreover, the
steadily increasing human population in Florida, the associated increasing
urban/industrial development pressures, and the corresponding release
and establishment of hundreds of competing exotic species, especially in
southern Florida, further exacerbate such vulnerability. And not only can
populations be affected, but if they are endemic or largely confined to the
state, entire taxa (i.e., species or subspecies) can be affected as well.

Also, ecological systems naturally and gradually progress over time
toward "maturity" through successional stages of vegetative characteristics following events retarding that progression. And over the millennia,
individual species have competitively carved out niches to take advantage

of, and therefore have an evolved dependence on, certain stages in that successional progression.

Historically, periodic successional retardation was primarily due to weather events, especially storm-related fires, and other natural phenomena, although the agricultural activities of Native Americans played a minor role in that respect. But since the arrival in Florida of Europeans in 1565, successional retardation has increasingly been due primarily to landscape-altering activities accommodating human habitation, resulting in few natural systems currently being allowed to progress into the later stages of ecological succession. In fact, most landscapes are currently maintained at some early successional stage that is most beneficial to a given human-related objective. Species dependent on early to mid-successional ecological stages, then, thrive, but those dependent on mature or near-mature stages are essentially relegated to geo-ecological islands and are thus particularly vulnerable.

How the state's wildlife resources have fared in the wake of ecological changes over the course of the 20th century reflects that circumstance. The most significant changes have been widespread alterations of the landscape to accommodate agricultural and urban/suburban development. In central, north, and northwest Florida, the most profound alteration has been a gradual deforestation of vast areas of both pine and hardwood forests, while in southern Florida an intricate network of canals and dikes has drained about half of the original extent of wetlands there, amounting to millions of acres.

As a result, at least 12 native taxa are known to have been rendered extinct over the past 100 years, at least four have been extirpated from the state (table 1), and more than 100 native Florida species are listed by the U.S. Fish and Wildlife Service as endangered or threatened (50 CFR 17.11 and 17.12). The number similarly listed by the State of Florida (Chapter 39–27, Florida Administrative Code) is even higher.

The fragility of Florida's native wildlife resources is further exemplified in the Florida Committee on Rare and Endangered Plants and Animals' authoritative, multivolume *Rare and Endangered Biota of Florida* publications (Deyrup and Franz 1994; Gilbert 1992; Humphrey 1992; Moler 1992; Rodgers et al. 1996; Ward 1979). Collectively, those works encompass 198 vertebrate species (72 birds, 37 mammals, 39 fish, and 50 amphibians and reptiles) and more than 600 invertebrates and plants categorized as endangered, threatened, rare, special concern, status undeter-

Table 1. Known extinctions/extirpations of native Florida species during the 20th century

Species	Disappearance time frame
Extinct	
Passenger pigeon (*Ectopistes migratorius*)	1900–1910
Carolina parakeet (*Conuropsis carolinensis*)	1900–1910
Florida black wolf (*Canis rufus floridanus*)	1920s
Caribbean monk seal (*Monachus tropicalis*)	1920s
Pallid beach mouse (*Peromyscus polionotus decoloratus*)	1940s
Chadwick Beach cotton mouse (*Peromyscus gossypinusrestrictus*)	1940s
Goff's pocket gopher (*Geomys pinetus goffi*)	1950s
American ivory-billed woodpecker (*Campephilus principalis principalis*)	1960s
Smyrna seaside sparrow (*Ammodramus maritimus pelonota*)[a]	1970s
Bachman's warbler (*Vermivora bachmanii*)	1970s
Squirrel Chimney cave shrimp (*Palaemonetes cummingi*)	1970s
Dusky seaside sparrow (*Ammodramus maritimus nigriscens*)[b]	1975–80
Extirpated	
Key West quail dove (*Geotrygon chrysia*)	1890–1910
Zenaida dove (*Zenaida aurita*)[c]	1890–1910
Whooping crane (*Grus americana*)[d]	1930s
Eskimo curlew (*Numenius borealis*)[e]	1960s

Note: Five species also either known or thought to have occurred historically in Florida disappeared from the state in the 19th century: the painted vulture (*Sarcorhamphus sacra*), great auk (*Pinguinus impennis*), Atlantic grey whale (*Eschrichtius gibbosus*), bison (*Bison bison*), and gray wolf (*Canis lupus*).

a. The validity of the Smyrna seaside sparrow as a distinct subspecies is subject to debate. Some consider it to have been synonymous with MacGillivray's seaside sparrow (*A.m. macgillivraii*), which has a range separated from the historic range of *A.m. pelonota* by the mouth of the St. Johns River (see chap. 13, "Saltmarsh Songbirds").

b. The sole surviving dusky seaside sparrows, six males, were taken into captivity for safekeeping in 1979–80. The last of those died in captive facilities at Walt Disney World in 1987 (see chap. 13, "Saltmarsh Songbirds").

c. Zenaida doves still occasionally, albeit rarely, wander to the Florida Keys, likely due to prevailing storm winds, but neither breeding nor presence of substantial numbers has been confirmed there for ≈100 years.

d. Reestablishment of the whooping crane in Florida was initiated by the Florida Game and Fresh Water Fish Commission in 1993 via long-term annual releases of 20–40 young birds secured from captive breeding facilities elsewhere. A total of 204 had been released through 2000. The first nesting occurred in spring 1999 (eggs were laid but failed), and the first production of young occurred in spring 2000, representing the first successful whooping crane breeding in the wild in the United States in at least 60 years and the first east of the Mississippi River since the 19th century.

e. All evidence of Eskimo curlews once regularly occurring in Florida (as stopovers during fall migration) consists of sighting reports and is thereby subject to question because of the close resemblance of the species to the whimbrel (*Numenius phaeopus*).

mined, recently extinct, and recently extirpated. Similarly, the Nature Conservancy's likewise authoritative *Precious Heritage: The Status of Biodiversity in the United States* (Stein et al. 2000) lists 570 Florida species as at risk.

Socio-environmental concerns are often triggered when such vulnerable native taxa are put at risk due to an impending or proposed land use change. Such concerns are further heightened, in part because of inherent legal ramifications, when taxa listed by state and/or federal agencies as endangered or threatened, or as otherwise in jeopardy (and thereby protected), are involved. However, those concerns can be ameliorated, often fully accommodated, with respect to most vulnerable species, with minimal if not negligible impacts on other management priorities. The status of only a very few species is so precarious as to preclude their being accommodated in multipurpose land management regimes. Moreover, certain biogeographic factors render a number of species particularly responsive to management accommodation, thus the overall survival potential of such species can even be improved in the course of accommodating other management objectives.

This book is focused on such species and is intended as an informational resource not only for the public but also for biological personnel of state, federal, and local governments whose land stewardship priorities include at least accommodating nongame species, if not promoting the welfare of wildlife at the field level. Landowners and other land-controlling entities with corresponding priorities or objectives may also find the work informative and applicable.

The species encompassed (or, in some cases, arrays of closely allied species) were selected on the basis of collective consideration of three criteria: (1) how amenable they may be, considering their life history and habitat requirements, to benefiting from feasible, practical management initiatives; (2) the frequency with which the Florida Fish and Wildlife Conservation Commission (formerly the Florida Game and Fresh Water Fish Commission), U.S. Fish and Wildlife Service, and local and regional governments having jurisdiction over wildlife resources receive requests for technical guidance or assistance involving their welfare; and (3) the incidence of their occurrence on public lands in Florida. A conscious effort was also made to ensure that the habitats required by the selected species, collectively, represented a broad spectrum of native Florida habitats.

The intent of this book in terms of field applicability is to provide users with fundamental biological information on which management decisions can be based or implemented in the field, and strategic management scenarios that would either sustain a targeted species' status quo in a given area or promote environmental conditions that would enhance its welfare by increasing population numbers, distribution, and/or densities. Supplemental to those primary utilitarian functions, relevant literature references are included in each chapter should users require more detailed information or wish to expand upon or otherwise deviate from the recommended management strategies.

Finally, all of the targeted species are protected to varying degrees by an array of state and federal laws and regulations. Not only are such statutory/regulatory proscriptions and other constraints often integral to making management decisions, but permits from appropriate jurisdictional agencies are required to engage in a number of management-related actions (e.g., capturing and handling for banding/marking purposes, etc.). Accordingly, an appendix is included individually referencing and summarizing the most salient of those legal accommodations and their applicability to the targeted species.

References

Agey, H. N., and G. M. Heinzmann. 1971. The ivory-billed woodpecker found in central Florida. *Florida Naturalist* 44:46–47, 64.

Anderson, B. H. 1996. Bachman's warbler. Pp. 124–27 in *Rare and Endangered Biota of Florida,* vol. 5: *Birds,* ed. J. A. Rodgers, Jr., et al.

Austin, O. L., Jr. 1968. Smyrna seaside sparrow. Pp. 835–38 in *Life Histories of North American Cardinals, Grosbeaks, Buntings, Towhees, Finches, Sparrows, and Allies,* ed. O. L. Austin. United States National Museum Bulletin 237[2].

Baker, J. L. 1978. Smyrna seaside sparrow. Pp. 115–16 in *Rare and Endangered Biota of Florida,* vol. 2: *Birds,* ed. H. W. Kale II. University Presses of Florida.

Banks, R. C. 1977. The decline and fall of the Eskimo curlew. *American Birds* 31:127–34.

Barber, R. D. 1985. A recent record of the Bachman's warbler in Florida. *Florida Field Naturalist* 13:64–66.

Blake, N. M. 1980. *Land into Water—Water into Land: A History of Water Management in Florida.* University Presses of Florida. 344 pp.

Bowman, R. 1996. Key West quail-dove. Pp. 17–22 in *Rare and Endangered Biota of Florida,* vol. 5: *Birds,* ed. J. A. Rodgers, Jr., et al.

Bowman, R. 1996. Zenaida dove. Pp. 24–30 in *Rare and Endangered Biota of Florida,* vol. 5: *Birds,* ed. J. A. Rodgers, Jr., et al.

Boyd, M. F. 1936. The occurrence of the American bison in Alabama and Florida. *Science* 84:203.

Bucher, E. H. 1992. The causes of extinction of the passenger pigeon. *Current Ornithology* 9:1–36.

Carter, L. J. 1974. *The Florida Experience: Land and Water Policy in a Growth State.* Johns Hopkins University Press.

Cox, J. A., and R. S. Kautz. 2000. *Habitat Conservation Needs of Rare and Imperiled Wildlife in Florida.* Florida Fish and Wildlilfe Conservation Commission. 156 pp.

Cox, J. A., R. S. Kautz, M. MacLaughlin, and T. Gilbert. 1994. *Closing the Gaps in Florida's Wildlife Habitat Conservation System.* Florida Game and Fresh Water Fish Commission. 239 pp.

Dahne, B. 1950. Now they are gone. *Florida Wildlife* 5(5):6–7, 30.

Davis, S. M., and J. C. Ogden, eds. 1994. *Everglades: The Ecosystem and Its Restoration.* St. Lucie Press. 826 pp.

Day, D. 1981. *The Doomsday Book of Animals.* Viking Press. 288 pp. (Includes accounts on the passenger pigeon, Eskimo curlew, painted vulture, Carolina parakeet, ivory-billed woodpecker, Florida black wolf, eastern bison, and Caribbean monk seal.)

Deyrup, M., and R. Franz, eds. 1994. *Rare and Endangered Biota of Florida,* vol. 4: *Invertebrates.* University Press of Florida. 798 pp.

Duda, M. D. 1987. *Floridians and Wildlife: Sociological Implications for Wildlife Conservation in Florida.* Florida Game and Fresh Water Fish Commission Nongame Wildlife Program Technical Report no. 2. 130 pp.

Faanes, C. A., and S. E. Senner. 1991. Status and conservation of the Eskimo curlew. *American Birds* 45:237–39.

Fernald, E. A., and E. D. Purdum, eds. 1992. *Atlas of Florida.* University Press of Florida. 280 pp.

Florida Natural Areas Inventory and Florida Department of Natural Resources. 1990. *Guide to the Natural Communities of Florida.* Florida Natural Areas Inventory. 111 pp.

Folk, M. 2000. Florida's first family. *Florida Wildlife* 54(4):2–5.

Forys, E. A., and C. R. Allen. 1999. Biological invasions and deletions: Community change in south Florida. *Biological Conservation* 87:341–47.

Franz, R. 1994. Squirrel Chimney cave shrimp. Pp. 181–82 in *Rare and Endangered Biota of Florida,* vol. 4: *Invertebrates,* ed. M. Deyrup and R. Franz.

Gilbert, C. R., ed. 1992. *Rare and Endangered Biota of Florida,* vol. 2: *Fishes.* University Press of Florida. 247 pp.

Gill, R. E., Jr., P. Canevari, and E. H. Iversen. 1998. *Eskimo Curlew.* Birds of North America no. 347, American Ornithologists' Union. 27 pp.

Gleason, P. J., ed. 1974. *Environments of South Florida: Present and Past.* Miami Geological Society Memoirs 2. 452 pp.

Gollop, J. B. 1988. The Eskimo curlew. *Audubon Wildlife Report* 1988:583–95.

Gollop, J. B. 1997. Comments on Eskimo curlew sightings. *Blue Jay* 55(1):75–78.

Gore, R. 1976. Florida, Noah's Ark for exotic newcomers. *National Geographic* 150:538–59.

Halliday, T. R. 1980. The extinction of the passenger pigeon *Ectopistes migratorius* and its relevance to contemporary conservation. *Biological Conservation* 17:157–62.

Hamel, P. B. 1981. *Bachman's Warbler: A Species in Peril.* Smithsonian Institution Press. 109 pp.

Hamel, P. B. 1988. Bachman's warbler. *Audubon Wildlife Report* 1988:625–35.

Hamel, P. B. 1995. *Bachman's Warbler.* Birds of North America no. 150, American Ornithologists' Union. 16 pp.

Hamel, P. B., and S. A. Gauthreaux, Jr. 1982. The field identification of Bachman's warbler. *American Birds* 36:235–40.

Heinrich, G., and C. Welch. 1983. A natural history and current conservation projects to save the ivory-billed woodpecker, *Campephilus principalis principalis. American Association of Zoological Parks and Aquariums Annual Conference Proceedings* 1983:224–29.

Hooper, R. G., and P. B. Hamel. 1977. Nesting habitat of Bachman's warbler: A review. *Wilson Bulletin* 89:373–79.

Humphrey, S. R. 1981. Goff's pocket gopher (*Geomys pinetus goffi*) is extinct. *Florida Scientist* 44:250–52.

Humphrey, S. R. 1992. Chadwick Beach cotton mouse. Pp. 24–28 in *Rare and Endangered Biota of Florida,* vol. 1: *Mammals,* ed. S. R. Humphrey.

Humphrey, S. R. 1992. Goff's pocket gopher. Pp. 11–18 in *Rare and Endangered Biota of Florida,* vol. 1: *Mammals,* ed. S. R. Humphrey.

Humphrey, S. R. 1992. Pallid beach mouse. Pp. 19–23 in *Rare and Endangered Biota of Florida,* vol. 1: *Mammals,* ed. S. R. Humphrey.

Humphrey, S. R. 1992. Plains bison. Pp. 47–53 in *Rare and Endangered Biota of Florida,* vol. 1: *Mammals,* ed. S. R. Humphrey.

Humphrey, S. R., ed. 1992. *Rare and Endangered Biota of Florida,* vol. 1: *Mammals.* University Press of Florida. 392 pp.

Humphrey, S. R., W. H. Kern, Jr., and M. E. Ludlow. 1988. The Anastasia Island cotton mouse (Rodentia: *Peromyscus gossypinus anastasae*) may be extinct. *Florida Scientist* 51:150–55.

Jackson, J. A. 1996. Ivory-billed woodpecker. Pp. 103–12 in *Rare and Endangered Biota of Florida,* vol. 5: *Birds,* ed. J. A. Rodgers, Jr., et al.

Johnsgard, P. A. 1980. Where have all the curlews gone? *Natural History* 89(8):30–33.

Johnson, A. F., and J. W. Muller. 1993. *An Assessment of Florida's Remaining Coastal Upland Natural Communities: Final Summary Report.* Florida Natural Areas Inventory. 37 pp.

Kale, H. W. II. 1996. Dusky seaside sparrow. Pp. 7–12 in *Rare and Endangered Biota of Florida,* vol. 5: *Birds,* ed. J. A. Rodgers, Jr., et al.

Kautz, R. S. 1993. Trends in Florida wildlife habitat 1936–1987. *Florida Scientist* 56:7–24.

Kautz, R. S. 1998. Land use and land cover trends in Florida, 1936–1995. *Florida Scientist* 61:171–87.

Kenyon, K. W. 1977. Caribbean monk seal extinct. *Journal of Mammalogy* 58:97–98.

Knudson, P. M. 1977. The case of the missing monk seal. *Natural History* 86(8):78–83.

LeBoeuf, K., W. Kenyon, and B. Villa-Ramirez. 1986. The Caribbean monk seal is extinct. *Marine Mammal Scientist* 2:70–72.

Lodge, T. E. 1994. *The Everglades Handbook: Understanding the Ecosystem.* St. Lucie Press. 228 pp.

Marshall, M. 1996. The dusky's demise: The extinction of *Ammodramus maritimus nigriscens. Wild Earth* 6(2):24–25.

Marshall, T. 1998. The Carolina parakeet mystery. *A.F.A. Watchbird* 25(2):42–43.

Moler, P. E., ed. 1992. *Rare and Endangered Biota of Florida,* vol. 3: *Amphibians and Reptiles.* University Press of Florida. 291 pp.

Morris, T., and P. L. Butt. 1994. *A Re-survey for the Squirrel Chimney (Florida) Cave Shrimp, Other Species, and the Condition of the Environment Within the Chimney Cave System, Alachua County, Florida.* Karst Environmental Service (Gainesville). 12 pp.

Myers, R. L., and J. J. Ewell, eds. 1990. *Ecosystems of Florida.* University of Central Florida Press. 765 pp.

Neill, W. T. 1957. The vanished sea wolves. *Florida Wildlife* 10(9):16–17, 38.

Nesbitt, S. A. 1982. The past, present, and future of the whooping crane in Florida. Pp. 151–54 in *Proceedings of the 1981 Crane Workshop,* ed. J. C. Lewis. National Audubon Society.

Nesbitt, S. A. 1996. Whooping crane. Pp. 13–16 in *Rare and Endangered Biota of Florida,* vol. 5: *Birds,* ed. J. A. Rodgers, Jr., et al.

Neumann, T. W. 1985. Human-wildlife competition and the passenger pigeon: Population growth from system destabilization. *Human Ecology* 13:389–410.

Nicholson, D. J. 1950. Disappearance of Smyrna seaside sparrow from its former haunts. *Florida Naturalist* 23:104.

Pearlstine, L. G., L. A. Brandt, W. M. Kitchens, and F. J. Mazzotti. 1995. Impacts of citrus development on habitats of southwest Florida. *Conservation Biology* 9:1020–32.

Ray, C. E. 1961. The monk seal in Florida. *Journal of Mammalogy* 42:113.

Repenning, R. W., and S. R. Humphrey. 1986. The Chadwick Beach cotton mouse (Rodentia: *Peromyscus gossypinus restrictus*) may be extinct. *Florida Scientist* 49:259–62.

Robson, M. S. 1992. Florida red wolf. Pp. 29–34 in *Rare and Endangered Biota of Florida*, vol. 1: *Mammals*, ed. S. R. Humphrey.

Rodgers, J. A., Jr. 1996. Carolina parakeet. Pp. 4–6 in *Rare and Endangered Biota of Florida*, vol. 5: *Birds*, ed. J. A. Rodgers, Jr., et al.

Rodgers, J. A., Jr. 1996. Passenger pigeon. Pp. 1–3 in *Rare and Endangered Biota of Florida*, vol. 5: *Birds*, ed. J. A. Rodgers, Jr., et al.

Rodgers, J. A., Jr., H. W. Kale II, and H. T. Smith, eds. 1996. *Rare and Endangered Biota of Florida*, vol. 5: *Birds*. University Press of Florida. 688 pp.

Schorger, A. W. 1973. *The Passenger Pigeon: Its Natural History and Extinction*. Norman: University of Oklahoma Press. 424 pp.

Schwartz, M. W., and J. Travis. 1995. *The Distribution and Character of Natural Habitats in Pre-settlement Northern Florida, as Recorded by Public Land Survey Records*. Florida Game and Fresh Water Fish Commission Nongame Wildlife Program Project GFC-86-020 Final Report. 50 pp.

Sherman, H. B. 1952. A list and bibliography of the mammals of Florida, living and extinct. *Quarterly Journal of the Florida Academy of Science* 15(2):85–126.

Smith, P. W., and S. A. Smith. 1989. A Zenaida dove in Florida, with comments on the species and its appearance here. *Florida Field Naturalist* 17:67–69.

Sorrie, B. A. 1979. A history of the Key West quail dove in the United States. *American Birds* 33:728–31.

Stein, B. A., L. S. Kutner, and J. S. Adams. 2000. *Precious Heritage: The Status of Biodiversity in the United States*. Oxford University Press. 416 pp.

Stevenson, H. M. 1972. A recent history of Bachman's warbler. *Wilson Bulletin* 84:344–47.

Sykes, P. W., Jr. 1980. Decline and disappearance of the dusky seaside sparrow from Merritt Island, Florida. *American Birds* 34:728–37.

Tanner, J. T. 1941. Three years with the ivory-billed woodpecker, America's rarest bird. *Audubon Magazine* 43(1):5–14.

Tanner, J. T. 1966. *The Ivory-billed Woodpecker*. Dover Publishing. 111 pp.

Timm, R. M., R. M. Salazar, and P. A. Townsend. 1997. Historical distribution of the extinct tropical seal, *Monachus tropicalis*. *Biological Conservation* 11:549–51.

Wallace, R. L. 1999. Solving problems in endangered species conservation: an introduction to problem orientation. *Endangered Species Update* 16(2):28–34.

Walters, M. J. 1992. *A Shadow and a Song: The Struggle to Save an Endangered Species*. Chelsea Green Publishing. 238 pp.

Ward, D. B., ed. 1979. *Rare and Endangered Biota of Florida*, vol. 5: *Plants*. University Presses of Florida. 175 pp.

Wiley, J. W. 1991. Ecology and behavior of the Zenaida dove. *Ornithology in the Neotropics* 2:49–75.

Wing, E. S. 1992. West Indian monk seal. Pp. 35–40 in *Rare and Endangered Biota of Florida*, vol. 1: *Mammals,* ed. S. R. Humphrey.

Wood, D. A. 1987. The realities of extinction. *Florida Wildlife* 41(3):5–9.

Wood, D. A. 1990. Delicate balance: Red wolf. *Florida Wildlife* 44(4):10.

Wood, D. A., and N. Eichholz. 1986. Florida's endangered woodpeckers. *Florida Wildlife* 40(2):20–23.

Zink, R. M., and H. W. Kale II. 1995. Conservation genetics of the extinct dusky seaside sparrow, *Ammodramus maritimus nigriscens. Biological Conservation* 74:69–71.

1

∞ ∞

Red-Cockaded Woodpecker

Status

Twenty-two species of woodpeckers (Order Piciformes; Family Picidae) are native to North America, nine of which are *Picoides* congeners. Three of the *Picoides* woodpeckers occur in Florida—the hairy woodpecker (*P. villosus*), downy woodpecker (*P. pubescens*), and red-cockaded woodpecker (*P. borealis*).

The red-cockaded woodpecker historically occurred throughout the southeastern United States, from eastern Texas and Oklahoma eastward and northeastward to New Jersey. It was characterized as "abundant" in 19th-century literature, but during the 20th century the species' distribution within its historic range has become profoundly fragmented, and total population numbers have declined precipitously due to destruction of habitat, primarily in association with timbering operations. Because of that continuing trend, the U.S. Fish and Wildlife Service federally listed the species as endangered in 1970. The Florida Game and Fresh Water Fish Commission listed it as threatened in 1974, reclassified it to endangered in 1975, then again reclassified it in 1979, returning it to the threatened category. The primary threat to the remaining red-cockaded woodpecker populations continues to be destruction or degradation of habitat via timbering and other land-clearing operations.

Red-cockaded woodpeckers once occurred in all 67 Florida counties. There are no records of the species from the Keys, but there are records from as far south as the Florida City (Dade County) area. The species' range still encompasses most of the state (fig. 1), but except in the panhandle—primarily Apalachicola National Forest—its distribution within that range consists of a patchwork pattern of scattered, isolated subpopulations. The statewide breeding population is estimated to number 1,500–1,800 pairs, ≈75 percent of that total concentrated in the panhandle. The

1

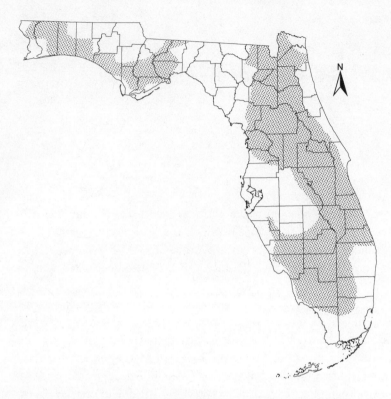

Fig. 1. Current range of the red-cockaded woodpecker in Florida.

population centered in the Apalachicola National Forest (550–600 breeding pairs) is the most substantial in the species' entire remaining range.

Distinguishing Characteristics

Adult red-cockaded woodpeckers measure 7.1–7.3 in (18–20 cm) in total length, wingspan is 13.8–14.8 in (36–38 cm), and weight is ≈1.6 ounces (45 g). Males are slightly larger than females. The nearest woodpecker in size to the red-cockaded in Florida is the congeneric hairy woodpecker, which is somewhat larger. Red-cockaded woodpeckers are easily distinguished from hairy woodpeckers, however, as well as from other Florida woodpeckers, by having conspicuous white cheek patches and black-and-white, horizontally barred backs (figs. 2a and 2b). The only other woodpecker in Florida with a black-and-white barred back is the red-bellied

Fig. 2. Adult red-cockaded
woodpeckers (Todd Engstrom,
above; Barry Mansell, right).

woodpecker (*Melanerpes carolinus*), but red-bellieds are substantially larger than red-cockadeds and have a considerable amount of red visible on the head and nape; no red at all is readily visible on adult red-cockadeds. The white cheek patches, coupled with the black crown and nape, make the red-cockaded woodpecker appear, when viewed dorsally, to have a "mohawk" haircut (fig. 2b).

Male red-cockadeds do have a few red feathers slightly above and behind each eye (the "cockades"), but those red spots are essentially covered by black feathers and are rarely visible in the field, usually only when the male is displaying. Otherwise, adult males and females are black and white in color and essentially indistinguishable from each other. The sex of nestlings and fledglings, however, can be distinguished; young males have a scarlet crown patch until their first molt in the fall, whereas females lack any red coloration at all throughout life.

Red-cockadeds have a wider vocal array than most other North American woodpeckers, a reflection of their sociality. The most common call has been phonetically characterized as a *jilp, sklit, shrit,* or *szrek* and is uttered at several-second intervals and almost constantly in association with foraging and other routine activities. A "welcoming" rattle, similar to the rattle of the hairy woodpecker, is typically uttered when two or more group members congregate, and a shrill, extended *keeeeek* is the primary predator alarm call. When the presence of raptors precipitates the alarm, the distress call is typically uttered, whereupon each member of the group flattens itself against a tree trunk or large branch and remains motionless and silent until the danger has passed.

Habitat

Pine stands of primarily old growth stems, or pine-hardwood stands dominated by old growth pines, with a low or sparse understory constitute red-cockaded woodpecker nesting and roosting habitat. Nest and roost cavities are excavated almost exclusively in mature (>60 years old) living pines. Sand pine (*Pinus clausa*) and spruce pine (*P. glabra*) are not selected, but all other species of southern pine found in Florida are used, although longleaf pine (*P. palustris*) is preferred to some degree where available, and pond pine (*P. serotina*) is rarely selected. The low or sparse understory affords unimpeded flight access to cavities and as such is an important habitat characteristic. Red-cockadeds will abandon individual cavity trees, as well as entire nesting/roosting areas, when the surrounding understory approaches heights of cavities.

Old growth pines also constitute high quality foraging substrates, but younger pines are used for foraging as well, although pines <30 years old are not used to any appreciable degree. Red-cockadeds also forage to some extent on hardwood trees and even in bayheads and cypress domes.

Life History and Behavior

Red-cockaded woodpeckers are nonmigratory and aggressively territorial. They occur in cooperative breeding social units called groups or clans, typically consisting of a breeding pair and up to three "helpers," which are nearly always male offspring of the mated pair from previous years. Juvenile females disperse or are expelled from the breeding unit prior to the onset of the breeding season following their births.

Helpers assist in defending territories from neighboring groups and in feeding and otherwise caring for the young. Breeding units typically number 2–4 birds prior to breeding and 4–6 afterward, but groups numbering 8–10 have been observed. Mated pairs usually remain together until one dies, but some intergroup movement of breeding adults does occur. The red-cockaded woodpecker and the acorn woodpecker (*Melanerpes formicivorus*), which occurs in western North America, are the only cooperatively breeding woodpeckers in North America. However, acorn woodpecker breeding units commonly have more than one breeding male and/or female.

Picoides borealis is the only North American woodpecker that virtually always excavates its roost and nest cavities in living trees. Cavities can be excavated to completion within a matter of a few months, but more typically it takes 1–3 years. Cavities are most commonly situated on the west to southwest side of mature pine trees, 3–10 feet (1–3 m) below the lowest crown branches. Once a cavity is completed, small, conical "resin wells" are excavated above, alongside, and below the cavity, on the opposite side of the tree, and sometimes even on closely adjacent trees. Resin wells are continuously maintained so as to sustain exudation of sap. The resulting resin flow gives the tree a glazed, candle-like appearance, which makes it unmistakably recognizable as a red-cockaded woodpecker cavity tree (fig. 3). The resin flow is an effective deterrent to rat snakes (*Elaphe guttata*) and perhaps to other predators of cavity-nesting birds. Red-cockadeds

Fig. 3. Active red-cockaded woodpecker cavity trees (Don A. Wood).

also chip away the bark from the immediate vicinity of cavities, creating a smooth "plate."

There are usually more cavity trees in the cluster (also called a colony) of trees occupied by a given group or clan than there are birds making up that particular breeding unit. It is also typical for a cluster to include a number of trees with "start holes," which are uncompleted cavities, and several abandoned cavity trees. The latter are often trees that have died and/or trees with cavities that have been usurped and enlarged by other species. Start holes can be initiated but then abandoned and may remain unattended for several months or even years before excavation is resumed. In such instances, it may be that the heartwood was initially too hard for successful cavity completion but softened up over time. Many cavity trees are infected with a heartwood-softening "red heart" fungus (*Phellinus pini*), which is an affliction of mature pines.

There is considerable competition for cavities from other species, primarily southern flying squirrels (*Glaucomys volans*), pileated woodpeckers (*Dryocopus pileatus*), red-bellied woodpeckers, red-headed woodpeckers (*Melanerpes erythrocephalus*), and eastern bluebirds (*Sialia sialis*). Those species can usurp red-cockaded woodpecker cavities, either temporarily or permanently (in the latter case, particularly if the invading species enlarges the cavity).

The spatial extent needed to sustain a given breeding unit depends primarily on habitat quality in terms of the abundance and density of mature pines. Home ranges in optimal quality habitat in the Carolinas average 175–215 acres (70–90 ha) in extent, but in most of Florida habitat quality is considerably lower than the more optimal conditions in the Carolinas, or, in fact, in many other areas within the species' total range. Habitat quality in southern and central Florida is particularly marginal in that respect. Home ranges there average 350–400 acres (140–160 ha) in extent, with some measuring ≥500 acres (200 ha). Habitat conditions are somewhat better in northern Florida, where home ranges average 300–350 acres (120–140 ha).

The breeding season in Florida commences in mid- to late April and extends through early June. Red-cockadeds are essentially single-brooded, but rare instances of double-brooding in a given year have been reported. The nest cavity is usually the roost cavity of the breeding male. Clutch size is 2–5 eggs, usually 3 or 4, and incubation lasts 10–11 days, one of the shortest incubation periods among birds. The young fledge at 27–28 days

of age but are dependent to some degree on their parents and any helpers present for up to several months thereafter. Red-cockadeds are long-lived for birds their size, with known ages of banded birds in the wild having been documented at >14 years.

Red-cockadeds forage primarily on the adults, larvae, and eggs of tree surface and subsurface arthropods and to a much lesser extent on such vegetative matter as pine mast and fruits. They have also been observed taking flying insects on the wing. Subsurface foods are taken by chipping away the outer layer of bark and gleaning what they find underneath. Males tend to forage more on the branches and upper trunks of trees, whereas females usually forage at lower elevations and more restrictively on the trunk.

Survey and Monitoring Techniques

Active red-cockaded woodpecker cavity trees are so conspicuous and unmistakable that whether a particular area is being used for breeding and roosting is relatively obvious. Habitats warranting surveying in that respect are mature (>50 years old) pinelands or pine-dominated pine-hardwood stands or younger stands that have scattered mature pines. Often, the scattered mature trees in that latter type of habitat are "cat face" relict trees once used for extracting turpentine (the "cat face" refers to the scar left by turpentiners). Walking linear transects, spaced according to the visibility afforded by the vegetation present, usually 100–250 feet (30–80 m) apart, is the most effective technique in that regard, but helicopter transects can also be effective to some degree.

Cavities can be categorized as currently in use if the tree is living and the resin is freshly flowing from resin wells. Cavities in living trees that have not been enlarged by other species but with dry, caked, and dully discolored (usually grayish or greenish) resin can be categorized as inactive. Such cavities, however, can be reactivated by red-cockadeds, even after several years of inactivity. Cavities in dead trees and enlarged cavities have little direct benefit to red-cockadeds, and for most purposes these can be categorized as permanently abandoned. Such cavities do benefit competing cavity-nesting species, however, in that they provide nest/roost sites, and therefore should be taken into account in red-cockaded management strategies.

Determining whether red-cockaded woodpeckers are using a given area for foraging is more complex. Any stand dominated by pines at least 30 years old and near nesting/roosting habitat has potential in that regard. There are subtle indications of red-cockadeds foraging in an area, particularly if the area is heavily used. The most obvious evidence is trees with smoother bark and a more reddish appearance (caused by the birds chipping away bark in the course of foraging) than would be the case otherwise. A more definitive technique, although not altogether effective, is to play a tape recording of red-cockaded foraging calls at stations throughout potential nesting/roosting or foraging habitat. Such calling will often elicit territorial responses by any red-cockadeds within hearing distance, but that is effective only during morning hours and only during the breeding season. This technique requires repetition each day for several consecutive days, as on any given day a group may be foraging out of hearing distance.

The number of birds comprising a given group can be determined by positioning observers at cavity trees during morning departure times, shortly before dawn, and/or at evening return times, near dusk. Several observers would normally be needed to ensure that all occupied trees in a given cluster are under observation.

For leg banding, marking, or other purposes, adults can be captured most effectively by deploying a mist net or mosquito net hoop connected to a pole over an occupied cavity, either prior to the resident bird's morning departure or just after its evening return. Striking the tree with a solid object will usually induce the bird to exit the cavity into the netting. Adults can also be captured, although much less effectively, by deploying a mist net in a cavity tree cluster area and playing a tape recording of red-cockaded calls under or very near the net. Resident birds will attempt to seek out and expel the "intruders" and in so doing may fly into the net.

Banding nestlings or inspecting nest contents requires scaling cavity trees with climbing spikes and belt or employing Swedish climbing ladders to reach cavities. A mirror and flashlight or small drop light can be used to view the contents, as can a micro-video camera probe, such as a TreeTop Peeper II (see Richardson et al. 1999b). Nestlings can be extracted with monofilament line snares or modified commercial four-pronged pick-up tools. Jackson (1982) describes the snare technique in detail, and D. M. Richardson et al. (1999a) describe the pick-up tool technique

The appropriate U.S. Fish and Wildlife Service aluminum leg band size for red-cockaded woodpeckers is 1A. Red bands should not be used when color-banding red-cockaded woodpeckers (or any other species of woodpecker). The color red is a behavioral trigger for most woodpecker species and as such can disrupt social behavior patterns.

Management

Fundamental Management Considerations

- Both habitat quality and carrying capacity are directly correlated with the availability and abundance of >60-year-old pines for nesting/roosting in combination with the availability and abundance of >30-year-old pines for foraging, and the more concentrated such resources are in a given area, the more red-cockaded woodpeckers that area can sustain over time. The most critical factor in that respect, however, is the abundance and density of >60-year-old pines. Not only do such trees constitute ideal foraging substrates, they are required in abundance for nesting/roosting because red-cockadeds will abandon a cavity tree soon after it dies, so suitable potential replacement trees must be available. Red-cockadeds will not persist where the abundance of mature pines is insufficient to offset the loss of cavity trees that die, regardless of the amount of otherwise suitable foraging habitat that may be available.

- Red-cockaded woodpeckers will abandon not only individual cavity trees but entire cavity tree cluster areas should the height of the understory in their immediate vicinities approach the height of active cavities.

- The length of time required to excavate cavities, coupled with the availability of pines suitable for cavity excavation, either to replace cavity trees that die or establish new clusters, can be a significant limiting factor in terms of both population stability and population expansion into vacant habitat.

- The quality of pines as foraging substrates increases with tree age, with ≈30-year-old pines being minimal and ≥60-year-old pines being optimal.

- Nest predators and/or interspecific cavity usurpers can be significant limiting factors in small populations and localized situations.

- Red-cockaded woodpeckers fly at altitudes below tree canopy height and are averse to flying over open terrain or open water. Structures extending above prevailing tree heights and areas of open water or terrain, then, could restrict foraging movements and/or effectively isolate groups from one another.

- Isolation of population segments from others renders them vulnerable to extirpation because of loss of genetic diversity and other demographic factors, and the smaller the isolated segment, the higher the extirpation potential.

- Red-cockaded woodpeckers can coexist with human presence and human activities, including construction of homes and other structures, timbering, agricultural operations, and recreational pursuits, as long as the intrusiveness of those activities is tailored to accommodate that coexistence.

Proactive Management

1. Understory Control

Nesting/roosting habitat should be subjected to prescribed burning every 2–5 years to retard understory growth. Cavity trees, including abandoned trees and trees with start holes, should be afforded some degree of protection during such burns by manual removal of fuel from their vicinity, creating fire lanes (but not so near cavity trees as to damage root systems), and/or by using only back fires and by executing burns when climatic conditions would minimize the trees' vulnerability to fire. Any snags present should likewise be afforded the same protection so as to provide nest/roost substrates for other cavity-nesting species that would otherwise compete with red-cockadeds for theirs. Such tree-protection precautions may be logistically prohibitive in areas supporting large numbers of cavity tree clusters, but in such instances the loss of a few cavity trees would be offset by the benefits of burning. Manual removal of understory and midstory vegetation may be needed in cavity tree cluster areas or in the immediate vicinity of individual cavity trees when such vegetation is approaching cavity heights and burning has been ineffective in eliminating them. Foraging habitat should be similarly burned to reduce fuel that could eventually result in a devastating crown fire and to promote potential nesting/roosting habitat conditions.

2. Nesting Habitat Enhancement

Excavating artificial start holes in selected trees to provide a "head start" in terms of cavity excavation, both in cavity tree cluster areas and in suitable but unoccupied nesting/roosting habitat, would significantly increase nesting habitat quality. Such targeted trees should be >50 years old and/or >9 in (23 cm) in diameter at breast height (dbh), and the hole should be situated on the southwesterly side of the tree, 3–10 feet (1–3 m) below the lower crown branches. Individual holes should be ≈2.25 in (58 cm) in diameter and well into the heartwood. In active cluster areas, selected trees should be near active cavity trees, and in unoccupied areas selected trees should be grouped into a simulated cluster. When the availability of trees suitable for cavity excavation in a cavity tree cluster area is severely restricted, or when a management objective is to induce colonization of an unoccupied but suitable area within a short period of time, artificial cavities can be excavated in available trees, or artificial cavity inserts can be deployed. Either technique can be effective in terms of red-cockadeds adopting them, although both are much more labor intensive and logistically onerous than merely excavating start holes. Moreover, the cavity insert technique requires relatively large trees, ≥15 in (38 cm) in diameter at the height of the planned insert, and the cavity excavation technique requires trees ≥75 years old with ≥10 in (25 cm) of heartwood, and such trees are relatively scarce in the state except in certain areas of northern Florida. Allen (1991) describes in detail the artificial cavity excavation technique, and Taylor and Hooper (1991) provide similar detail about the cavity insert technique.

3. Foraging Habitat Enhancement

Dense stands of young pines (<30 years old) should be thinned to enhance their potential for foraging by opening up the habitat and increasing the growth rate of the remaining trees.

4. Interspecific Competition Control

Where competition for cavities from other species is a significant problem, either or both of two techniques can be employed to minimize that problem. First, abandoned cavities that have been enlarged by competitors (but are situated in living trees) can be rehabilitated by constructing and deploying cavity restrictor devices at cavity entrances. Such devices can render previously unsuitable (= enlarged) cavities once more suitable for red-cockaded occupancy and, conversely, unsuitable for most cavity competitors. Carter et al. (1989) describe in detail the cavity restrictor technique. Second, artificial nest boxes can be deployed near active cavity trees to accommodate other cavity-nesting species, thereby mitigating, at least to some degree, the propensity of those species to usurp red-cockaded cavities. Southern flying squirrels and eastern bluebirds, in particular, have been demonstrated to prefer nest boxes over natural cavities, and where such boxes have been used, productivity in target red-cockaded woodpecker groups has increased.

5. Terrestrial Nest Predator Control

Predation on eggs and nestlings by rat snakes or other tree-climbing predators can be minimized or precluded by installing smooth aluminum flashing or by shaving bark (with a drawknife) around the trunks of cavity trees. Rat snakes can overcrawl relatively narrow flashing or areas of smooth bark, so flashing or shaved areas ≥36 in (92 cm) wide should be employed when applying either of these strategies. Withgott et al. (1995) and Neal et al. (1998) provide additional details about the aluminum flashing technique, and Saenz et al. (1999) describe the shaved bark technique.

6. Genetic Rehabilitation

To rescue small and irreversibly isolated populations, genetic rehabilitation, via translocations of individual birds, would be needed. Most effective in that regard is capturing juvenile females and relocating them to clusters occupied by bachelor males, but relocating juvenile males to cluster areas occupied by single females and relocating juvenile pairs have also been successful. Moving adults of either sex has limited efficacy, if any; adults have a strong homing instinct. When isolated populations are so small (≤3 groups) that even such extraordinary measures would be futile in forestalling extinction, the annual production of juveniles in those populations, as long as they persist, should be "harvested" and introduced into more secure populations. Not only would such a strategy preclude the loss of whatever genetic characteristics those isolated individuals possess, it would enhance the survival potential of recipient populations by increasing their genetic diversity. DeFazio et al. (1987), Rudolph et al. (1992), Allen et al. (1993), Hess and Costa (1995), Carrie et al. (1999), Edwards et al. (1999), and Franzreb (1999) can be consulted for detailed capture, translocation, and release strategies and methodologies.

Accommodative Management

Primary land use prerogatives often conflict with promoting red-cockaded woodpecker welfare, and in such instances the management objective for the species is necessarily accommodative rather than proactive. Most often, such conflicting management priorities involve either timbering operations or development projects. But in either case, or to integrate other multiple-use land management exigencies when the objective is merely to minimize, if not preclude, legal vulnerability under the array of laws and regulations protecting red-cockaded woodpeckers (see appendix), they can be accommodated using an integrated, stratified management approach focusing on individual groups rather than broad, holistic applications.

1. Cluster Zone Accommodation

This zone would provide the immediate nesting and roosting requirements of a given clan as well as high quality foraging habitat in the immediate vicinity of the cluster. It should encompass all active cavity trees occupied/utilized by the resident group as well as all living trees having inactive cavities that are not enlarged. It should be delineated with a polygon connecting all the outermost cavity trees, plus a buffer extending ≥200 feet (60 m) outward from that polygon. Considering normal sizes of cluster areas in Florida, such zones would typically encompass 8–20 acres (3–8 ha). However, when a delineated polygon plus the 200-foot buffer measures <12 acres (5 ha), the buffer should be extended to encompass at least that minimum area to ensure that sufficient short-term nesting and roosting resources are retained. Tree cutting in the Cluster Zone should be limited to (1) removal of understory hardwood stems, (2) no more than 20 percent of the 35–45-year-old pine stems present, (3) no more than 40 percent of the 25–35-year-old pines present, and (4) no more than 60 percent of the <25-year-old pines present. All >45-year-old pines within the zone should be retained, as should all inactive cavity trees and all snags (for use by interspecific cavity competitors). Construction in the Cluster Zone should be limited to nature trails, single-lane primitive roads, primitive campsites, and primitive shelters.

2. Primary Foraging Zone Accommodation

This zone would provide the primary foraging resources for a given group, as well as future cavity trees as clusters "drift" over time, and should extend ≥1,000 feet (365 m) outward from the perimeter of the Cluster Zone. Tree cutting in the zone should be restricted to (1) hardwood stems, (2) no more than 15 percent of the 45–60-year-old pines present, (3) no more than 30 percent of the 35–45-year-old pines, (4) no more than 45 percent of the 25–35-year-old pines, and (5) no more than 75 percent of the ≤25-year-old pines. All >60-year-old pines encompassed within the zone should be retained. Construction in the Primary Foraging Zone should be limited to low-density housing, with construction of one- and two-story structures consigned to areas where forest clearing is necessary and taller structures restricted to preexisting open areas. Infrastructure construction should be limited to two-lane streets and relatively small retention ponds. In most cases, the Primary Foraging Zone, inclusive of the Cluster Zone, would measure 125–150 acres (60–73 ha).

3. Secondary Foraging Zone Accommodation

This zone would provide the secondary and supplemental foraging resources needed by a given group as well as facilitate the dynamic, seasonal expansion and constriction of the areal extent of home ranges, and it should extend ≥1,000 feet outward from the perimeter of the Primary Foraging Zone. Tree cutting in the Secondary Foraging Zone should be restricted to (1) hardwood stems, (2) no more than 25 percent of the >60-year-old pines present, (3) no more than 50 percent of the 45–60-year-old pines, (4) no more than 60 percent of the 35–45-year-old pines present, (5) no more than 75 percent of the 25–35-year-old pines, and (6) no more than 90 percent of the <25-year-old pines. Construction and development should be limited by the same constraints as those observed in the Primary Foraging Zone. In most instances, the Secondary Foraging Zone would approximate 300 acres (100 ha) in size, therefore the entire treatment unit of the Cluster Zone, Primary Foraging Zone, and Secondary Foraging Zone would normally measure 400–450 acres (160–185 ha).

4. Connector Zone Accommodation

When the perimeter of a treatment unit is within 1.5 miles (2.5 km) of the perimeter of another (or, if off site, the estimated perimeter), efforts should be made to minimize the potential for the groups occupying those clusters to become isolated from each other as a result of the accommodative management strategies applied. Connecting those units with a corridor ≥500 feet (150 m) wide in which the Secondary Foraging Zone accommodative strategy is employed would be effective in that respect.

Relevant Literature

Allen, D. H. 1991. *Constructing Artificial Red-cockaded Woodpecker Cavities.* U.S. Forest Service Southeastern Forest Experiment Station General Technical Report SE-73. 19 pp.

Allen, D. H., K. E. Franzreb, and R. E. Escano. 1993. Efficacy of translocation strategies for red-cockaded woodpeckers. *Wildlife Society Bulletin* 21:155–59.

Baggett, D. L. 1995. Improved installation of artificial cavities for red-cockaded woodpeckers. *Wildlife Society Bulletin* 23:101–2.

Baker, W. W. 1983. A non-clamp patagial tag for use on red-cockaded woodpeckers. Pp. 110–11 in *Red-cockaded Woodpecker Symposium II Proceedings,* ed. D. A. Wood.

Beever, J. W., and K. A. Dryden. 1992. Red-cockaded woodpeckers and hydric slash pine flatwoods. *Transactions of the North American Natural Resources Conference* 57:693–700.

Beyer, D. E., Jr., R. Costa, R. G. Hooper, and C. A. Hess. 1996. Habitat quality and reproduction of red-cockaded woodpecker groups in Florida. *Journal of Wildlife Management* 60:826–35.

Bonnie, R. 1997. Safe harbor for the red-cockaded woodpecker. *Journal of Forestry* 95(4):17–22.

Bowman, R., D. L. Leonard, Jr., L. K. Backus, and A. R. Mains. 1999. Interspecific interactions with foraging red-cockaded woodpeckers in south-central Florida. *Wilson Bulletin* 111:346–53.

Bowman, R., D. L. Leonard, Jr., L. K. Backus, P. M. Barber, A. R. Mains, L. M. Lichman, and D. Swan. 1998. *Demography and Habitat Characteristics of the Red-cockaded Woodpecker at the Avon Park Air Force Range.* Archbold Biological Station. 149 pp.

Carrie, N. R., R. N. Conner, D. C. Rudolph, and D. K. Carrie. 1999. Reintroduction and postrelease movements of red-cockaded woodpecker groups in eastern Texas. *Journal of Wildlife Management* 63:824–32.

Carrie, N. R., K. R. Moore, S. A. Stephens, and E. L. Keith. 1998. Influence of cavity availability on red-cockaded woodpecker group size. *Wilson Bulletin* 110:93–99.

Carter, J. H. III, J. R. Walters, S. H. Everhart, and P. D. Doerr. 1989. Restrictors for red-cockaded woodpecker cavities. *Wildlife Society Bulletin* 17:68–72.

Conner, R. N. 1989. *Injection of 2,4-D to Remove Hardwood Midstory within Red-cockaded Woodpecker Colony Areas.* U.S. Forest Service Research Paper SO-251. 4 pp.

Conner, R. N., and K. A. O'Halloran. 1987. Cavity-tree selection by red-cockaded woodpeckers as related to growth dynamics of southern pines. *Wilson Bulletin* 99:398–412.

Conner, R. N., and D. C. Rudolph. 1991. Effects of mid-story reduction and thinning in red-cockaded woodpecker cavity tree clusters. *Wildlife Society Bulletin* 19:63–66.

Conner, R. N., D. C. Rudolph, D. Saenz, and R. R. Schaefer. 1984. Heartwood, sapwood, and fungal decay associated with red-cockaded woodpecker cavity trees. *Journal of Wildlife Management* 58:728–34.

Conner, R. N., D. C. Rudolph, R. R. Schaefer, D. Saenz, and C. E. Shackelford. 1999. Relationships among red-cockaded woodpecker group density, nestling provisioning rates, and habitat. *Wilson Bulletin* 111:494–98.

Conner, R. N., D. Saenz, D. C. Rudolph, W. G. Ross, and D. L. Kulhavy. 1998. Red-cockaded woodpecker nest-cavity selection: relationships with cavity age and resin production. *Auk* 115:447–54.

Copeyon, C. K., J. R. Walters, and J. H. Carter III. 1991. Induction of red-cockaded woodpecker group formation by artificial cavity construction. *Journal of Wildlife Management* 55:549–56.

Costa, R. 1999. Safe harbor: A private lands conservation strategy for longleaf pine habitat and red-cockaded woodpeckers. *Proceedings of the Longleaf Pine Alliance Conference* 2:42–44.

Costa, R., and E. Kennedy. 1994. Red-cockaded woodpecker translocations 1989–1994: State-of-our-knowledge. *Proceedings of the Annual Conference of the American Zoo and Aquarium Association* 1994:74–81.

Coulson, R. N., M. D. Guzman, K. Skordinski, J. W. Fitzgerald, R. N. Conner, D. C. Rudolph, F. L. Oliveria, D. F. Wunneburger, and P. E. Pulley. 1999. Forest landscapes: Their effect on the interaction of the southern pine beetle and red-cockaded woodpecker. *Journal of Forestry* 97:4–10.

Cox, J., W. W. Baker, and D. A. Wood. 1995. Status, distribution, and conservation of the red-cockaded woodpecker in Florida: A 1992 update. Pp. 457–64 in *Red-cockaded Woodpecker: Recovery, Ecology, and Management,* ed. D. L. Kulhavy et al.

DeFazio, J. T., Jr., M. A. Hunnicutt, M. R. Lennartz, G. L. Chapman, and J. A. Jackson. 1987. Red-cockaded woodpecker translocation experiments in South Carolina. *Proceedings of the Annual Conference of the Southeastern Association of Fish and Wildlife Agencies* 41:311–17.

DeLotelle, R. S., and R. J. Epting. 1992. Reproduction of the red-cockaded woodpecker in central Florida. *Wilson Bulletin* 104:285–94.

DeLotelle, R. S., R. J. Epting, and G. Demuth. 1995. A 12-year study of red-cockaded woodpeckers in central Florida. Pp. 259–69 in *Red-cockaded Woodpecker: Recovery, Ecology, and Management,* ed. D. L. Kulhavy et al.

DeLotelle, R. S., R. J. Epting, and J. R. Newman. 1987. Habitat use and territory characteristics of red-cockaded woodpeckers in central Florida. *Wilson Bulletin* 99:202–17.

DeLotelle, R. S., J. R. Newman, and A. E. Jerauld. 1983. Habitat use by red-cockaded woodpeckers in central Florida. Pp. 59–67 in *Red-cockaded Woodpecker Symposium II Proceedings,* ed. D. A. Wood.

Doerr, P. D., J. R. Walters, and J. H. Carter III. 1989. Reoccupation of abandoned clusters of cavity trees (colonies) by red-cockaded woodpeckers. *Proceedings of the Annual Conference of the Southeastern Association of Fish and Wildlife Agencies* 43:326–36.

Edwards, J. W., C. A. Dachelet, and W. M. Smathers. 1999. A mobile aviary to enhance translocation success of red-cockaded woodpeckers. *Proceedings of the Annual Meeting of the Canadian Society of Environmental Biologists* 37:48–53.

Edwards, J. W., E. E. Stevens, and C. A. Dachelet. 1997. Insert modifications improve access to artificial red-cockaded woodpecker nest cavities. *Journal of Field Ornithology* 68:228–34.

Engstrom, R. T., and G. Mikusinski. 1998. Ecological neighborhoods in red-cockaded woodpecker populations. *Auk* 115:473–78.

Engstrom, R. T., and E. J. Sanders. 1997. Red-cockaded woodpecker foraging ecology in an old-growth longleaf pine forest. *Wilson Bulletin* 109:203–217.

Engstrom, R. T., L. A. Brennan, W. L. Neel, R. M. Farrar, S. T. Lindeman, W. K. Moser, and S. M. Hermann. 1996. Silvicultural practices and red-cockaded woodpecker management: A reply to Rudolph and Conner. *Wildlife Society Bulletin* 24:334–38.

Epting, R. J., R. S. DeLotelle, and T. Beaty. 1995. Red-cockaded woodpecker territory and habitat use in Georgia and Florida. Pp. 270–76 in *Red-cockaded Woodpecker: Recovery, Ecology, and Management,* ed. D. L. Kulhavy et al.

Ferral, D. P., J. W. Edwards, and A. E. Armstrong. 1997. Long-distance dispersal of red-cockaded woodpeckers. *Wilson Bulletin* 109:154–57.

Franzreb, K. E. 1997. Success of intensive management of a critically imperiled population of red-cockaded woodpeckers in South Carolina. *Journal of Field Ornithology* 68:458–70.

Franzreb, K. E. 1999. Factors that influence translocation success in the red-cockaded woodpecker. *Wilson Bulletin* 111:38–45.

Glitzenstein, J. S., W. J. Platt, and D. R. Streng. 1995. Effects of fire regime and habitat on tree dynamics in north Florida longleaf pine savannas. *Ecological Monographs* 65:441–76.

Haig, S. M., J. R. Belthoff, and D. H. Allen. 1993. Population viability analysis for a small population of red-cockaded woodpeckers and an evaluation of enhancement strategies. *Conservation Biology* 7:289–301.

Hanula, J. L., K. E. Franzreb, and W. P. Pepper. 2000. Longleaf pine characteristics associated with arthropods available for red-cockaded woodpeckers. *Journal of Wildlife Management* 64:60–70.

Hardesty, J. L., and C. Kindell. 1997. Conserving ecosystems at Eglin AFB. *Endangered Species Bulletin* 22(1):8–9.

Hardesty, J. L., K. E. Gault, and H. F. Percival. 1997. *Ecological Correlates of Red-cockaded Woodpecker Foraging Preference, Habitat Use, and Home Range Size in Northwest Florida (Eglin Air Force Base)*. Florida Cooperative Fish and Wildlife Research Unit. 80 pp.

Hardesty, J. L., K. E. Gault, and H. F. Percival. 1997. *Trends, Status, and Aspects of Demography of the Red-cockaded Woodpecker in the Sandhills of Florida's Panhandle*. Florida Cooperative Fish and Wildlife Research Unit. 61 pp.

Harlow, R. F., R. G. Hooper, and M. R. Lennartz. 1983. Estimating numbers of red-cockaded woodpecker colonies. *Wildlife Society Bulletin* 11:360–63.

Hedrick, L. D., R. G. Hooper, D. L. Krusac, and J. M. Dabney. 1998. Silvicultural systems and red-cockaded woodpecker management: Another perspective. *Wildlife Society Bulletin* 26:138–47.

Hendricks, B. 1999. The long coattails of the red-cockaded woodpecker. *Quail Unlimited Magazine* 9(2):14–15.

Heppell, S. S., J. R. Walters, and L. B. Crowder. 1994. Evaluating management alternatives for red-cockaded woodpeckers: A modeling approach. *Journal of Wildlife Management* 58:479–87.

Hess, C. A. 1997. Stomach flushing: Sampling the diet of red-cockaded woodpeckers. *Wilson Bulletin* 109:535–39.

Hess, C. A., and R. Costa. 1995. Augmentation from the Apalachicola National Forest: The development of a new management technique. Pp. 385–88 in *Red-cockaded Woodpecker: Recovery, Ecology, and Management*, ed. D. L. Kulhavy et al.

Hess, C. A., and F. C. James. 1998. Diet of the red-cockaded woodpecker in the Apalachicola National Forest. *Journal of Wildlife Management* 62:509–17.

Hooper, R. G. 1983. Colony formation by red-cockaded woodpeckers: Hypotheses and management implications. Pp. 72–77 in *Red-cockaded Woodpecker Symposium II Proceedings*, ed. D. A. Wood.

Hooper, R. G., and R. F. Harlow. 1986. *Forest Stands Selected by Foraging Red-cockaded Woodpeckers*. U.S. Forest Service Southeastern Forest Experiment Station Research Paper SE-259. 10 pp.

Hooper, R. G., and H. D. Muse. 1989. *Sequentially Observed Periodic Surveys of Management Compartments to Monitor Red-cockaded Woodpecker Populations*. U.S. Forest Service Southeastern Forest Experiment Station Research Paper SE-276. 13 pp.

Hooper, R. G., A. F. Robinson, Jr., and J. A. Jackson. 1980. *The Red-cockaded Woodpecker: Notes on Life History and Management*. U.S. Forest Service. 8 pp.

Hovis, J. A. 1996. Status and management of the red-cockaded woodpecker on Goethe State Forest, Florida. *Proceedings of the Annual Conference of the Southeastern Association of Fish and Wildlife Agencies* 50:254–63.

Hovis, J. A., and R. F. Labisky. 1985. Vegetative associations of red-cockaded woodpecker colonies in Florida. *Wildlife Society Bulletin* 13:307–14.

Hovis, J. A., and R. F. Labisky. 1996. Red-cockaded woodpecker. Pp. 81–102 in *Rare and Endangered Biota of Florida,* vol. 5: *Birds,* ed. J. A. Rodgers, Jr., et al. University Press of Florida.

Hunter, W. C., A. J. Mueller, and C. L. Hardy. 1994. Managing for red-cockaded woodpeckers and neotropical migrants: Is there a conflict? *Proceedings of the Annual Conference of the Southeastern Association of Fish and Wildlife Agencies* 48:383–94.

Jackson, J. A. 1977. Determination of the status of red-cockaded woodpecker colonies. *Journal of Wildlife Management* 41:448–52.

Jackson, J. A. 1978. Competition for cavities and red-cockaded woodpecker management. Pp. 103–12 in *Endangered Birds: Management Techniques for the Preservation of Threatened Species,* ed. S. A. Temple. University of Wisconsin Press.

Jackson, J. A. 1978. Pine bark redness as an indicator of red-cockaded woodpecker activity. *Wildlife Society Bulletin* 6:171–72.

Jackson, J. A. 1982. Capturing woodpecker nestlings with a noose: A technique and its limitations. *North American Bird Bander* 7:90–93.

Jackson, J. A. 1985. An evaluation of aerial survey techniques for red-cockaded woodpeckers. *Journal of Wildlife Management* 49:1083–88.

Jackson, J. A. 1987. The red-cockaded woodpecker. Pp. 478–93 in *Audubon Wildlife Report 1987,* ed. R. L. DiSilvestro. Academic Press.

Jackson, J. A. 1994. *Red-cockaded Woodpecker.* Birds of North America no. 85, American Ornithologists' Union. 19 pp.

Jackson, J. A., and S. D. Parris. 1991. A simple, effective net for capturing cavity roosting birds. *North American Bird Bander* 16:30–31.

James, F. C., C. A. Hess, and D. Kufrin. 1997. Species-centered environmental analysis: Indirect effects of fire history on red-cockaded woodpeckers. *Ecological Applications* 7:118–29.

Kappes, J. J., Jr. 1997. Defining cavity-associated interactions between red-cockaded woodpeckers and other cavity-dependent species: Interspecific competition or cavity kleptoparasitism? *Auk* 114:778–80.

Khan, M. Z., and J. R. Walters. 1997. Is helping a beneficial learning experience for red-cockaded woodpecker (*Picoides borealis*) helpers? *Behavioral Ecology and Sociobiology* 41:69–73.

Krusac, D. L., J. M. Dabney, and J. J. Petrick. 1994. An ecological approach to managing southern national forests for red-cockaded woodpecker recovery. *Proceedings of the Annual Conference of the Southeastern Association of Fish and Wildlife Agencies* 48:374–82.

Kulhavy, D. L., R. G. Hooper, and R. Costa, eds. 1995. *Red-cockaded Woodpecker: Recovery, Ecology, and Management.* Stephen F. Austin University College of Forestry. 551 pp.

Lennartz, M. R., and J. D. Metteauer. 1987. Test of a population estimation technique for red-cockaded woodpeckers. *Proceedings of the Annual Conference of the Southeastern Association of Fish and Wildlife Agencies* 40:320–24.

Lennartz, M. R., R. G. Hooper, and R. F. Harlow. 1987. Sociality and cooperative breeding of red-cockaded woodpeckers. *Behavioral Ecology and Sociobiology* 20:77–88.

Letcher, B. H., J. A. Priddy, J. R. Walters, and L. B. Crowder. 1998. An individual-based, spatially-explicit simulation model of the population dynamics of the endangered red-cockaded woodpecker, *Picoides borealis. Biological Conservation* 86:1–14.

Ligon, J. D. 1970. Behavior and breeding biology of the red-cockaded woodpecker. *Auk* 87:255–78.

Lipscomb, D. J., and T. M. Williams. 1995. Use of geographic information systems for determination of red-cockaded woodpecker management areas. Pp. 137–44 in *Red-cockaded Woodpecker: Recovery, Ecology, and Management,* ed. D. L. Kulhavy et al.

Locke, B. A., R. N. Conner, and J. C. Kroll. 1983. Factors influencing colony site selection by red-cockaded woodpeckers. Pp. 46–50 in *Red-cockaded Woodpecker Symposium II Proceedings,* ed. D. A. Wood.

Loeb, S. C. 1993. Use and selection of red-cockaded woodpecker cavities by southern flying squirrels. *Journal of Wildlife Management* 57:329–35.

Loeb, S. C. 1996. Effectiveness of flying squirrel excluder devices on red-cockaded woodpecker cavities. *Proceedings of the Annual Conference of the Southeastern Association of Fish and Wildlife Agencies* 50:303–11.

Loeb, S. C., and R. H. Hooper. 1997. An experimental test of interspecific competition for red-cockaded woodpecker cavities. *Journal of Wildlife Management* 61:1268–80.

Loeb, S. C., W. D. Pepper, and A. T. Doyle. 1992. Habitat characteristics of active and abandoned red-cockaded woodpecker colonies. *Southern Journal of Applied Forestry* 16:120–25.

McConnell, W. V. 1999. Red-cockaded woodpecker cavity excavation in seedtree-shelterwood stands in the Wakulla (Apalachicola National Forest, Florida) sub-population. *Wildlife Society Bulletin* 27:509–13.

McFarlane, R. W. 1992. *A Stillness in the Pines: The Ecology of the Red-cockaded Woodpecker.* W. W. Norton Publishing. 270 pp.

Mitchell, L. R., L. D. Carlile, and C. R. Chandler. 1999. Effects of southern flying squirrels on nest success of red-cockaded woodpeckers. *Journal of Wildlife Management* 63:538–45.

Montague, W. G., J. C. Neal, J. E. Johnson, and D. A. James. 1995. Techniques for excluding southern flying squirrels from cavities of red-cockaded woodpeckers. Pp. 401–9 in *Red-cockaded Woodpecker: Recovery, Ecology, and Management,* ed. D. L. Kulhavy et al.

Neal, J. C., W. G. Montague, D. M. Richardson, and J. H. Withgott. 1998. Exclusion of rat snakes from red-cockaded woodpecker cavities. *Wildlife Society Bulletin* 26:851–54.

Nesbitt, S. A., A. E. Jerauld, and B. A. Harris. 1983. Red-cockaded woodpecker summer range sizes in southwest Florida. Pp. 68–71 in *Red-cockaded Woodpecker Symposium II Proceedings*, ed. D. A. Wood.

Nesbitt, S. A., B. A. Harris, R. W. Repenning, and C. B. Brownsmith. 1982. Notes on red-cockaded woodpecker study techniques. *Wildlife Society Bulletin* 10:161–63.

New, K. C., and J. L. Hanula. 1998. Effect of time elapsed after prescribed burning in longleaf pine stands on potential prey of the red-cockaded woodpecker. *Southern Journal of Applied Forestry* 22:175–83.

Phillips, L. F., Jr., J. Tomcho, Jr., and J. R. Walters. 1998. Double-clutching and double-brooding in red-cockaded woodpeckers in Florida. *Florida Field Naturalist* 26:109–13.

Plentovich, S., J. W. Tucker, Jr., N. R. Holler, and G. E. Hill. 1998. Enhancing Bachman's sparrow habitat via management of red-cockaded woodpeckers. *Journal of Wildlife Management* 62:347–54.

Porter, M. L., and R. F. Labisky. 1986. Home range and foraging habitat of red-cockaded woodpeckers in northern Florida. *Journal of Wildlife Management* 50:239–47.

Porter, M. L., M. W. Collopy, R. F. Labisky, and R. C. Littell. 1985. Foraging behavior of red-cockaded woodpeckers: An evaluation of research methodologies. *Journal of Wildlife Management* 49:505–7.

Raulston, B. E., D. A. James, and J. E. Johnson. 1996. Effects of cavity-entrance restrictors on red-cockaded woodpeckers. *Wildlife Society Bulletin* 24:694–98.

Reed, J. M., P. D. Doerr, and J. R. Walters. 1988. Minimum viable population size of the red-cockaded woodpecker. *Journal of Wildlife Management* 52:385–91.

Reed, J. M., J. H. Carter III, J. R. Walters, and P. D. Doerr. 1988. An evaluation of indices of red-cockaded woodpecker populations. *Wildlife Society Bulletin* 16:406–10.

Richardson, D. M., and D. L. Smith. 1992. Hardwood removal in red-cockaded woodpecker colonies using a shear V-blade. *Wildlife Society Bulletin* 20:428–33.

Richardson, D. M., M. Copeland, and J. W. Bradford. 1999. Translocation of orphaned red-cockaded woodpecker nestlings. *Journal of Field Ornithology* 70:400–3.

Richardson, D. M., R. Costa, and R. Boykin. 1998. *Strategy and Guidelines for the Recovery and Management of the Red-cockaded Woodpecker and Its Habitats on National Wildlife Refuges*. U.S. Fish and Wildlife Service. 51 pp.

Richardson, D. M., J. W. Bradford, B. J. Gentry, and J. L. Hall. 1999. Evaluation of a pick-up tool for removing red-cockaded woodpecker nestlings from cavities. *Wildlife Society Bulletin* 26:855–58.

Richardson, D. M., J. W. Bradford, P. G. Range, and J. Christensen. 1999. A video probe system to inspect red-cockaded woodpecker cavities. *Wildlife Society Bulletin* 27:353–56.

Ross, W. G., D. L. Kulhavy, and R. N. Conner. 1997. Stand conditions and tree characteristics affect quality of longleaf pine for red-cockaded woodpecker cavity trees. *Forest Ecological Management* 91:145–54.

Rudolph, D. C., and R. N. Conner. 1991. Cavity tree selection by red-cockaded woodpeckers in relation to tree age. *Wilson Bulletin* 103:458–67.

Rudolph, D. C., and R. N. Conner. 1996. Red-cockaded woodpeckers and silvicultural practices: Is uneven-age silviculture preferable to even-aged? *Wildlife Society Bulletin* 24:330–33.

Rudolph, D. C., R. N. Conner, and J. Turner. 1990. Competition for red-cockaded woodpecker roost and nest cavities: Effects of resin age and entrance diameter. *Wilson Bulletin* 102:23–36.

Rudolph, D. C., R. N. Conner, D. K. Carrie, and R. R. Schaefer. 1992. Experimental reintroduction of red-cockaded woodpeckers. *Auk* 109:914–16.

Saenz, D., C. S. Collins, and R. N. Conner. 1999. A bark-shaving technique to deter rat snakes from climbing red-cockaded woodpecker cavity trees. *Wildlife Society Bulletin* 27:1069–73.

Seagle, S. W., R. A. Lancia, P. A. Adams, M. R. Lennartz, and H. A. Devine. 1987. Integrating timber management and red-cockaded woodpecker habitat management. *Transactions of the North American Wildlife and Natural Resources Conference* 52:41–52.

Shapiro, A. E. 1983. Characteristics of red-cockaded woodpecker cavity trees and colony areas in southern Florida. *Florida Scientist* 46:84–95.

Smith, M. W. 1981. Comments on herbicide injection for habitat maintenance of red-cockaded woodpecker colonies. *Mississippi Kite* 11:52–53.

Taylor, W. E., and R. G. Hooper. 1991. *A Modification of Copeyon's Drilling Technique for Making Artificial Red-cockaded Woodpecker Cavities.* U.S. Forest Service Southeastern Forest Experiment Station General Technical Report SE-72. 31 pp.

U.S. Fish and Wildlife Service. 1985. *Red-cockaded Woodpecker Recovery Plan.* U.S. Fish and Wildlife Service. 88 pp.

U.S. Fish and Wildlife Service. 1999. Red-cockaded woodpecker. Pp. 4/473–93 in *South Florida Multi-Species Recovery Plan.* U.S. Fish and Wildlife Service.

VanBalen, J. B., and P. D. Doerr. 1978. The relationship of understory vegetation to red-cockaded woodpecker activity. *Proceedings of the Annual Conference of the Southeastern Association of Fish and Wildlife Agencies* 32:82–92.

Walters, J. R. 1991. Application of ecological principles to the management of endangered species: The case of the red-cockaded woodpecker. *Annual Review of Ecology and Systematics* 22:505–23.

Walters, J. R., P. D. Doerr, and J. H. Carter III. 1988. The cooperative breeding system of the red-cockaded woodpecker. *Ethology* 78:275–305.

Walters, J. R., P. P. Robinson, W. Starnes, and J. Goodson. 1995. The relative effectiveness of artificial cavity starts and artificial cavities in inducing the formation of new groups of red-cockaded woodpeckers. Pp. 367–71 in *Red-cockaded Woodpecker: Recovery, Ecology, and Management,* ed. D. L. Kulhavy et al.

Wigley, T. B., S. W. Sweeney, and J. R. Sweeney. 1999. Habitat attributes and reproduction of red-cockaded woodpeckers in intensively managed forests. *Wildlife Society Bulletin* 27:801–9.

Wilson, C. W., R. E. Masters, and G. A. Bukenhofer. 1995. Breeding bird response to pine-grassland community restoration for red-cockaded woodpeckers. *Journal of Wildlife Management* 59:56–67.

Withgott, J. H., J. C. Neal, and W. G. Montague. 1995. A technique to deter rat snakes from climbing red-cockaded woodpecker cavity trees. Pp. 394–400 in *Red-cockaded Woodpecker: Recovery, Ecology, and Management,* D. L. Kulhavy et al.

Wood, D. A., ed. 1983. *Red-cockaded Woodpecker Symposium II Proceedings.* Florida Game and Fresh Water Fish Commission.

Wood, D. A., and N. Eichholz. 1986. Florida's endangered woodpeckers. *Florida Wildlife* 40(2):20–23.

Wood, D. R., L. W. Burger, Jr., F. J. Vilella, and B. E. Raulston. 2000. Long-term effects of red-cockaded woodpecker cavity-entrance restrictors. *Wildlife Society Bulletin* 28:105–9.

Zwicker, S. M., and J. R. Walters. 1999. Selection of pines for foraging by red-cockaded woodpeckers. *Journal of Wildlife Management* 63:843–52.

2

∾ ᛞ

Bald Eagle

Status

The bald eagle (*Haliaeetus leucocephalus*) is among 59 species of eagles (Order Falconiformes; Family Accipitridae) worldwide, and one of eight *Haliaeetus* congeners (the "fish eagles"). It occurs throughout the United States (including Alaska), Canada, and northern Mexico. The only other eagle native to North America, the golden eagle (*Aquila chrysaetos*), likewise occurs over much of that range but not in Florida except as an occasional wanderer. Florida's bald eagle population constitutes ≈70 percent of the total numbers in the Southeast and ≈19 percent of the total in the entire conterminous United States.

The U.S. Department of the Interior included the bald eagle on the first federal endangered species list, issued in 1967, reclassified it to threatened in August 1995, and in 1999 initiated the process by which to delist it altogether. The Florida Game and Fresh Water Fish Commission included the species on its first endangered species list, issued in 1972, but reclassified it to threatened in 1974.

Dramatic declines in bald eagle numbers and distribution occurred in the conterminous United States from the 1940s through the early 1970s, due primarily to environmental contamination by the lipid-soluble pesticide DDT and its metabolites. DDT does not biodegrade and therefore accumulated in eagle body tissues over time, inhibiting calcium deposition, which resulted in thin, fragile eggshells. Reproductive success declined accordingly, and by the time DDT was banned in the United States in 1972, breeding populations had been effectively eliminated in the conterminous states except for Florida, the Southwest, the Chesapeake Bay area, and the northernmost tier of states.

The species has, however, been slowly recovering nationwide since the 1972 pesticide ban. The current primary mortality factors are shooting,

Fig. 4. Distribution of active bald eagle nests in Florida.

electrocution on power line structures, vehicular impact injuries, and lead poisoning. The current primary limiting factor is loss of habitat to incompatible land use changes, mainly urban and suburban development.

Although Florida's bald eagle population was not systematically monitored during the era of DDT use, anecdotal information from that period indicates that numbers did not decline nearly as precipitously in the state as occurred elsewhere. Florida Game and Fresh Water Fish Commission personnel initiated systematic, aerial annual monitoring of all known nests shortly after the 1972 pesticide ban. From that point until 1997, all known nests were overflown twice each nesting season, once early in the breeding cycle (December–January) to document territory occupancy and once late in the cycle (March–April) to document reproductive success (nestling and fledgling numbers). Having resulted in a substantial database on eagle productivity over the years, and because of rising costs of aircraft operations, the March–April flights were discontinued in 1997.

Results of the survey efforts through the early 1980s reflected a fairly stable annual statewide population of ≈350 mated pairs, but at that point population numbers began increasing steadily, and as of the 1999–2000 breeding season, the population had approximately tripled, reaching ≥1,050 pairs.

Nesting territories are distributed throughout the state, but concentrations occur in areas associated with abundant foraging habitat (expanses of open water)—in coastal areas, near lakes, and along major rivers (fig. 4). Particularly populous in that respect are Osceola and Polk counties (>115 active territories each), but substantial numbers also occur in Lake County (>65 territories) and Alachua, Brevard, Lee, Monroe, Putnam, Seminole, and Volusia counties (35–50 territories each). Among the remainder of Florida's 67 counties, only Baker, Escambia, Holmes, Lafayette, Madison, Nassau, Santa Rosa, and Washington counties are devoid of active nesting territories.

Distinguishing Characteristics

Although *bald* commonly means hairless, at the time the bald eagle was scientifically described as a species, *bald* meant "white" or "white-faced," hence its common name. Both the head and tail of adults are altogether white (fig. 5), with the remainder of the plumage dark brown. The eyes, bill, and feet are yellow. Juveniles and subadults are brown-and-white

Fig. 5. Adult bald eagle (Stephen A. Nesbitt).

mottled, lacking the white head and tail, and the eyes and bill are dark rather than yellow. Full adult plumage is not reached until the fifth or sixth year, but white head and/or tail feathers can begin appearing in the third or fourth year.

Florida's eagles have wingspans of 6–7 feet (1.8–2.1 m) and weigh 8–10 lb (3.6–4.5 kg), smaller than those breeding in Alaska, Canada, and the northern states (wingspan 8 feet; weight 14 lb). Typical of most raptors, females are substantially larger than males, but otherwise the sexes are not readily distinguishable.

Habitat

Florida's bald eagles are essentially riparian, nesting primarily very near coasts, large bodies of water, and major rivers. Except in the extreme southern Everglades and in Florida Bay, a dominant living tree, most commonly a pine (*Pinus* spp.) or cypress (*Taxodium distichum*), is selected for nesting. Nesting territories are typically forested, with up to several frequented perch sites—most often snags—and an unimpeded line of sight usually exists from the nest to the resident birds' primary feeding area. Pine and cypress trees are not present in the southern Everglades or Florida Bay, so nesting there occurs in mangroves. Open water areas constitute the primary foraging habitat.

Life History and Behavior

Bald eagles reach sexual maturity at age four years and are perennially monogamous, but when a pair member dies, the survivor usually secures another mate. Once a nesting territory is established, the resident pair will return to that territory annually unless changing habitat conditions render it no longer suitable or one pair member dies and the survivor relocates to the territory of a new mate.

The breeding season in Florida commences when adults return to their nesting territories, usually sometime from early September to mid-November, somewhat earlier in the south than the north. Courtship/pair bond reinforcement is repeated at the initiation of the breeding cycle each year and is highly ritualistic, comprising a number of aerial displays. Particularly spectacular is the grasping of each other's feet at high altitudes and cartwheeling downward, wings outstretched, separating just above the ground.

Bald eagles are territorial during the breeding season, defending their nesting home ranges not only from other eagles but also from ospreys (*Pandion haliaetus*) and other raptors. The minimum distance between nests of neighboring eagle pairs is ≈1 mile (1.6 km), but distances between nests can be smaller if substantial visual barriers are present and/or open water foraging habitat is abundant.

Nests are constructed primarily of sticks and small branches and nearly always in living trees, although when a nest tree dies, the resident pair may persist in that tree for several years. Nests are typically situated within the tree crown such that a canopy of branches is overhead (fig. 6). Nest construction can take as little as a few days, but usually 1–2 weeks, and nests can be ≥6 feet (2 m) in diameter and weigh hundreds of pounds. Osprey nests are sometimes mistaken for bald eagle nests, but as a rule ospreys nest in dead trees or on man-made structures and situate their nests as high in a tree or other structure as possible (fig. 7). Constructing artificial nesting platforms is, consequently, a viable management strategy for ospreys but not for bald eagles.

Nests are used year after year by the resident pair, but each year new nesting material is added, culminating with the addition of some green foliage, often Spanish moss (*Tillandsia usneoides*) or pine boughs. When a nest is destroyed, the resident pair typically renests in the same tree, if it is undamaged, or in one nearby. If a nest loss is early in the breeding cycle, renesting and successful reproduction will likely occur that same season. Otherwise, renesting will be deferred to the following annual cycle. Nesting territories sometimes contain more than one nest (though rarely more than two), with nests used alternately by the resident pair over time but at unpredictable interval frequencies. In such multinest territories, nesting occurs in only one nest at any given time, but if an early nesting attempt in the primary nest fails, an alternate nest may be used in a subsequent effort that season, or occasionally a new alternate nest may be constructed for the second nesting effort.

Egg laying can occur as early as mid-October and as late as late February, but the peak egg-laying period is December through early January. If the initial clutch is lost, a second clutch is typically laid 25–35 days later, but only if the loss is relatively early in the nesting season, no later than

Fig. 6. Active bald eagle nest (Don A. Wood).

Fig. 7. Utility pole osprey nest (Stephen A. Nesbitt).

mid-January. Clutch size is 1–3 eggs, most often 2, laid at intervals 2–4 days apart. Incubation lasts 32–35 days, both sexes incubate, and the nestlings fledge at 11–12 weeks of age. Parental feeding usually continues for 4–6 weeks after fledging but may continue for 10–11 weeks.

In any given year, ≈75 percent of Florida's breeding pairs successfully fledge young, averaging ≈1.5 fledglings per successful nest. Nesting territories are typically vacated by late May or early June, earlier in the south than the north, but occasionally both adults and fledglings continue associating with their nests through June or July.

Considering the nesting chronology of bald eagles in Florida, the breeding season in the state can be generically viewed as extending from early September through mid-May. But for strategic management purposes, the breeding season as that term applies to individual territories in fact commences when the adults arrive in the fall and lasts until the adults and young disperse in the spring or early summer. Also in that same provincial context, the breeding season in individual territories would end at any point when the resident adults aborted their nesting efforts and dispersed, which might happen at any time in the breeding cycle. Such distinctions can be important in terms of management strategies that involve imposing special breeding season accommodations.

Dispersing fledglings wander widely, with band recoveries and radiotelemetry records having come from Canada, along the length of the Atlantic Coast, and several northern tier states. Movement patterns of adults in the non-nesting season are not well known. Some remain in or near their nesting territories year-round, but most depart to little-known destinations. Juveniles typically return to Florida each fall and upon sexual maturity establish nesting territories in the vicinity of their natal areas. Bald eagles have lived >50 years in captivity, but life span in the wild is not known. Reproductive life span is estimated to be 20–30 years of age.

Bald eagles feed primarily on fish, which are taken by swooping to grasp prey from water surfaces with their talons, but are opportunistic to some extent and occasionally feed on turtles, snakes, birds, mammals, and carrion. Eagles also commonly "pirate" fish from ospreys and other eagles, harassing them in flight until their prey is released. Primary prey fish in Florida are catfish, mullet (*Mugil* spp.), shad (*Dorosoma* spp.), pickerel (*Esox* spp.), sea trout (*Cynoscion nebulosus*), needlefish (*Strongylura marina*), and American eels (*Anguilla rostrata*). Prey is usually carried to perch sites or nests to be eaten.

Survey and Monitoring Techniques

Monitoring of bald eagles in Florida should focus on the nesting season. Eagles do not congregate into large overwintering concentrations, conducive to making population counts, in Florida as they do in more northerly states. Early observations (October–December) to determine if a given territory is active (= occupied) can be made by approaching nests from the ground. However, to avoid undue disturbance to the resident breeders, such visits should be restricted to the amount of time necessary to determine the presence or absence of adults. Adults can arrive on territory as late as late December, so when early observations in a given season indicate that a nest is not being used, the nest should not necessarily be categorized as inactive that year. Additional nest checks, at least through December, should be made to confirm that the territory is indeed vacant.

Aircraft overflights are necessary for effective observation of incubation or to count eggs, nestlings, or fledging-age young present. Rotary-blade aircraft are more efficient than fixed-wing craft in that respect because of the relatively slower speeds and lower altitudes possible. Incubation/egg count overflights should be made between early January and early February to achieve the best results. Nestling counts should be made from early March through April, and fledgling counts should be made from mid-March through early May. Such flights have little disruptive impact on adults, provided that repeated "buzzing" does not occur and that rotary-blade aircraft do not hover directly over nests.

Adult bald eagles can be captured for leg banding, wing-marking, or other purposes with some success using monofilament snares attached to floating fish. The technique entails a system of four monofilament loop snares attached to a fish ≈8–9 in (20–24 cm) long, which is in turn attached with monofilament line and shock cord to a free-floating log. When an eagle strikes the bait in a swoop, the loops close and the weight of the log prevents the snared bird from flying away. The shock cord minimizes potential injury. Cain and Hodges (1989) describe the floating fish snare technique in detail. Baited hoop and bow traps deployed on the ground have also been used to capture adult eagles. Bloom (1987) describes those techniques and an array of others in detail.

Handling or banding nestlings requires scaling nest trees to reach nests. Because nest trees are typically formidable in stature—often >180 feet (60 m) in height—and configuration, only skilled, experienced tree climbers should attempt nest access operations. Any nest access should be undertaken well before nestlings reach eight weeks of age, at which time they would be susceptible to leaving the nest prematurely due to the intrusion. The appropriate U.S. Fish and Wildlife Service aluminum leg band size for bald eagles is 9. The USFWS assigns or approves leg band and wing-marker color schemes for bald eagles, so any operations involving these techniques should be coordinated with that agency to preclude compromising similar operations elsewhere.

Management

Fundamental Management Considerations

• The breeding season is the most critical time of year in terms of bald eagle welfare in Florida, and the breeding territory is the most important habitat component. Accommodating eagles or foraging habitat at the field level during the nonbreeding season is not a critical need, as it is in more northerly states, although some precautions can be taken to maximize a feeding area's potential for eagle use.

• There is considerable interpair variation in what nesting bald eagles will tolerate in terms of human-related intrusion into nesting territories. Most, however, are highly sensitive in that respect and will abort nesting attempts or permanently abandon territories when their tolerance threshold is exceeded.

• Bald eagles select nesting sites based primarily on the characteristics of the surrounding habitat. Significantly altering that habitat, then, especially when the density and/or abundance of snags and dominant trees is affected, can in effect destroy a nesting territory, resulting in abandonment.

• Bald eagles nesting in settings where nearby human activity is essentially constant at some level (e.g., in agricultural areas, near highways and other roadways, or in suburban areas) are de facto tolerant of that activity and the level at which it occurs. But significantly exceeding that level or expanding or changing the nature of the activity so as to be more intrusive, especially when such changes occur over a short period, will likely result in aborted breeding efforts or permanent territory abandonment.

Proactive Management

1. Breeding Season Privacy and Security

Human access should be restricted within a 750-foot (260 m) primary zone around active nests during the breeding season (from the time adults arrive on the territory in the fall until dispersal in the spring or early summer) except for infrequent incursions of short duration, such as biological personnel conducting brief monitoring visits. An exception would be vehicular traffic along existing roads, but stopping a vehicle within the primary zone during the breeding season should be avoided. Eagles can be disturbed by vehicles stopping, especially if someone gets out of them, even if they are tolerant of vehicular traffic. In a secondary zone extending an additional 750 feet (260 m) outward from the primary zone, human presence need not be restricted, but activities necessitating excessive noise should be relegated to the non-nesting season. Also, any prescribed burning in that zone during the nesting season should be done on days when prevailing winds would not carry smoke toward nests. However, in the case of a pair that is demonstrably tolerant of a more intense level of human intrusion or presence near the nest than are most bald eagles, zone sizes can justifiably be adjusted. Such high-tolerance "suburban eagles" (so-called because of the relatively close proximity of their nests to housing or other human habitation) are relatively rare, but requirements for effectively accommodating their nesting privacy and security need not be as stringent as is appropriate with most nesting eagles. The prevailing objective in determining appropriate zone sizes in association with such "suburban nests" should be not to exceed the level and/or nature of the demonstrated tolerance.

2. Nesting Habitat Maintenance

Manipulation of habitat conditions within designated primary zones via prescribed burning, roller chopping, and/or timber thinning (except that snags and dominant trees should not be cut) can enhance nesting habitat quality. Such work, however, should be relegated to the non-nesting season. When prescribed burning is used, nest trees should be protected by raking or using other mechanical means prior to ignition to minimize fuel in their vicinity and also by back-burning and executing burns under climatic conditions when nest tree vulnerability to fire would be minimal. Habitat manipulation in a given primary zone for the benefit of other species, either wild or domestic, would not necessarily be incompatible with eagle welfare, as long as such manipulation is likewise limited to low-impact activities and relegated to the non-nesting season. Activities in primary zones serving other land use exigencies also would not necessarily be incompatible with eagle welfare, but should be similarly low-impact in nature (e.g., trail construction, primitive camp maintenance, minimal land clearing) and relegated to the non-nesting season.

3. Foraging Habitat Maintenance

Snags and other perching and roosting sites near bodies of water known to be eagle foraging areas should not be cut. Aquatic weed control measures, if needed to clear open water expanses, would also be beneficial in such areas.

4. Temporal Considerations

An "unused" territory should be considered active and subject to management consideration until nesting eagles have been absent from that territory through five consecutive breeding seasons. Nesting territories occupied by pairs that undergo a mate loss commonly remain vacant until the survivor secures a new mate. Moreover, even intact pairs do not necessarily nest every year. Also, abandoned territories are not uncommonly inherited by young breeders or dispossessed older breeders seeking a nesting niche. Unused territories can thus remain vacant for several years before reoccupancy, and as such should not necessarily be considered abandoned until sufficient time elapses as to determine conclusively that such is indeed the case.

Accommodative Management

Promoting bald eagle welfare in a given area sometimes conflicts with other land use prerogatives, most often timbering and other agricultural operations or development/construction projects that encroach into eagle nesting territories. Accordingly, merely accommodating bald eagle presence, rather than employing a proactive strategy, is often necessary. Moreover, because of the array of statutory and regulatory protection afforded bald eagles in Florida (see appendix), in many such instances, local, regional, state, and/or federal permits are required to effect the change. The regulatory agencies involved issue such permits only upon acceptable accommodation of the affected eagles or, in some cases, mitigation for impacting them adversely. And even when such permits are not required, the party effecting a given land use change is nevertheless legally vulnerable under those statutes and regulations should any be violated in the course of or as a result of that change.

1. Development/Construction Projects

The U.S. Fish and Wildlife Service's (1987) *Habitat Management Guidelines for the Bald Eagle in the Southeast Region* have been demonstrated to be successful in terms of accommodating nesting bald eagles on development/construction sites (see Lincer et al. 1988 and Nesbitt et al. 1993). The guidelines are not legally binding, but they are predicated on existing laws and regulations. Thus when permits are required to initiate a given land use change, they represent the definitive instrument in terms of acceptability in that respect, as interpreted by the permitting agencies involved. The guidelines, in part, call for a primary, no-development zone extending, except under extraordinary circumstances, from 750 to 1,500 feet (260–460 m) outward from an active nest, the exact distance to be set depending on site-specific circumstances. A secondary zone is further called for, to extend similarly variable distances from 750 feet (230 m) to 1 mile (1.6 km) outward from the perimeter of the primary zone, within which acceptable development is conditioned on a number of factors (e.g., structure density and/or height and construction timetables).

2. Timbering Operations

Because they do not result in the perpetual presence of humans or human-related structures and facilities, timbering operations can be much less intrusive in terms of bald eagle tolerance, provided certain precautions are taken, than are development and other construction projects. Encroachment into bald eagle nesting territories for timber harvest purposes would likely have negligible adverse impacts on the resident eagles provided that (1) all cutting operations, including heavy equipment operation, within 1,500 feet (460 m) of nests are consigned to the time of year when eagles are not in residence on the affected territory; (2) clear-cutting does not encroach any nearer the active nest than ≈500 feet (150 m); (3) shelterwood and/or seed tree cuts do not encroach any nearer the nest than ≈350 feet (105 m) and the uncut trees are not subsequently cut (i.e., after a seed crop has been established); and (4) selective cutting does not encroach any nearer the nest than ≈200 feet (60 m) and not more than 25 percent of the canopy trees in that area are cut.

3. Farming/Ranching Operations

Although bald eagles coexisting with farming or ranching operations are demonstrably tolerant of those operations, when the nature of a given operation is to be significantly changed, the resident eagles could be adversely impacted. To preclude that potential, any new or expanded operations necessitating total or near total clearing of forested lands should not encroach any nearer active nests than ≈500 feet (150 m). Any such operations not requiring forest clearing should not encroach any nearer nests than ≈350 feet (105 m), and all land clearing associated with the operation should be relegated to the time of year when eagles are not in residence.

Relevant Literature

Bloom, P. H. 1987. Capturing and handling raptors. Pp. 99–123 in *Raptor Management Techniques Manual*, ed. B. G. Pendleton et al.

Broley, C. L. 1947. Migration and nesting of the Florida bald eagle. *Wilson Bulletin* 59:3–20.

Brown, B. T., G. S. Mills, C. Powels, W. A. Russell, G. D. Therres, and J. T. Pottie. 1999. The influence of weapons-testing noise on bald eagle behavior. *Journal of Raptor Research* 33:227–32.

Buehler, D. A. 1995. A geographic information system to identify potential bald eagle breeding habitat for southeastern United States rivers and reservoirs. *Proceedings of the Annual Conference of the Southeastern Association of Fish and Wildlife Agencies* 49:292–302.

Buehler, D. A., T. J. Mersmann, J. D. Fraser, and J. K. D. Seegar. 1991. Effects of human activity on bald eagle distribution on the northern Chesapeake Bay. *Journal of Wildlife Management* 55:282–90.

Buehler, D. A., J. D. Fraser, M. R. Fuller, L. S. McAllister, and J. K. D. Seegar. 1995. Captive and field-tested radio transmitter attachments for bald eagles. *Journal of Field Ornithology* 66:173–80.

Cain, S. L., and J. I. Hodges. 1989. A floating-fish snare for capturing bald eagles. *Journal of Raptor Research* 23:10–13.

Chandler, S. K., J. D. Fraser, D. A. Buehler, and J. K. D. Seegar. 1995. Perch trees and shoreline development as predictors of bald eagle distribution on Chesapeake Bay. *Journal of Wildlife Management* 59:325–32.

Curnutt, J. 1996. Southern bald eagle. Pp. 179–87 in *Rare and Endangered Biota of Florida*, vol. 5: *Birds*, ed. J. A. Rodgers, Jr., et al. Gainesville: University Press of Florida.

Duda, M. D. 1990. The public and raptor conservation in the southeast: An approach to human management. Pp. 121–26 in *Proceedings of the Southeastern Raptor Management Symposium and Workshop*, ed. B. G. Pendleton. National Wildlife Federation Scientific and Technical Series no. 14.

Fraser, J. D. 1983. The impact of human activities on bald eagle activities: A review. Pp. 68–84 in *Proceedings of the 1983 Bald Eagle Days*, ed. J. M. Gerrard and T. M. Ingram. Manitoba: White Horse Plains Publishing.

Gerrard, J. M.. and G. R. Bortolotti. 1988. *The Bald Eagle*. Smithsonian Institution Press. 177 pp.

Grier, J. W. 1980. Modeling approaches to bald eagle population dynamics. *Wildlife Society Bulletin* 8:316–22.

Grubb, T. G., and W. W. Bowerman. 1997. Variations in breeding bald eagle responses to jets, light planes and helicopters. *Journal of Raptor Research* 31:213–22.

Grubb, T. G., and R. M. King. 1991. Assessing human disturbance of breeding bald eagles with classification tree models. *Journal of Wildlife Management* 55:500–511.

Jackman, R. E., W. G. Hunt, D. E. Driscoll, and F. J. Lapansky. 1994. Refinements to selective trapping techniques: A radio-controlled bow net and power snare for bald and golden eagles. *Journal of Raptor Research* 28:268–73.

Kinard, F. W., Jr. 1999. Expanding urban/suburban bald eagle nest sites. *Bulletin of the South Carolina Academy of Science* 61:80.

Knight, R. L., and S. K. Knight. 1984. Responses of wintering bald eagles to boating activity. *Journal of Wildlife Management* 48:999–1004.

Lincer, J. L., B. A. Millsap, and G. L. Holder. 1988. Bald eagle nest buffer zones: Do they work in Florida? *Papers of the 1988 Annual Meeting of the Raptor Research Foundation.*

Mathisen, J. E. 1968. Effects of human disturbance on nesting of bald eagles. *Journal of Wildlife Management* 32:1–6.

Mathisen, J. E., L. D. Frenzel, and T. C. Dunstan. 1977. Management strategy for bald eagles. *Transactions of the North American Wildlife and Natural Resources Conference* 42:86–92.

McEwan, L. C., and D. H. Hirth. 1979. Southern bald eagle productivity and nest site selection. *Journal of Wildlife Management* 43:585–94.

McEwan, L. C., and D. H. Hirth. 1980. Food habits of the bald eagle in north-central Florida. *Condor* 82:229–31.

McGarigal, K., R. G. Anthony, and F. B. Isaacs. 1991. *Interactions of Humans and Bald Eagles.* Wildlife Monographs no. 115. 47 pp.

Montopoli, G. J., and D. A. Anderson. 1991. A logistic model for the cumulative effects of human intervention on bald eagle habitat. *Journal of Wildlife Management* 55:290–93.

Nesbitt, S. A., M. J. Folk, and D. A. Wood. 1993. Implementation and effects of bald eagle management guidelines in Florida. *Proceedings of the Annual Conference of the Southeastern Association of Fish and Wildlife Agencies* 47:333–38.

Nesbitt, S. A., G. L. Holder, D. A. Mager, and S. T. Schwikert. 1990. Use of aerial surveys to evaluate bald eagle nesting in Florida. Pp. 207–10 in *Proceedings of the Southeastern Raptor Management Symposium and Workshop,* ed. B. G. Pendleton.

Pendleton, B. G., ed. 1990. *Proceedings of the Southeastern Raptor Management Symposium and Workshop.* National Wildlife Federation Scientific and Technical Series no. 14.

Pendleton, B. G., B. A. Millsap, K. W. Cline, and D. M. Bird, eds. 1987. *Raptor Management Techniques Manual.* National Wildlife Federation Science and Technical Series no. 10. 420 pp.

Shapiro, A. E., F. Montalbano III, and D. Mager. 1982. Implications of construction of a flood control project upon bald eagle nesting activity. *Wilson Bulletin* 94:55–63.

Shea, D. S., and W. B. Robertson, Jr. 1979. Unusual observations of nesting bald eagles in south Florida. *Florida Field Naturalist* 7:3–5.

Snow, C. 1973. *Southern Bald Eagle and Northern Bald Eagle.* U.S. Bureau of Land Management Habitat Management Series Endangered Species Report no. 5. 58 pp.

Stalmaster, M. V. 1987. *The Bald Eagle.* Universe Books. 227 pp.

Stalmaster, M. V., and J. R. Newman. 1978. Behavioral responses of wintering bald eagles to human activity. *Journal of Wildlife Management* 42:506–13.

Steenhof, K. 1978. *Management of Wintering Bald Eagles.* U.S. Fish and Wildlife Service Publication FWS/OBS-78/79. 59 pp.

Stolen, E. D. 1996. Black and turkey vulture interactions with bald eagles in Florida. *Florida Field Naturalist* 24:43–45.

U.S. Fish and Wildlife Service. 1987. *Habitat Management Guidelines for the Bald Eagle in the Southeast Region.* U.S. Fish and Wildlife Service. 9 pp.

U.S. Fish and Wildlife Service. 1989. *Southeastern States Bald Eagle Recovery Plan.* U.S. Fish and Wildlife Service. 100 pp.

U.S. Fish and Wildlife Service. 1999. Bald eagle. Pp. 4/237–60 in *South Florida Multi-Species Recovery Plan.* U.S. Fish and Wildlife Service.

Van Meter, V. B. 1999. *The Bald Eagle in Florida.* Florida Power and Light Company. 38 pp.

Williams-Walls, N., S. McCuskey, W. Marion and J. R. Wilcox. 1986. Productivity and changes in nest utilization in four central Florida bald eagle nesting territories. *Florida Field Naturalist* 14(2):29–52.

Wood, P. B. 1987. *Distribution, Ownership Status, and Habitat Characteristics of Bald Eagle Nest Sites in Florida.* Florida Game and Fresh Water Fish Commission Nongame Wildlife Program Project GFC-85-020 Final Report. 39 pp.

Wood, P. B. 1990. The wandering eagles. *Florida Wildlife* 44(5):19–21.

Wood, P. B. 1991. Habitat use and movement patterns of subadult bald eagles in Florida. *Journal of Raptor Research* 25:163.

Wood, P. B. 1999. Bald eagle response to boating activity in northcentral Florida. *Journal of Raptor Research* 33:97–101.

Wood, P. B., and M. W. Collopy. 1995. *Population Ecology of Subadult Southern Bald Eagles in Florida: Post-fledging Ecology, Migration Patterns, Habitat Use, and Survival.* Florida Game and Fresh Water Fish Commission Nongame Wildlife Program Project NG87-026 Final Report. 111 pp.

Wood, P. B., D. A. Buehler, and M. A. Byrd. 1990. Bald eagle. Pp. 13–21 in *Proceedings of the Southeastern Raptor Management Symposium and Workshop,* ed. B. G. Pendleton.

Wood, P. B., M. W. Collopy, and C. M. Sekerak. 1998. Postfledgling nest dependence period for bald eagles in Florida. *Journal of Wildlife Management* 62:333–39.

Wood, P. B., T. C. Edwards, Jr., and M. W. Collopy. 1989. Characteristics of bald eagle nesting habitat in Florida. *Journal of Wildlife Management* 53:441–49.

Young, L. S., and M. N. Kochert. 1987. Marking techniques. Pp. 125–156 in *Raptor Management Techniques Manual,* ed. B. G. Pendleton et al.

3

Gopher Tortoise

Status

Four species of tortoises (Order Testudines; Family Testudinidae) are native to North America, but only the gopher tortoise (*Gopherus polyphemus*) occurs east of the Mississippi River; the other three are collectively distributed over the southwestern United States and Mexico. The range of *G. polyphemus* encompasses the southeastern United States from extreme eastern Louisiana to southern South Carolina.

Gopher tortoises occur in all 67 Florida counties but in the southernmost counties are found only in near-coastal areas. Total numbers have declined dramatically and the species' distribution has become exceedingly fragmented in recent decades, primarily due to habitat destruction or degradation associated with phosphate mining, citrus farming enterprises, and urban and suburban development. Human predation was also a significant factor historically in depleting populations, particularly in the panhandle. Such predation, however, has been curtailed, although not altogether eliminated, by a regulatory prohibition on all taking of gopher tortoises, imposed by the Florida Game and Fresh Water Fish Commission in 1988. Current population numbers are estimated to be only ≈20 percent of historic numbers, and habitat destruction continues to be the primary threat to the species, although poaching is a contributory limiting factor.

The gopher tortoise was listed as threatened by the Game and Fresh Water Fish Commission in 1975 but reclassified to the species of special concern category in 1979. The species is federally listed, on a geographic basis, as threatened in Louisiana, Mississippi, and southwestern Alabama but not in Florida.

Fig. 8. Adult gopher tortoise (Joan E. Berish).

Distinguishing Characteristics

Gopher tortoises can attain ≈15 in (39 cm) in carapace length and ≈24 lb (11 kg) in weight (fig. 8). The carapace is oblong and somewhat flattened on top. The plastron of adult males is somewhat concave, whereas female plastrons are flat, but otherwise the sexes are essentially indistinguishable. The forelimbs are shovel-like for digging, but the hind feet are elephantine. Adults are grayish to brownish in color. Hatchlings (fig. 9) are yellowish orange and ≈1.5–2.0 in (3.8–5.0 cm) in length at hatching.

Habitat

Gopher tortoises occur primarily in habitat characterized by well-drained sandy soils with low-growing herbs and other vegetation (the primary food source) and with interspersed open areas. Longleaf pine (*Pinus palustris*)–xeric scrub oak (*Quercus* spp.) sandhills constitute optimal habitat in that respect, but tortoises also occur in sand pine (*P. clausa*) scrub, pine flatwoods, dry prairies, and mixed pine-hardwood communities and also, often in high densities, in disturbed habitats (e.g., old fields,

roadsides, fencerows). High quality habitat (open canopy, abundant herbaceous forage) can sustain up to ≈4 tortoises per acre (10/ha), while poor quality or marginal habitat (closed canopy, thick shrub cover, minimal herbaceous forage) can support ≤1 tortoise within that same areal extent.

Life History and Behavior

As their common name implies, gopher tortoises excavate burrows, which provide refuge from temperature extremes, moisture loss, and predators. Burrows can extend ≥30 feet (9 m) in length, but average 14–15 feet (4–5 m), and reach ≈10 feet (3 m) in depth (average 6–7 feet). A gopher tortoise burrow is recognizable and distinguished from burrows excavated by other species in being shaped roughly like a half circle at the entrance and in having distinctive soil mounds extending up to several feet outward from the entrance (fig. 10). Burrows of other species are essentially round in configuration. Tortoise burrows provide habitat and/or refuge to some degree for >300 other species, including the threatened eastern indigo snake (*Drymarchon corais couperi*), the gopher frog (*Rana capito*), a species of special concern, and several invertebrate species occurring nowhere else but in association with tortoises or their burrows.

Fig. 9. Hatchling gopher tortoise (Joan E. Berish).

Fig. 10. (*Above and right*): Active gopher tortoise burrows (Don A. Wood).

Home range size of adults is highly variable, depending primarily on the availability of foraging resources. Average range sizes as reported in the literature vary from 0.5 acres (0.2 ha) to 3 acres (1.2 ha) in size, with male home ranges typically larger than those of females. Feeding is confined to diurnal hours and normally restricted to within 150 feet (46 m) of burrows. Foods include gopher apples (*Licania michauxii*), legumes, sedges, grasses, and fruits. Feeding activity and other movements are very limited when temperatures are <50°F (28°C). Long-range movements are infrequent but do occur, with distances of up to ≈3 miles (5 km) having been documented. Some tortoises exhibit homing behavior when artificially displaced.

The breeding season in Florida is roughly April–July, but males may attempt to breed throughout the active season (spring–summer–fall). Nesting occurs from May through June. One clutch of 3–12 eggs (average 6) is deposited annually. Females typically excavate a hole outside the mouth of the burrow in which to deposit eggs, but egg deposition can also occur away from burrows. Incubation lasts 80–110 days, depending on prevailing temperatures. Predation on both eggs and hatchlings is heavy, primarily by raccoons (*Procyon lotor*), foxes (*Urocyon cinereoargenteus* and *Vulpes vulpes*), skunks (*Mephitis mephitis* and *Spilogale putorius),* and a variety of snakes.

Females reach sexual maturity at 10–20 years (depending on latitude), males at a somewhat younger age. Life span is estimated to be 40–60 years.

Gopher tortoises have a well-defined social structure, typically occurring in loose colonies consisting of a few dominant males in association with a number of reproductive females. The males establish dominance-submissive hierarchies within colonies via ceremonial combat. Courtship is ritualistic, with head bobbing the most typical display.

A highly contagious upper respiratory tract disease (URTD), which is ultimately fatal to at least some infected individuals, poses a serious threat to gopher tortoises in Florida. The exact mortality rate among infected gopher tortoises is not yet known, but in at least one population of the closely related desert tortoise (*Gopherus agassizii*) in the southwestern United States, URTD was apparently the primary factor in a 90 percent decline in numbers (from 200 per square mile to 20 per square mile). The disease has been found in scattered populations in Florida but undoubtedly occurs in more than is currently known. External signs of the infection—runny nose, swollen eyelids, reddened and teary eyes, and emaciation—are cyclical in nature and are thus not necessarily apparent at any given time.

Survey and Monitoring Techniques

Because gopher tortoise burrows are so conspicuous, tortoise presence in a given area is relatively obvious. Grid transects can be established to locate burrows, spaced depending on visibility afforded by the density of the vegetation. A rough estimate of population numbers in an area can be derived by multiplying the number of burrows found in the area (excluding caved-in burrows or burrows filled with debris) by 0.6.

A more accurate, although more time-consuming, method of determining not only population numbers but also the occupancy status of individual burrows is by employing a video camera system to inspect burrow contents. Equipment necessary for this technique is a small video camera attached to the end of a long, flexible tube or cable for insertion into burrows, with a mechanical control at the other end, a light source accompanying the camera, a monitor for viewing burrow contents, and a power source for the system (see Guyer et al. 1997 and Kent et al. 1997).

Gopher tortoises can be readily captured for marking or other purposes by hand or by burying bucket traps near burrow entrances. Bucket traps should be covered with cloth or a similar material and covered with a thin layer of soil. Drainage of buckets should be accommodated by drilling bottom holes. Traps should be checked daily to minimize prolonged exposure of captured tortoises to the elements and should remain in place for at least 30 consecutive days to ensure that at least most potential burrow users are captured. A standard technique employed to mark tortoises for future identification purposes is the scute-notching scheme of Cagle (1939), using the eight rearmost and three right front scutes (fig. 11).

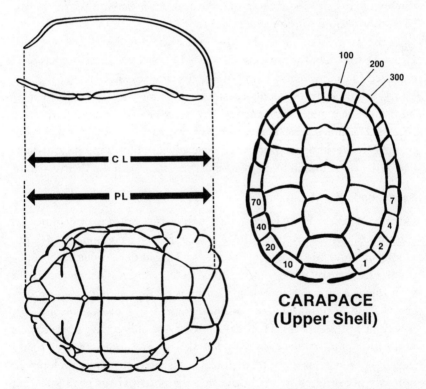

CARAPACE (Upper Shell)

Fig. 11. The gopher tortoise scute-notching technique of Cagle (1939). The scheme is additive: the tortoise to be marked no. 1 would be notched in the right rearmost scute, no. 2 would be notched in the scute to the right of that one, no. 3 would be notched in both those scutes, and so on.

Marking tortoises with paint is prohibited pursuant to Chapter 39–25.003(12) of the Florida Administrative Code.

Management

Proactive Management

Because gopher tortoises feed on early successional vegetation, habitat management strategies for the species should be designed to set back vegetative succession periodically. The conceptual management goal in that respect should be to produce a mosaic of vegetation density, ranging from small treeless areas to scattered areas of 30–40 percent tree canopy cover. Prescribed burning is the most effective technique for this, but manual tree thinning may be necessary to attain the appropriate canopy cover. Exotic vegetation should routinely be removed.

Burn treatments at intervals of 2–5 years would achieve the best results. Growing-season burns are most effective, but on sites where fire has been excluded for many years, an initial nongrowing-season burn may be necessary, followed by a growing-season burn 18 months later. Also, winter burns may be more feasible in sand pine scrub. Roller chopping to retard succession is much less effective but may be necessary when burning is not possible. Roller chopping, however, especially double-chopping, can damage burrows, although in many instances tortoises can dig their way out.

Accommodative Management

Gopher tortoises cannot coexist with high density housing or commercial enterprises. In such instances, the only recourse for accommodating populations or population segments onsite is to avoid developing where they occur. Low density development, however, is not necessarily inconsistent with tortoise presence, provided that construction activities do not encroach, and resulting facilities are not situated, any nearer tortoise burrows than >50 feet (9 m). There can, however, be indirect negative impacts on tortoise populations even from low density development. Free-roaming dogs not uncommonly kill tortoises upon encounter, and development not only necessitates streets, increasing the potential for road kills, but also increases the potential for poaching and other forms of harm.

When development plans cannot accommodate onsite tortoises, either the entire resident population or some segment of it must be dealt with by sanctioned "taking," as legally defined (see appendix), through the regulatory process administered by the Florida Fish and Wildlife Conservation Commission. Under that process, the options available are (1) mitigating for the take of tortoises by providing an acceptable degree of habitat protection, either onsite or elsewhere, or (2) capturing and relocating affected tortoises to an acceptable recipient site, either on- or offsite. Relocation, however, should be regarded as a last resort, a cosmetic resolution to any conflict between development and tortoise welfare. Relocation of any species of wildlife normally has negative impacts on both the relocated and the affected resident populations in terms of stress, disease and parasite transmission, social structure disruption, and increased competition. And the gopher tortoise, considering its social structure and the fact that the highly infectious and potentially fatal URTD occurs in some populations, is particularly vulnerable in that respect. Moreover, unoccupied areas which superficially appear suitable as recipient sites for displaced wildlife are in fact likely not so. Otherwise, except under extraordinary circumstances, the affected species would already be there.

Regardless of the option selected, permits from the Fish and Wildlife Conservation Commission are required to "take" any and all affected tortoises. The commission's *Ecology and Habitat Protection Needs of Gopher Tortoise* (Gopherus polyphemus) *Populations Found on Lands Slated for Large-Scale Development in Florida* (Cox et al. 1987) provides further and more detailed guidance relative to mitigation in association with major projects, but the commission should be contacted prior to opting for either mitigation or relocation.

Relevant Literature

Alford, R. A. 1980. Population structure of *Gopherus polyphemus* in northern Florida. *Journal of Herpetology* 14:177–82.

Arescim M. J., and C. Guyer. 1999. Burrow abandonment by gopher tortoises in slash pine plantations of the Conecuh National Forest. *Journal of Wildlife Management* 63:26–35.

Aresco, M. J., and C. Guyer. 1998. Efficacy of using scute annuli to determine growth histories and age of *Gopherus polyphemus* in southern Alabama. *Copeia* 1998:1094–1100.

Auffenberg, W., and R. Franz. 1982. The status and distribution of the gopher tortoise (*Gopherus polyphemus*). Pp. 95–126 in *North American Tortoises:*

Conservation and Ecology, ed. R. B. Bury. U.S. Fish and Wildlife Service Wildlife Research Report no. 12.

Belzer, W. R., and D. A. Reese. 1995. Radio transmitter attachment for turtle telemetry. *Herpetological Review* 26:191–92.

Berish, J. E. 1991. *Identification of Critical Gopher Tortoise Habitat in South Florida.* Florida Game and Fresh Water Fish Commission Study 7539 Final Report. 23 pp.

Berish, J. E., and C. T. Moore. 1993. Gopher tortoise response to large-scale clearcutting in northern Florida. *Proceedings of the Annual Conference of the Southeastern Association of Fish and Wildlife Agencies* 47:419–27.

Breininger, D. R., P. A. Schmalzer, and C. R. Hinkle. 1991. Estimating occupancy of gopher tortoise (*Gopherus polyphemus*) burrows in coastal scrub and slash pine flatwoods. *Journal of Herpetology* 25:317–21.

Breininger, D. R., P. A. Schmalzer, and C. R. Hinkle. 1994. Gopher tortoise densities in coastal scrub and slash pine flatwoods in Florida. *Journal of Herpetology* 28:60–65.

Breininger, D. R., P. A. Schmalzer, D. A. Rydene, and C. R. Hinkle. 1988. *Burrow and Habitat Relationships of the Gopher Tortoise in Coastal Scrub and Slash Pine Flatwoods on Merritt Island, Florida.* Florida Game and Fresh Water Fish Commission Nongame Wildlife Program Project GFC-84-016 Final Report. 238 pp.

Burke, R. L. 1989. Burrow-to-tortoise conversion factors: Comparison of three gopher tortoise survey techniques. *Herpetological Review* 20:92–94.

Burke, R. L., and J. Cox. 1988. Evaluation and review of field techniques used to study and manage gopher tortoises. Pp. 205–15 in *Management of Reptiles, Amphibians and Small Mammals in North America.* U.S. Forest Service General Technical Report RM-166.

Burke, R. L., M. A. Ewert, J. B. McLemore, and D. R. Jackson. 1996. Temperature-dependent sex determination and hatching success in the gopher tortoise (*Gopherus polyphemus*). *Chelonian Conservation Biology* 2:86–88.

Bury, R. B., and D. J. Germano, eds. 1994. *Biology of North American Tortoises.* National Biological Survey Fish and Wildlife Research Report no. 13.

Butler, J. A., and T. W. Hull. 1996. Reproduction of the tortoise, *Gopherus polyphemus,* in northeastern Florida. *Journal of Herpetology* 30:14–18.

Butler, J. A., and S. Sowell. 1996. Survivorship and predation of hatchling and yearling gopher tortoises, *Gopherus polyphemus. Journal of Herpetology* 30:455–58.

Butler, J. A., R. D. Bowman, T. W. Hull, and S. Sowell. 1995. Movements and home range of hatchling and yearling gopher tortoises, *Gopherus polyphemus. Chelonian Conservation Biology* 1:173–80.

Cagle, F. R. 1939. A system of marking turtles for future identification. *Copeia* 1939:170–72.

Cox, J., D. Inkley, and R. Kautz. 1987. *Ecology and Habitat Protection Needs of*

Gopher Tortoise Populations Found on Lands Slated for Large-Scale Development in Florida. Florida Game and Fresh Water Fish Commission Nongame Wildlife Program Technical Report no. 4. 75 pp.

Diemer, J. E. 1986. The ecology and management of the gopher tortoise in the southeastern United States. *Herpetologica* 42:125–33.

Diemer, J. E. 1992. Demography of the tortoise *Gopherus polyphemus* in northern Florida. *Journal of Herpetology* 26:281–89.

Diemer, J. E. 1992. Gopher tortoise. Pp. 123–27 in *Rare and Endangered Biota of Florida,* vol. 3: *Amphibians and Reptiles,* ed. P. E. Moler. University Press of Florida.

Diemer, J. E. 1992. Home range and movements of the tortoise *Gopherus polyphemus* in northern Florida. *Journal of Herpetology* 26:158–65.

Diemer, J. E., and P. E. Moler. 1982. Gopher tortoise response to site preparation in northern Florida. *Proceedings of the Annual Conference of the Southeastern Association of Fish and Wildlife Agencies* 36:634–37.

Diemer, J. E., and C. T. Moore. 1994. Reproduction of gopher tortoises in north-central Florida. Pp. 129–37 in *Biology of North American Tortoises,* ed. R. B. Bury and D. J. Germano.

Diemer, J. E., D. R. Jackson, J. L. Landers, J. N. Layne, and D. A. Wood. 1989. *Gopher Tortoise Relocation Symposium Proceedings.* Florida Game and Fresh Water Fish Commission. 109 pp.

Doonan, T. J., and I. J. Stout. 1994. Effects of gopher tortoise (*Gopherus polyphemus*) body size on burrow structure. *American Midland Naturalist* 131:273–80.

Douglass, J. F. 1990. Patterns of mate-seeking and aggression in a southern Florida population of the gopher tortoise, *Gopherus polyphemus. Proceedings of the Desert Tortoise Council Symposium* 1986:155–99.

Douglass, J. F., and J. N. Layne. 1978. Activity and thermoregulation of the gopher tortoise (*Gopherus polyphemus*) in southern Florida. *Herpetologica* 34:359–74.

Douglass, J. F., and C. E. Winegarner. 1977. Predators of eggs and young of the gopher tortoise in southern Florida. *Journal of Herpetology* 11:236–38.

Guyer, C., and S. M. Hermann. 1997. Patterns of size and longevity of gopher tortoise (*Gopherus polyphemus*) burrows: Implications for the longleaf pine ecosystem. *Chelonian Conservation Biology* 2:507–13.

Guyer, C., K. E. Nicholson, and S. Baucom. 1996. Effects of tracked vehicles on gopher tortoises (*Gopherus polyphemus*) at Fort Benning Military Installation, Georgia. *Georgia Journal of Science* 54:195–203.

Guyer, C., C. T. Meadows, S. C. Townsend, and G. L. Wilson. 1997. A camera device for recording vertebrate activity. *Herpetological Review* 28:138–40.

Hardesty, J. L., and C. Kindell. 1997. Conserving ecosystems at Eglin AFB. *Endangered Species Bulletin* 22(1):8–9.

Iverson, J. B. 1980. The reproductive biology of *Gopherus polyphemus*. *American Midland Naturalist* 103:353–59.

Jackson, D. R., and E. G. Milstrey. 1989. The fauna of gopher tortoise burrows. Pp. 86–98 in *Gopher Tortoise Relocation Symposium Proceedings,* ed. J. E. Diemer et al.

Jackson, D. R., and R. J. Bryant, eds. 1984. *Proceedings of the 5th Annual Meeting of the Gopher Tortoise Council: The Gopher Tortoise and Its Community.* Florida State Museum. 93 pp.

Kaczor, S. A., and D. C. Hartnett. 1990. Gopher tortoise (*Gopherus polyphemus*) effects on soils and vegetation in a Florida sandhill community. *American Midland Naturalist* 123:100–111.

Kent, D. M., M. A. Langston, D. W. Hanf, and P. M. Wallace. 1997. Utility of a camera system for investigating gopher tortoise burrows. *Florida Scientist* 60:193–96.

Kushlan, J. A., and F. J. Mazzotti. 1984. Environmental effects on a coastal population of gopher tortoises. *Journal of Herpetology* 18:231–39.

Landers, J. L., and J. L. Buckner. 1981. *The Gopher Tortoise: Effects of Forest Management and Critical Aspects of Its Ecology.* Southlands Forest Experiment Station Technical Note no. 56. 7 pp.

Macdonald, L. A., and H. R. Mushinsky. 1988. Foraging ecology of the gopher tortoise, *Gopherus polyphemus,* in a sandhill habitat. *Herpetologica* 44:345–53.

Martin, P. L., and J. N. Layne. 1987. Relationship of gopher tortoise body size to burrow size in a southcentral Florida population. *Florida Scientist* 50:264–67.

McCoy, E. D., and H. R. Mushinsky. 1992. Studying a species in decline: Gopher tortoises and the dilemma of the "correction factors." *Herpetologica* 48: 402–7.

McCoy, E. D., and H. R. Muchinsky. 1995. *The Demography of Gopherus polyphemus* (Daudin) *in Relation to Size of Available Habitat.* Florida Game and Fresh Water Fish Commission Nongame Wildlife Program Project GFC-86-013 Final Report. 71 pp.

McRae, W. A., J. L. Landers, and J. A. Garner. 1981. Movement patterns and home range of the gopher tortoise. *American Midland Naturalist* 106:165–79.

Mushinsky, H. R., and L. A. Esman. 1994. Perceptions of gopher tortoise burrows over time. *Florida Field Naturalist* 22:1–7.

Mushinsky, H. R., and E. D. McCoy. 1994. Comparison of gopher tortoise populations on islands and on the mainland in Florida. Pp. 39–47 in *Biology of North American Tortoises,* ed. R. B. Bury and D. J. Germano.

Mushinsky, H. R., D. S. Wilson, and E. D. McCoy. 1994. Growth and sexual dimorphism of *Gopherus polyphemus* in central Florida. *Herpetologica* 50:119–28.

Reid, G. K. 1991. The gopher tortoise: Landlord of the sandhills. *Florida Naturalist* 64:3–5.

Smith, R. B., D. R. Breininger, and V. L. Larson. 1997. Home range characteristics of radiotagged gopher tortoises on Kennedy Space Center, Florida. *Chelonian Conservation Biology* 2:358–62.

Smith, R. B., R. A. Seigel, and K. R. Smith. 1998. Occurrence of upper respiratory tract disease in gopher tortoise populations in Florida and Mississippi. *Journal of Herpetology* 32:426–30.

Tanner, G., and W. Terry. 1981. Effect of roller chopping and web plowing on gopher tortoise burrows in southern Florida. Pp. 66–73 in *Proceedings of the 2nd Annual Meeting of the Gopher Tortoise Council*, ed. R. Lohoefener et al.

U.S. Fish and Wildlife Service. 1990. *Gopher Tortoise Recovery Plan*. U.S. Fish and Wildlife Service. 28 pp.

Voris, S. M. 1998. *Alligator mississippiensis* (American alligator) and *Gopherus polyphemus* (gopher tortoise) commensalism. *Herpetological Review* 29:166.

Williams, T. 1999. The terrible turtle trade. *Audubon* 101(2):44–51.

Wilson, D. S., H. R. Mushinsky, and E. D. McCoy. 1994. Home range, activity, and use of juvenile gopher tortoises in central Florida. Pp. 147–60 in *Biology of North American Tortoises*, ed. R. B. Bury and D. J. Germano.

Witz, B. W., D. S. Wilson, and M. D. Palmer. 1992. Estimating population size and hatchling mortality of *Gopherus polyphemus*. *Florida Scientist* 55:14–19.

4

∽ ∾

Florida Scrub-jay

Status

The Florida scrub-jay (*Aphelocoma coerulescens*) is among eight species of jays (Order Passeriformes; Family Corvidae) native to North America. It is one of three *Aphelocoma* congeners comprising the scrub-jay assemblage, the others being the western scrub-jay (*A. californica*) and island scrub-jay (*A. insularis*), which are collectively distributed through much of western North America, from Oregon through central Texas to southern Mexico. The three species had long been considered a single species, subdivided into a number of subspecies (the Florida form was designated *A. coerulescens coerulescens*), but the *Aphelocoma* assemblage was taxonomically reevaluated in 1995, resulting in full-species status designations for the three congeners. As a consequence, the Florida scrub-jay is now Florida's only endemic bird of full-species status. It is morphologically and behaviorally as well as geographically distinct from the other two species.

The Florida scrub-jay's historic range is essentially the Florida Peninsula, but its distribution within that range was always fragmented, corresponding to the fragmented distribution of its scrub habitat, and is exceedingly so today. Only ≈60 percent of the known historic subpopulations remain, and ≈50 percent of those are declining in numbers, mostly due to destruction of habitat for citrus conversion and other agricultural operations and to fire suppression and suburban development.

The species' current range encompasses scattered subpopulations from Clay County southward to northern Collier County, but substantial numbers occur only in Putnam, Marion, Lake, and Brevard counties (fig. 12). The species' overall range is also shrinking, particularly along the Atlantic Coast, where it has been altogether extirpated from Duval and St. Johns counties (the northern extremity of the species' historic range) and Dade and Broward counties (the southern extremity). The statewide population is estimated to number 7,000–11,000 birds, but ≈80 percent of that total occurs in only two areas—on Merritt Island (Brevard County) and in the Ocala National Forest and immediate vicinity (southern Putnam, eastern Marion, and northern Lake counties). Of the remaining total, ≈50 percent occurs on public lands and ≈50 percent on private lands.

The Florida Game and Fresh Water Fish Commission included the Florida scrub-jay on the first State of Florida endangered species list, issued in 1972, but reclassified it to threatened in 1975. The U.S. Fish and Wildlife Service federally listed it as threatened in 1987. Bills were introduced in the Florida Legislature in 1999 and again in 2000 to replace the northern mockingbird (*Mimus polyglottos*) with the Florida scrub-jay as the official state bird, but those initiatives failed.

Fig. 12. Current range (*between the solid lines*) and distribution (*dots/stippling*) of the Florida scrub-jay.

Fig. 13. Adult Florida scrub-jay (Barry Mansell).

Distinguishing Characteristics

Adult Florida scrub-jays (fig. 13) measure ≈10 in (26 cm) in total length and weigh ≈2.5 oz (females) to ≈2.7 oz (males) (72.5–77.3 g). The crown, nape, wings, rump, and tail are dull blue, the back is pale straw, and the underparts are grayish. The forecrown and eyebrows are frosted with white, the throat is white, and a necklace of blue feathers separates the white throat from the grayish underparts. Males are slightly larger than females, but otherwise the sexes are indistinguishable in appearance. Immatures are similar but have a dusky brown rather than dull blue head and neck, and the overall body colors are duller. Florida scrub-jays approximate the much more common blue jay (*Cyanocitta cristata*) in size, but unlike blue jays they have no crest, are much duller in overall coloration, have no bold black markings, and lack white-tipped wings and tail feathers. They also have somewhat longer tails and legs than do blue jays.

The most common scrub-jay vocalization is a loud *weep*, uttered both intermittently, typically from sentinel perches, and in a rapid series of 3–10 notes, typically while in flight. *Weep* calls are mostly used in association with territorial disputes and as predator warnings. Females (but not males) utter rapidly repeated, mechanical *hiccup* calls, perhaps homologous with the "rattles" of other corvids, when alarmed by territorial intruders. Other vocalizations include an emphatic, grating screech (which attracts other scrub-jays) uttered in association with intruding predators, especially snakes and owls, and during intense territorial disputes; a short, guttural "growl" uttered during intense territorial disputes; a raspy note uttered when physically defending nest contents from predators (sometimes with accompanying beak jabs); a soft *chiop* indicating anxiety; a distress screech uttered when in physical combat with a territorial intruder or when in the grasp of a predator; a low-amplitude warble of whistles, chirps, and twitters—resembling the warble of the gray catbird (*Dumetella carolinensis*)—uttered in association with courtship and in a variety of other contexts; and a guttural, raspy *kuk* uttered in association with courtship feeding, feeding nestlings, and delivering nesting material.

Predator alarm calls are normally uttered from high, exposed sentinel perches. Territorial vocalizing is usually from sentinel perches near territory boundaries and in flight toward intruders and is most intense from dawn to mid-morning. Low-amplitude calls are uttered from within or atop shrubs, and courtship warbling normally occurs on the ground.

Habitat

Florida scrub-jays are exceedingly habitat specific, exclusively associated with thickets of oak scrub <10 feet (3 m) in height, interspersed with areas of bare sand. In scrubs with scattered taller, nonscrub vegetation, such as sand pine (*Pinus clausa*) or turkey oak (*Quercus laevis*), the taller vegetation must have <50 percent canopy cover to be suitable for scrub-jay occupancy.

Landscapes suitable for scrub-jays, however, are not necessarily homogeneous. Scrub habitat often occurs as just one element making up a larger-scale matrix of several habitat types, although only the scrub component in such matrices is used by scrub-jays.

Oak scrubs are distributed along both coastlines and on interior dunes deposited during the Pleistocene high sea level era and as such occur primarily in association with well-drained, fine, white, siliceous sands. The typical oak species comprising scrub, usually in various combinations, are sand live oak (*Quercus geminata*), myrtle oak (*Q. myrtifolia*), Archbold oak (*Q. inopina*), Chapman oak (*Q. chapmanii*), and runner oak (*Q. minima*). Other species also often present in scrub are turkey oak, saw-palmetto (*Serenoa repens*), scrub palmetto (*Sabal etonia*), sand pine, rosemary (*Ceratiola ericoides*), crookedwood (*Lyonia ferruginea*), silkbay (*Persea humilis*), and garberia (*Garberia fruticosa*).

Florida oak scrub is often referred to as "scrubby flatwoods" and can be characteristically subdivided into turkey oak scrub, sand pine scrub, palmetto scrub, and rosemary scrub. Abrahamson et al. (1984), Myers (1990), and Laessle (1958) provide considerable detail on scrub distribution, composition, and dynamics.

Life History and Behavior

Florida scrub-jays are nonmigratory and monogamous and breed cooperatively, with nonbreeding adults, called helpers, usually associated with a mated pair (≈52 percent of mated pairs have helpers, but with high annual variation). Helpers typically comprise ≈35 percent of a given scrub-jay subpopulation and assist their respective breeding pairs in all territorial and young-rearing activities except nest construction, egg laying, and incubation. Most helpers are two years of age or younger and the offspring of the resident breeding pair. Helping to age seven years does occur, but rarely, with helping beyond age two years more common among males than females.

The average breeding unit size is three, but breeding pairs sometimes have up to six helpers. Most have one or two, with three or more present only ≈10 percent of the time. Pairs with helpers average fledging ≈2.4 young per year, whereas pairs without helpers fledge ≈1.6 annually, so from an evolutionary/ecological standpoint, helping constitutes reproductive insurance. The cooperative breeding social structure in the Florida scrub-jay is probably an evolutionary adaption to surviving in Florida's fragmented scrub (the western scrub-jay species are not cooperative breeders) and is not substantially dissimilar to the cooperative breeding social structure of the red-cockaded woodpecker (*Picoides borealis*).

Although intrafamily pecking order disputes are rare, a dominance hierarchy does exist within breeding units. Males dominate females, breeders dominate helpers, and older helpers dominate younger helpers. Helpers of like sex and age have linear dominance-subordinate relationships. Juveniles join the hierarchy during their first summer. When breeding units break up due to loss of both breeders, helpers usually either inherit the territory or relocate to unrelated families.

Although scrub-jays are sexually mature at age one year physiologically, breeding rarely occurs before the second year and often not until three or four years and occasionally even later. Reproductive vigor peaks at four years but remains high through age 14. Females >5 years of age produce >50 percent of the annual offspring in a given population. The breeding season lasts ≈90 days, extending from early March to late June (peaking in April–May), but the breeding cycle can be delayed in years of unusually cold or wet weather in February–early March.

Courtship/pair bond reinforcement consists of the male hopping (sometimes walking) in an arc around the female, tail fanned widely and dragging the ground and tilted toward her, and with the eyebrows and posterior auricular patch extended. The male also sometimes nibbles gently at the toes of the female. Copulation is secretive and infrequent.

Sand live oaks are preferred for nesting, but various other oaks, and occasionally other species, are used. Nests measure 7–8 in (18–20 cm) in diameter and are constructed 3–6 feet (1–2 m) above ground, typically at the edge of a clump of dense shrubs and usually shaded from above. Nest material is typically oak twigs of varying shapes and thickness, formed into a thick-walled cup and lined with sabal palmetto fibers. Both pair members gather nest material, construct the nest, and feed and attend the young, but only the female incubates and broods, during which the male brings her food. Clutch size is 2–5 eggs, averaging 3.4. The eggs are greenish with irregularly shaped cinnamon spots, and measure ≈1.1 × ≈0.8 in (2.7 × 2.0 cm). The incubation period is ≈18 days, and fledging usually occurs ≈18 days after that, although fledging has been recorded as early as age 12 days and as late as 25 days. Scrub-jays normally are single-brooded but can produce three or four clutches in a given season.

Snakes, especially eastern coachwhips (*Masticophis flagellum*) and indigo snakes (*Drymarchon corais*), are the primary predators of eggs and nestlings. Adults attack large snakes by mobbing and diving and pecking fiercely, but small snakes are eaten. Nests are defended from other potential predators, often other corvids, by chasing them from the vicinity. Large snakes are also important predators of adults, as are sharp-shinned hawks (*Accipiter striatus*), Cooper's hawks (*A. cooperii*), merlins (*Falco columbarius*), great horned owls (*Bubo virginianus*), and bobcats (*Lynx rufus*).

Nestling survival rate to independence is ≈59 percent, and the annual survival rate of breeding adults is ≈78 percent. Most fledglings remain in the natal territory for at least one year before dispersing. The maximum recorded dispersal distance for males is 4.3 miles (7 km), and the maximum for females is 23.6 miles (38 km), but most remain within ≈2 miles (3.5 km) of their natal territory throughout life. The maximum recorded life span is 15.5 years.

Territories are well-defined and maintained and defended year-round by all group members, with territorial defense most vigorous immediately before nesting (in late winter–early spring) and after the autumn molt. Territorial displays consist of bobbing motions, undulating flight displays, sideways hopping on the ground toward intruders, and a "flat-headed" threat display, a result of extended neck, nape, sides of head, and eyebrow feathers.

Territories can persist for many years, with ownership often passed on by mate replacement or inheritance by helpers, although they can merge with neighboring territories or disappear with the loss of one or both breeders. Territory size increases to some degree with family size but averages ≈24 acres (10 ha). Territory density is 2–6 per ≈100 acres (40 ha).

Florida scrub-jays forage by hopping (occasionally walking) along bare sand or by jumping from shrub to shrub within oak foliage or palmetto fronds. They are omnivorous, with ≈60 percent of the diet being animal matter and ≈40 percent plant material. Insects, primarily orthopterans and lepidopteran larvae, form the bulk of the diet over most of the year. Many other insects and other arthropods are also taken, however, including ticks removed from cattle, pigs, and deer, as are a variety of small vertebrates (>20 species recorded), carrion, and eggs of small birds.

Considerable time in late summer through December is spent gathering ripening acorns, the principal plant food. Many are eaten immediately, but the majority are cached in the sand, husks intact, to be recovered, husked, and eaten throughout the remainder of the year. Scrub-jays open acorns by bracing them against a hard substrate with the inner toes, then hammering them with their chisel-shaped mandible. Other small nuts, fruits, and seeds are also occasionally taken, and such human-offered foods as corn, peanuts, and sunflower seeds are readily taken.

Survey and Monitoring Techniques

Florida scrub-jays are sedentary in their home ranges, conspicuous when present, and relatively unafraid of humans. Their presence in an area is therefore often obvious and can be confirmed by mere visual observation. A more definitive technique to determine presence or absence, as well as to calculate population numbers, is to play tape recordings of scrub-jay territorial scolding in appropriate habitat. Any resident birds within hearing distance will respond, but because scrub-jays are reluctant to fly on windy days and will not readily respond to distant territorial calls when temperatures are high, surveys should be conducted on clear, calm (<9 mph winds) days and initiated shortly after sunrise, terminating sometime before midday.

Seasonally, the most advantageous times for surveying are February–March (just prior to the nesting season), July (when young of the year are still distinguishable in appearance), and September (when territorial behavior is particularly intense). Scrub-jay behavior and movements are subdued during the fall Accipiter migration period; foraging foray distances are maximal during late winter; and in late spring the young are quiet and adults are occupied with molting and feeding fledglings. Surveys during such times, then, would yield marginal results.

Surveys should be conducted by systematically traversing, by walking or driving (if logistically feasible), along parallel transects spaced 300–600 ft (100–200 m) apart, the exact distance determined by topography, density of vegetation, and, in the case of the tape recording playback method, the power of the speaker being used. Tape recordings should be played at intervals of 300–600 feet (100–200 m) along each transect and for at least one minute toward each of the four primary compass directions (assuming potential habitat occurs in all four directions from the observer).

Capturing scrub-jays for leg banding, marking, or other purposes is best accomplished using Potter traps baited with peanuts. The appropriate U.S. Fish and Wildlife Service aluminum leg band size for scrub-jays is 2.

Management

Fundamental Management Considerations

• Scrub-jays occur exclusively in oak scrub, and oak scrub 3–6 feet (1–2 m) in height constitutes optimal habitat quality. Scrub typically attains that height sometime between 8 and 15 years following a fire, but at any height, habitat quality begins declining dramatically at ≈20 years.

• In scrub habitats with sand pines, turkey oak, or other taller vegetation interspersed within the scrub, the canopy cover of that taller vegetation must be <50 percent for the scrub to be suitable scrub-jay habitat.

• Scrub-jays require open areas, typically consisting of bare sand, interspersed throughout their territories.

• Scrub-jays will not fly either through or over forested lands. Forested habitats, then, regardless of size, would tend to isolate scrub-jay subpopulations.

• Scrub areas separated by distances >7.5 miles (12.0 km) are altogether isolated from each other in terms of scrub-jay dispersal and colonization.

Proactive Management

1. Scrub Maintenance

Periodic burning is the most effective manipulative technique in maintaining habitat quality, in terms of both scrub height manipulation and control of sand pines, turkey oaks, and other invading taller vegetation. Burns should be executed before the target scrub approaches 10 feet (3 m) in height, but in any event not less frequently than every 20 years. From a temporal perspective, management units should be subdivided with fire lanes such that no more than 25 percent of a given unit is burned in a given year. Mechanical manipulation (e.g., roller chopping) of scrub succession is less effective but may be necessary where burning is not feasible or practical. Mechanical manipulation may also be necessary to control invading taller vegetation or as the initial step in rehabilitating old-growth scrubs or areas otherwise unsuitable as scrub-jay habitat.

2. Landscape Management

Management strategies for broad-scale landscapes comprising a matrix of several habitat types should promote scrub-jay dispersal access among the scrub components of the matrix by minimizing dispersal impediments, such as forested areas, between them.

3. Open Space Augmentation

Mowed areas can mirror natural openings in terms of their utility as foraging habitat, so keeping areas adjacent to scrub (e.g., roadsides) well mowed would supplement the natural openings inherent in the scrub.

4. Population Expansion/Reestablishment

Establishing scrub-jay populations in areas of suitable habitat not currently occupied, or where populations are so small and isolated that they are vulnerable to extirpation due to inbreeding or other genetic or demographic factors, would require translocating individuals from secure subpopulations to those areas. Translocating "surplus" nonbreeding helpers is most effective in that regard. Mumme and Below (1995; 1999) provide considerable detail relative to that technique.

Accommodative Management

Scrub-jays are among the most tolerant of North American birds in terms of human presence. They can and do coexist with humans in parks and other recreational facilities. They can also be accommodated within low density housing subdivisions and adjacent to higher density projects, but only at levels afforded by the extent of oak scrub habitat retained in the course of facility maintenance or project development. Accommodating scrub-jays when other land use prerogatives conflict with the birds' welfare, then, is directly related to accommodating oak scrub habitat to the maximum extent possible in the course of exercising those prerogatives. The Florida Fish and Wildlife Conservation Commission's *Ecology and Development-Related Habitat Requirements of the Florida Scrub Jay* (Fitzpatrick et al. 1991) provides specific, detailed guidance in that respect.

Relevant Literature

Abrahamson, W. G., A. F. Johnson, J. N. Layne, and P. A. Peroni. 1984. Vegetation of the Archbold Biological Station, Florida: An example of the southern Lake Wales Ridge. *Florida Scientist* 47:209–50.

Bowman, R., and G. E. Woolfenden. 1997. The scrub and the scrub-jay: Imperiled natural treasures of Florida. *Florida Naturalist* 71:10–11.

Breininger, D. R. 1992. *Habitat Model for the Florida Scrub Jay on John F. Kennedy Space Center.* NASA Technical Memorandum 107543. 95 pp.

Breininger, D. R. 1999. Florida scrub-jay demography and dispersal in a fragmented landscape. *Auk* 116:520–27.

Breininger, D. R., M. A. Burgman, and B. M. Smith. 1999. Influence of habitat quality, catastrophes, and population size on extinction risk of the Florida scrub-jay. *Wildlife Society Bulletin* 27:810–22.

Breininger, D. R., M. J. Provancha, and R. B. Smith. 1991. Mapping Florida scrub jay habitat for purposes of land-use management. *Photogrammetric Engineering and Remote Sensing* 57:1467–74.

Breininger, D. R., V. L. Larson, B. W. Duncan, and R. B. Smith. 1998. Linking habitat suitability to demographic success in Florida scrub-jays. *Wildlife Society Bulletin* 26:118–28.

Breininger, D. R., V. L. Larson, D. M. Oddy, R. B. Smith, and M. J. Barkaszi. 1996. Florida scrub-jay demography in different landscapes. *Auk* 113:617–25.

Breininger, D. R., V. L. Larson, B. W. Duncan, R. B. Smith, D. M. Oddy, and M. F. Goodchild. 1995. Landscape patterns of Florida scrub jay habitat use and demographic success. *Conservation Biology* 9:1442–53.

Cox, J. A. 1987. *Status and Distribution of the Florida Scrub Jay.* Florida Ornithological Society Special Publication no. 3. 110 pp.

DeGange, A. R., J. W. Fitzpatrick, J. N. Layne, and G. E. Woolfenden. 1989. Acorn harvesting by Florida scrub jays. *Ecology* 70:348–56.

Dreschel, T. W., R. B. Smith, and D. R. Breininger. 1990. Florida scrub jay mortality on roadsides. *Florida Field Naturalist* 18:82–83.

Fitzpatrick, J. W., and G. E. Woolfenden. 1986. Demographic routes of cooperative breeding in some New World jays. Pp. 137–60 in *Evolutionary Behavior,* ed. M. Nitecki and J. Kitchell. University of Chicago Press.

Fitzpatrick, J. W., G. E. Woolfenden, and R. L. Curry. 1994. Fire and conservation biology of the Florida scrub jay (*Aphelocoma coerulescens coerulescens*). *Journal of Ornithology* 135:493–94.

Fitzpatrick, J. W., G. E. Woolfenden, and M. T. Kopeny. 1991. *Ecology and Development-Related Habitat Requirements of the Florida Scrub Jay.* Florida Game and Fresh Water Fish Commission Nongame Wildlife Program Technical Report no. 8. 49 pp.

Francis, A. M., J. P. Hailman, and G. E. Woolfenden. 1989. Mobbing by Florida scrub jays: Behavior, sexual asymmetry, role of helpers and ontogeny. *Animal Behavior* 38:795–816.

Gipe, T. G., and J. G. Morris. 1987. Effects of prescribed burning on the suitability of habitat for the Florida scrub jay, *Aphelocoma coerulescens coerulescens. Florida Scientist* 50 (Supplement 1): 36.

Gould-Beierle, K. L., and A. C. Kamil. 1998. Use of landmarks in three species of food-storing corvids. *Ethology* 104:361–78.

Grubb, T. C., Jr., G. E. Woolfenden, and J. W. Fitzpatrick. 1998. Factors affecting nutritional condition of fledgling Florida scrub-jays: A ptilochronology approach. *Condor* 100:753–56.

Hailman, J. P., K. G. McGowan, and G. E. Woolfenden. 1994. Role of helpers in the sentinel behavior of the Florida scrub jay (*Aphelocoma c. coerulescens*). *Ethology* 97:119–40.

Hokit, D. G., B. M. Stith, and L. C. Branch. 1999. Effects of landscape structure in Florida scrub: a population perspective. *Ecological Applications* 9:124–34.

Laessle, A. M. 1958. The origin and successional relationships of sandhill vegetation and sand-pine scrub. *Ecological Monographs* 28:361–87.

McDonald, D. B., J. W. Fitzpatrick, and G. E. Woolfenden. 1996. Actuarial senescence and demographic heterogeneity in the Florida scrub jay. *Ecology* 77:2373–81.

McGowan, K. J., and G. E. Woolfenden. 1989. A sentinel system in the Florida scrub jay. *Animal Behavior* 37:1000–6.

Menges, E. S. 1998. Ecology and conservation of Florida scrub. Pp. 7–22 in *Savannas, Barrens, and Rock Outcrop Communities of North America,* ed. R. C. Anderson et al. Cambridge University Press.

Mumme, R. L. 1992. Do helpers increase reproductive success? An experimental analysis in the Florida scrub jay. *Behavioral Ecology and Sociobiology* 31:319–28.

Mumme, R. L., and T. H. Below. 1995. *Relocation as a Management Technique for the Threatened Florida Scrub Jay.* Florida Game and Fresh Water Fish Commission Nongame Wildlife Program Project NG88-043 Final Report. 48 pp.

Mumme, R. L., and T. H. Below. 1999. Evaluation of translocation for the threatened Florida scrub-jay. *Journal of Wildlife Management* 63:833–42.

Myers, R. L. 1990. Scrub and high pine. Pp. 154–93 in *Ecosystems of Florida,* ed. R. L. Myers and J. J. Ewel. University of Central Florida Press.

Ripple, J. 1994. Florida's scrub jays. *Florida Wildlife* 48(3):14–15.

Root, K. V. 1998. Evaluating the effects of habitat quality, connectivity, and catastrophes on a threatened species. *Ecological Applications* 8:854–65.

Schaub, R., R. L. Mumme, and G. E. Woolfenden. 1992. Predation on the eggs and nestlings of Florida scrub jays. *Auk* 109:585–93.

Schoech, S. J. 1996. The effect of supplemental food on body condition and the timing of reproduction in a cooperative breeder, the Florida scrub-jay. *Condor* 98:234–44.

Schoech, S. J. 1998. Physiology of helping in Florida scrub-jays. *American Scientist* 86:70–71.

Schoech, S. J., R. L. Mumme, and M. C. Moore. 1991. Reproductive endocrinology and mechanisms of breeding inhibition in cooperatively breeding Florida scrub jays. *Condor* 93:354–64.

Schoech, S. J., R. L. Mumme, and J. C. Wingfield. 1996. Delayed breeding in the cooperatively breeding Florida scrub-jay (*Aphelocoma coerulescens*): Inhibition or the absence of stimulation. *Behavioral Ecology and Sociobiology* 39:77–90.

Schoech, S. J., R. L. Mumme, and J. C. Wingfield. 1996. Prolactin and helping behavior in the cooperatively breeding Florida scrub-jay, *Aphelocoma c. coerulescens*. *Animal Behavior* 52:445–56.

Snodgrass, J. W., T. Townsend, and P. Brabitz. 1993. The status of scrub and scrub jays in Brevard County, Florida. *Florida Field Naturalist* 21:69–74.

Stallcup, J. A., and G. E. Woolfenden. 1978. Family status and contribution to breeding by Florida scrub jays. *Animal Behavior* 26:1144–56.

Thaxton, J. E., and T. M. Hingtgen. 1996. Effects of suburbanization and habitat fragmentation on Florida scrub-jay dispersal. *Florida Field Naturalist* 24:25–60.

U.S. Fish and Wildlife Service. 1990. *Florida Scrub Jay Recovery Plan.* U.S. Fish and Wildlife Service. 23 pp.

U.S. Fish and Wildlife Service. 1999. Florida scrub-jay. Pp. 4/261–90 in *South Florida Multi-Species Recovery Plan,* U.S. Fish and Wildlife Service.

Woolfenden, G. E. 1974. Nesting and survival in a population of Florida scrub jays. *Living Bird* 12:25–49.

Woolfenden, G. E., and J. W. Fitzpatrick. 1984. *The Florida Scrub Jay: Demography of a Cooperative-breeding Bird.* Princeton University Press Monographs in Population Biology no. 20. 406 pp.

Woolfenden, G. E., and J. W. Fitzpatrick. 1990. Florida scrub jay: A synopsis after 18 years of study. Pp. 241–66 in *Cooperative Breeding in Birds,* ed. P. B. Stacey and W. B. Koenig. Cambridge University Press.

Woolfenden, G. E., and J. W. Fitzpatrick. 1991. Florida scrub jay ecology and conservation. Pp. 542–65 in *Bird Population Studies: Relevance to Conservation and Management,* ed. C. M. Perrins et al. Oxford University Press.

Woolfenden, G. E., and J. W. Fitzpatrick. 1996. Florida scrub jay. Pp. 267–80 in *Rare and Endangered Biota of Florida,* vol. 5: *Birds,* ed. J. A. Rodgers, Jr., et al. University Press of Florida

Woolfenden, G. E., and J. W. Fitzpatrick. 1996. *Florida Scrub-jay.* Birds of North America no. 228, American Ornithologists' Union. 27 pp.

5

∾ ∾

Florida Grasshopper Sparrow

Status

The grasshopper sparrow (*Ammodramus savannarum;* Order Passeriformes; Family Emberizidae; Subfamily Emberizinae) occurs sporadically throughout much of North America, southward through Central America to Ecuador, and in the West Indies. Twelve subspecies are recognized, of which two occur in Florida: the eastern grasshopper sparrow (*A. s. pratensis*) and the Florida grasshopper sparrow (*A. s. floridanus*). The eastern subspecies is an overwintering migrant in the state, whereas the Florida grasshopper sparrow is a nonmigratory, year-round resident. Except during winter, Florida grasshopper sparrows are geographically disjunct from other *A. savannarum* subspecies by >300 miles (500 km). Four other congeneric *Ammodramus* species occur in Florida: the seaside sparrow (*A. maritimus*), sharp-tailed sparrow (*A. caudacutus*), Henslow's sparrow (*A. henslowii*), and LeConte's sparrow (*A. leconteii*).

The prairie region of the south-central peninsula, from central Polk and central Osceola counties southward into Hendry County, constitutes the historic range of the Florida grasshopper sparrow. Populations were characterized as large and widespread within that range in the early 1900s, but no quantitative data exist. Habitat loss in recent decades has resulted in both contraction of the overall range and fragmentation of suitable habitat within that range.

The known remaining range encompasses Glades, Highlands, and Okeechobee counties and portions of Osceola, Polk, Hardee, DeSoto, and Hendry counties, but only six breeding sites are known. Thirteen occurrence sites were known as recently as the mid-1970s, but six of those sites are no longer occupied. Based on systematic counts of singing males, and assuming a sex ratio of 1:1, the minimum number of breeding adults occupying the six known sites is ≈712. The number comprising the total population, however, is no doubt considerably higher than that minimum. An unknown percentage of the total population at any given time would be made up of juveniles and other nonbreeders, and unconfirmed (but credible) reports exist of occurrence sites on private lands both within and outside the known range. Other occurrence sites may also exist but thus far remain undetected.

The primary threat to the sparrow's welfare is conversion of prairie to farmland, pastureland, and pine plantations and degradation of habitat quality due to incompatible range management regimes, particularly fire exclusion.

The Florida Game and Fresh Water Fish Commission listed the Florida grasshopper sparrow as an endangered species in 1975, and the U.S. Fish and Wildlife Service federally listed it as endangered in 1986.

Distinguishing Characteristics

Florida grasshopper sparrows (fig. 14) attain ≈5 in (12.7 cm) in length and weigh ≈0.6 ounces (17.2 g). The top of the head is rather flattened and mostly black but with a light median stripe. The eyes are ringed in white, a gray to ochre stripe occurs over the eyes, and the lores are orange. The feathers on the upper parts of the body are black edged with gray, the bend of the wing is yellow, and the underparts are whitish and unstreaked, tinged with buff on the throat, breast, and sides. The feet are pinkish. The sexes are essentially indistinguishable in the field, but there are subtle dimorphic differences in wing length and in weight. Juvenile plumage is similar to that of adults but the breast is streaked. The other grasshopper sparrow subspecies, collectively, are dorsally lighter and ventrally darker in coloration. Grasshopper sparrows are relatively short-tailed compared to most other sparrows.

The male's primary song consists of two or three *chips* followed by a grasshopper-like buzz (hence the species' common name). A secondary song is a more sustained and more melodious series of rambling notes. Both songs are relatively indistinct and are among the weakest in any North American bird.

The only other breeding sparrow that would be encountered where Florida grasshopper sparrows breed is the Bachman's sparrow, but that species is grayer in color and has a longer tail, rounder head, and more melodious song.

Fig. 14. Male Florida grasshopper sparrow (Barry Mansell).

Habitat

Florida grasshopper sparrows occur in poorly drained, early successional bunchgrass grasslands that are sparsely vegetated, shrubby, and abundantly interspersed with small patches of bare ground (fig. 15). Saw-palmetto (*Serenoa repens*) is typically dominant where grasshopper sparrows occur, but dwarf live oak (*Quercus minima*), pawpaws (*Asimina* spp.), gopher apple (*Licania michauxii*), St. Johns worts (*Hypericum* spp.), wiregrass (*Aristida* spp.), yellow-eyed grass (*Xyris* spp.), and bluestems (*Andropogon* spp.) are also common.

From a microhabitat perspective, Florida grasshopper sparrows usually occur in those areas of a particular grassland where the palmettos and/

Fig. 15. Florida grasshopper sparrow habitat (Michael F. Delany).

or other shrubby vegetation such as dwarf live oaks are of relatively low height, ≈1–2 feet (0.3-0.6 m), the areal shrub cover is 10–34 percent, and the cumulative areal extent of bare ground totals 20–34 percent. Historically, such areas were most often the result of frequent fires, so the subspecies' distribution on a given grassland, and to some extent throughout its geographic range, was likely dynamic over time, dependent on the frequency and location of natural fires.

Natural fires still occur and affect grasshopper sparrow distribution, but certain areas under low-intensity fire maintenance as rangelands mirror natural conditions, and thereby support grasshopper sparrow populations (two of the six currently known occurrence sites are grazed by cattle). However, such management is compatible with grasshopper sparrow presence only so long as clumped or shrubby vegetation (necessary for nesting) is not altogether removed, and patches of bare ground (necessary for unrestricted movement during foraging and other activity) remain, and only so long as burning remains the primary management strategy and approximates natural frequencies (every 2–3 years).

Life History and Behavior

Florida grasshopper sparrows occur in scattered breeding aggregations of a few up to ≥200 pairs. Pairs are monogamous, the breeding season extends from mid-March through July, and 2–3 broods can be produced annually. Breeding territories are widely spaced throughout a breeding site and range from ≈1.5 acres (0.6 ha) to ≈12.0 acres (4.8 ha) in size, averaging ≈4.4 acres (1.8 ha). Nests are typically domed and constructed of grass and grasslike monocots and are situated on the ground in shallow depressions sheltered by saw-palmetto, dwarf live oak, or clumps of wiregrass, yellow-eyed grass, or other vegetation. The availability of small clumps of dense vegetation in a matrix with sparser vegetation apparently is an important factor influencing nest site selection.

Nest diameter is ≈4 in (10 cm) and height is ≈3 in (8 cm). Clutch size is 3–5 eggs, incubation lasts 11–12 days, and the young fledge at age nine days. The eggs are white with reddish brown speckles. Only the female incubates and broods, but both parents care for fledglings. Breeding territories are often adjacent to or overlap those of Bachman's sparrows, but Bachman's sparrows typically nest in areas with taller, denser saw-palmetto than do grasshopper sparrows.

Florida grasshopper sparrows forage on the ground, feeding ≈70 percent on animal matter, primarily insects and arachnids, and ≈30 percent on vegetable matter, mostly seeds of sedges and grasses. Animal matter dominates the diet during spring and summer; vegetable matter dominates during winter. Adults have atypically high annual survival rates (≈60 percent) and long life spans (average three years) compared to most other passerines. Those factors, in combination with a relatively high reproductive potential (2–3 broods annually), render the subspecies physiologically amenable to relatively rapid recovery from population ebbs. Nest predation and nests flooding, however, may be significant limiting factors in that respect. Known adult mortality factors include collisions with vehicles and predation.

Little is known about Florida grasshopper sparrow activity during winter, but adults apparently remain in the general vicinity of their breeding territories year-round. Winter movements of up to 2.2 miles (3.6 km) from breeding territories have been documented (via radiotelemetry). Contributing to that dearth of knowledge is the fact that eastern grasshopper sparrows are present in Florida during winter. Even mere observations of grasshopper sparrows in winter, then, would have minimal significance in terms of defining winter movements and other activity unless observers were exceptionally skilled in differentiating between these two similar subspecies.

Survey and Monitoring Techniques

Surveys to document presence or absence of grasshopper sparrows or to calculate population numbers and densities should be designed to take into account their secretive and otherwise inconspicuous behavior. The most effective method is to search for males during the time of year when they are singing (early April through July). Males sing throughout the day during that time but most frequently from sunrise to about 9:00 A.M. Surveying personnel should walk transects ≈150 feet (50 m) apart, stopping frequently for visual and auditory scans. Males usually sing perched atop shrubs, so visual scans should be focused on the tops of vegetation. Binoculars would be essential. Playbacks of a taped territorial song can also be useful in that males will seek out "intruders."

Nests are difficult to locate and are most often found only by diligently searching locations from which a female was flushed or to which adults have been observed carrying food items.

Mist netting is the most efficient and effective method of capturing grasshopper sparrows for leg banding or other purposes. For best results, nets should be deployed between two shrubs known to be used as singing perches by the resident male, and/or birds can be lured into nets by playing a taped territorial song. Following the modified net-deploying technique of Delany et al. (1992) would further increase efficiency. The appropriate U.S. Fish and Wildlife Service aluminum leg band size for grasshopper sparrows is 1.

Management

Fundamental Management Considerations

- Early successional, treeless (but shrubby) bunchgrass grassland, with bare ground cumulatively totaling 20–34 percent of a given area, constitutes optimum habitat for the Florida grasshopper sparrow.
- Florida grasshopper sparrows are apparently locally nomadic in

terms of seeking out and occupying suitable habitat and as such would likely colonize created or rehabilitated habitat, provided that such areas are near occupied habitat.

• From a genetic perspective, the six remaining subpopulations of Florida grasshopper sparrows can be considered a single management unit. Genetic similarities among them suggest either that they were isolated from one another relatively recently or that interpopulation emigration/immigration occurs, or has recently occurred, at some level.

Proactive Management

1. Habitat Maintenance

Periodic prescribed burning is the most effective and efficient strategy in terms of maintaining the grassland characteristics required by grasshopper sparrows. Although more research is needed as regards the most advantageous timing of prescribed burns, current knowledge indicates that they should be executed at intervals of two to three years, or whenever either the palmetto/shrub cover exceeds 2 feet (0.6 m) in height or significant grass litter has accumulated. Winter (November–January) burns would preclude loss of nests or nestlings to fire and would achieve the needed successional retardation, but experimental growing-season burns have been demonstrated to extend the breeding season. Spring–summer burning may, therefore, increase overall productivity in the treatment year and may perhaps have further benefits. However, should such growing-season burns be employed, precautions should be taken to minimize the potential for nest loss and nestling mortality. The core of the nesting period (May through June) should be avoided in that respect, back fires (burning against the wind) should be utilized, and the treatment area should be subdivided such that no more than one-third of its extent is burned in a given year.

2. Population Expansion

Although this has not so far been tested, it is likely that populations of grasshopper sparrows can be expanded and new subpopulations established via rehabilitating areas of previously suitable habitat. Should such targeted areas be pastures or abandoned farmlands, the desired prairie-like conditions should return <5 years after abandonment, at which time burning schedules can be initiated. However, roller chopping pretreatments and/or manual removal of woody vegetation may be necessary in areas where long-term fire exclusion has resulted in such advanced successional stages as to be nonconducive to retardation via fire. Growing-season (spring–summer) burns can also be effective in rehabilitating overgrown habitats. The size of areas targeted for rehabilitation would be unimportant where these are adjacent to occupied habitat (the outcome would be an expansion of the existing population), but targeted areas disjunct from occupied areas should be ≥600 acres (240 ha) in size. Areas of that size are required to sustain at least 50 breeding pairs, which is considered the minimum long-term viability threshold for grasshopper sparrow subpopulations.

3. Demographic Health

Wherever feasible, corridors of prairie-like habitat linking disjunct subpopulations should be created and/or maintained to enhance the potential for genetic interchange among those subpopulations.

Accommodative Management

Agricultural enterprises, primarily intense livestock grazing, constitute the primary conflicting land use in terms of grasshopper sparrow welfare. Grasshopper sparrows can, however, coexist in grasslands managed for grazing purposes, provided that burn schedules, stocking rates, and other management strategies are tailored to accommodate grasshopper sparrow presence. Such tailored range management is in place where grasshopper sparrows occur on Avon Park Air Force Bombing Range and, insofar as stocking strategies are concerned, indicates that one animal per 20 acres (8 ha) and grazing regimes of ≤21 days, followed by longer periods of stock exclusion, are compatible in that regard, although more research is needed to determine upper and lower limits with precision.

Relevant Literature

Abrahamson, W. G., and D. C. Hartnett. 1990. Pine flatwoods and dry prairies. Pp. 103–49 in *Ecosystems of Florida,* ed. R. L. Myers and J. J. Ewel. University of Central Florida Press.

Capece, J. C., M. Mozaffari, and G. T. Bancroft. 1998. Agroecology research for sustaining sub-tropical prairie ecosystems on beef cattle ranches of Florida.

Proceedings of the Annual Conference on Ecosystem Restoration and Creation 24:70–81.

Dean, T. F., M. F. Delany, E. W. Chapman, and P. D. Vickery. 1998. Longevity and site fidelity of Florida grasshopper sparrows. *Journal of Field Ornithology* 69:51–54.

Delany, M. F. 1992. Netting and banding Florida grasshopper sparrows. *North American Bird Bander* 17:45–47.

Delany, M. F. 1994. Banding together for the Florida grasshopper sparrow. *Endangered Species Technical Bulletin* 19(6):8–9.

Delany, M. F. 1995. Small wonders: Florida grasshopper sparrows. *Florida Naturalist* 68:11.

Delany, M. F. 1996. Florida grasshopper sparrow. Pp. 128–36 in *Rare and Endangered Biota of Florida,* vol. 5: *Birds,* ed. J. A. Rodgers, Jr., et al. University Press of Florida.

Delany, M. F. 1997. Florida's prairie. *Endangered Species Bulletin* 22(4):14–15.

Delany, M. F., and J. A. Cox. 1986. Florida grasshopper sparrow breeding distribution and abundance in 1984. *Florida Field Naturalist* 14:100–4.

Delany, M. F., and S. B. Linda. 1994. Characteristics of occupied and abandoned Florida grasshopper sparrow territories. *Florida Field Naturalist* 22:106–9.

Delany, M. F., and S. B. Linda. 1998. Characteristics of Florida grasshopper nests. *Wilson Bulletin* 110:136–39.

Delany, M. F., and S. B. Linda. 1998. Nesting habitat of Florida grasshopper sparrows at Avon Park Air Force Range. *Florida Field Naturalist* 26:33–39.

Delany, M. F., J. T. Giesel, and D. A. Brazeau. 2000. Genetic variability among populations of the Florida grasshopper sparrow. *Journal of Wildlife Management* 64:631–36.

Delany, M. F., C. T. Moore, and D. R. Progulske, Jr. 1994. Distinguishing gender of Florida grasshopper sparrows using body measurements. *Florida Field Naturalist* 22:48–51.

Delany, M. F., C. T. Moore, and D. R. Progulske, Jr. 1995. Territory size and movements of Florida grasshopper sparrows. *Journal of Field Ornithology* 66:305–9.

Delany, M. F., D. W. Perkins, and B. Pranty. 1998. *Florida Grasshopper Sparrow Demography: Avon Park Air Force Range.* U.S. Air Force/Florida Cooperative Fish and Wildlife Research Unit Research Work Order no. 175 Final Report. 64 pp.

Delany, M. F., D. R. Progulske, Jr., and S. D. Coltman. 1992. Netting and banding Florida grasshopper sparrows. *North American Bird Bander* 17:45–47.

Delany, M. F., H. M. Stevenson, and R. McCracken. 1985. Distribution, abundance, and habitat of the Florida grasshopper sparrow. *Journal of Wildlife Management* 49:626–31.

Karr, J. R. 1981. Surveying birds with mist nets. Pp. 62–67 in *Estimating Numbers of Terrestrial Birds,* ed. C. J. Ralph and J. M. Scott. Cooper Ornithological Society Studies in Avian Biology no. 6.

Perkins, D. W., P. D. Vickery, T. F. Dean, and M. D. Scheurell. 1998. Florida grasshopper sparrow reproductive success based on nesting records. *Florida Field Naturalist* 26:7–17.

Pranty, B. 2000. Three sources of Florida grasshopper sparrow mortality. *Florida Field Naturalist* 28:27–29.

Quinlan, S. E., and R. L. Boyd. 1976. Mist netting success in relation to weather. *North American Bird Bander* 1:168–70.

Shriver, W. G., and P. D. Vickery. 1999. Aerial assessment of potential Florida grasshopper sparrow habitat: Conservation in a fragmented landscape. *Florida Field Naturalist* 27:1–9.

Shriver, W. G., P. D. Vickery, and S. A. Hedges. 1996. Effects of summer burns on Florida grasshopper sparrows. *Florida Field Naturalist* 24:68–73.

Shriver, W. G., P. D. Viskery, and D. W. Perkins. 1999. The effects of summer burns on breeding Florida graasshopper and Bachman's sparrows. *Studies in Avian Biology* 19:144–48.

Smith, R. L. 1968. Grasshopper sparrow. Pp. 725–45 in *Life Histories of North American Cardinals, Buntings, Towhees, Sparrows, and Allies,* ed. O. L. Austin, Jr. U.S. National Museum Bulletin 237[2].

U.S. Fish and Wildlife Service. 1988. *Recovery Plan for the Florida Grasshopper Sparrow.* U.S. Fish and Wildlife Service. 22 pp.

U.S. Fish and Wildlife Service. 1999. Florida grasshopper sparrow. Pp. 4/371–92 in *South Florida Multi-Species Recovery Plan,* U.S. Fish and Wildlife Service.

Vickery, P. D. 1996. *Grasshopper Sparrow.* Birds of North America no. 239, American Ornithologists' Union. 23 pp.

Walsh, P. B., D. A. Darrow, and J. G. Dyess. 1995. Habitat selection by Florida grasshopper sparrows in response to fire. *Proceedings of the Annual Conference of the Southeastern Association of Fish and Wildlife Agencies* 49:340–47.

Whitmore, R. C. 1981. Structural characteristics of grasshopper sparrow habitat. *Journal of Wildlife Management* 45:811–14.

6

Fox Squirrel

Status

The fox squirrel (*Sciurus niger*) is among three species of squirrels (Order Rodentia; Family Sciuridae) native to Florida, the others being the gray squirrel (*S. carolinensis*) and the southern flying squirrel (*Glaucomys volans*). Fox squirrels occur over most of central and eastern North America, with ten subspecies recognized, three of which occur in Florida—the southern fox squirrel (*S. n. niger*), Sherman's fox squirrel (*S. n. shermani*), and Big Cypress fox squirrel (*S. n. avicennia*).

The generally accepted geographic range delineations for the three Florida subspecies (fig. 16) are based primarily on subtle differences in morphological characteristics rather than on genetic analyses. The prevailing thought is that the Florida Panhandle from the Aucilla River westward constitutes the range of the southern fox squirrel in the state; the subspecies' total range extends northerly and northeasterly through southeastern Alabama, most of Georgia, the Carolinas, to and including southern Virginia. The accepted range of the Sherman's fox squirrel extends from the Georgia piedmont southward through the Florida Peninsula (eastward from the Aucilla River) to a line roughly from Manatee County on the Gulf Coast to southeastern Palm Beach County on the Atlantic Coast. And the range of the Big Cypress fox squirrel is southwest Florida south of the Caloosahatchee River and west of the Everglades. The Big Cypress fox squirrel also formerly occurred east of the Everglades, in extreme eastern Dade and Broward counties, but that population, which included intergrades between Big Cypress and Sherman's fox squirrels, is now extirpated.

The taxonomic status of and distributional delineation for the Big Cypress fox squirrel seem irrefutable considering that its range is altogether disjunct from those of other fox squirrel subspecies and that it has distinc-

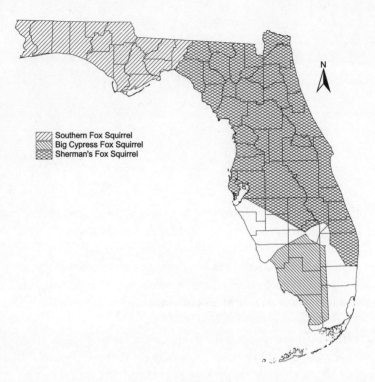

Southern Fox Squirrel
Big Cypress Fox Squirrel
Sherman's Fox Squirrel

Fig. 16. Ranges of the three subspecies of fox squirrels occurring in Florida.

tive morphological and behavioral characteristics. But with respect to the Sherman's and southern fox squirrels, it has been postulated that the more westerly Apalachicola River rather than the Aucilla River represents the range barrier between those two subspecies. Genetic (e.g., DNA) analyses are needed to confirm or adjust the accepted distributional delineations of the Sherman's and southern subspecies.

The Florida Game and Fresh Water Fish Commission designated the Big Cypress fox squirrel an endangered species in 1973 but reclassified it to threatened in 1979. The Sherman's fox squirrel was designated a threatened species in 1975 but reassigned to the species of special concern category in 1979. The southern fox squirrel is not listed in either category.

Only ≈10 percent of Florida's original longleaf pine (*Pinus palustris*) forestland and only ≈20 percent of the state's original slash pine (*P. elliottii*) forestland remain intact today, and mature longleaf pine- and slash pine–dominated forests constitute the primary fox squirrel habitats in Florida. At least inferentially, then, fox squirrel numbers and distribution in Florida, regardless of subspecies, have declined significantly over the past several decades, due primarily to conversion and degradation of habitat. As a result, fox squirrels now occur in the state in a patchwork pattern of isolated subpopulations, many of which are small and/or continuing to decline in numbers. Such isolation renders the individual subpopulations particularly vulnerable. Not only is extirpation or further decimation more likely due to localized single events (e.g., disease outbreaks, catastrophic storms, or profound land-use changes), but demographic erosion and a source/sink system can become established as a result of inbreeding, prevention of dispersal, and other problems associated with limited genetic variability. In large part because of those evolving factors, in 1991 the Florida Game and Fresh Water Fish Commission imposed a year-round closure on recreational fox squirrel hunting on all commission-administered wildlife management areas in the state, and in 1996 it expanded that closure to include the entire state. Fox squirrel hunting in the south Florida counties occupied by the threatened Big Cypress fox squirrel has been prohibited since 1973.

Distinguishing Characteristics

Although each of Florida's three fox squirrels has a black crown and cheeks, and white muzzle and ears (or ear tips), they are otherwise highly variable in pelage coloration, both within and between subspecies. Dominant body color patterns occur among the subspecies, however, as well as among individual populations. Big Cypress fox squirrels are most typically rust to orange-buffy with a dark back, less commonly uniformly tan or uniformly black. Tan is the most frequently appearing color in Sherman's fox squirrels (fig. 17), with most individuals being uniformly tan, tan with black underparts, or black with tan underparts. Some individuals, however, are uniformly black. Gray is the dominant color in southern fox squirrels, with most being silvery to dark gray with white or black underparts, but some individuals are uniformly black or black with rusty underparts.

The Big Cypress fox squirrel is the smallest of the three subspecies, averaging ≈21 in (54 cm) in total length (head + body + tail) and ≈2.0 lb (900 g) in weight. Sherman's fox squirrel is the largest, averaging ≈25 in (63 cm) in total length and ≈2.5 lb (1100 g) in weight, and the southern fox

Fig. 17. Adult Sherman's fox squirrel (Barry Mansell).

squirrel is intermediate in size. In each of the subspecies, tail length is roughly equal to head plus body length.

Habitat

Fox squirrel habitat in Florida can be generically characterized as a mixture of mast-producing tree species, primarily pine-oak assemblages. Sherman's and southern fox squirrels are essentially dependent on open, mature, upland pine-oak communities, most often dominated by longleaf pine and turkey oak (*Quercus laevis*) but with the oak component interspersed with post oaks (*Q. stellata*), live oaks (*Q. virginiana*), southern red oaks (*Q. falcata*), laurel oaks (*Q. hemisphaerica*), or bluejack oaks (*Q. incana*) or various combinations of these. Not uncommonly, however, loblolly pine (*P. taeda*), slash pine, or sand pine (*P. clausa*) is the dominant or codominant pine species present.

Other habitats used to some extent by Sherman's and southern fox squirrels are bottomland and upland hardwood forests and cypress (*Taxodium* spp.) domes and strands but only when they are adjacent to or interspersed within a pine-oak community. Suburban parks and golf courses are also used to some extent, and in south-central Florida a number of savanna-like (pine-oak) improved pastures mirror natural pine-oak habitats and are occupied by Sherman's fox squirrels.

Big Cypress fox squirrels occur in more diverse habitats, most typically slash pine flatwoods and cypress forest but also tropical hardwood hammocks, live oak woods, mangrove forest, and suburban habitats such as golf courses and parks. Cabbage palm (*Sabal palmetto*) is a common habitat component in most of those associations.

Life History and Behavior

Florida's fox squirrels have two pronounced breeding seasons per year, one extending from early May through August and the other from late November through January, although females usually produce only one litter per year. The sexes associate with each other only during breeding activity, at which times mating chases (i.e., ≥2 males chasing a single female) are frequent. Vocalizing is also frequent during breeding activity, although uncommon during nonbreeding periods.

Mean litter size is 2.3. The young remain in the brood nest for ≈75 days and wean at age ≈90 days. Sexual maturity is reached at age ≈9 months. Longevity in the wild is unknown, but captive fox squirrels have lived >13 years.

Although fox squirrels elsewhere commonly nest in tree cavities, especially during winter, in Florida they seldom do. Instead, they construct exposed nest platforms of leaves, Spanish moss (*Tillandsia usneoides*), twigs, pine needles, and other vegetative material. Big Cypress fox squirrels also commonly incorporate strips of cypress bark into nests. Southern and Sherman's fox squirrels typically situate their nests high in oaks, less frequently in longleaf pines, whereas Big Cypress fox squirrels construct their nests in slash pines, oaks, cabbage palms, and cypress trees. Nests in cypress often are within large clumps of bromeliads. Individuals may construct up to 30 nests in any given year, and each may be used for shelter from only once to >10 times. Any given nest, then, is of significant consequence in terms of fox squirrel welfare only when it is being occupied.

The primary food items of southern and Sherman's fox squirrels are longleaf and slash pine seeds, turkey oak acorns, and live oak acorns. Supplemental foods include acorns of other oak species, hickory nuts, bulbs, mushrooms and other fungi, vegetative buds, staminate pine cones, insects, and various farm crops, especially pecans, corn, and peanuts. Pine cones are cut while still green (May through October), and acorns are harvested beginning in late September, some of which may be cached for later retrieval.

Slash pine seeds are the primary food of the Big Cypress fox squirrel, with the male cones (microstrobili) harvested mostly during winter and the female cones (macrostrobili) mostly during summer. Supplemental foods include cypress cone seeds (especially during fall through early winter), cabbage palm fruits, bromeliad buds, acorns, mushrooms and other fungi, queen palm (*Cocos pamosa*) fruits, and fig (*Ficus* spp.) fruits. Food availability is a crucial habitat component for each subspecies. In years of poor acorn production, complete reproductive failures have occurred during the winter breeding season, and seasonal habitat use patterns can be profoundly affected by the abundance or paucity of food resources.

Fox squirrel home ranges in Florida average ≈100 acres (40 ha) in size for males and ≈50 acres (20 ha) for females, considerably larger than are typical in more northern and western populations. However, home range size, configuration, and use vary dramatically over time with seasonal availability of food resources, with reproductive activity, and with weather. Adjacent home ranges of males overlap extensively, but their core areas do not, although they are not aggressively defended. Female home ranges overlap to a much lesser degree, and their core areas are aggressively defended from other females.

Survey and Monitoring Techniques

Southern and Sherman's fox squirrels occupy open habitats, and the animals' size and striking color patterns render them relatively conspicuous where they occur. Mere presence or absence, then, can usually be determined by visual observation. Where there are enough roads, slow, vehicular road transects can yield results in that respect, but field transects may be necessary where roads are scarce. In pine flatwoods or open pine-oak habitats, such transects could be ≈300 feet (100 m) apart without loss of

areal coverage, but in denser habitats, transects should be spaced according to range of visibility.

In contrast, Big Cypress fox squirrels more commonly occupy habitats
with dense saw-palmetto (*Serenoa repens*) comprising the understory and
are thus more difficult to observe directly. Accordingly, road or field transects would yield more definitive results if supplemented with surveys for
stripped bark in cypress-dominated stands, which would indicate possible
fox squirrel presence. Gray squirrels, however, also strip bark from cypress trees, so casual observation of trees with stripped bark would require concentrated follow-up observations to confirm the presence or
absence of fox squirrels.

The presence of cored pine cones and/or leaf nests in a given area would
indicate possible fox squirrel presence (regardless of the subspecies), even
if the animals are not seen, but can also indicate gray squirrel presence.
Such areas might therefore be targeted for concentrated follow-up surveys.

Some degree of stealth and diligence is necessary when surveying for
any of the subspecies. Fox squirrels commonly react to disturbance either
by climbing high and remaining silent and motionless until the disturbance passes or by fleeing on the ground.

The most advantageous times of day to survey for fox squirrels is
shortly after dawn and before dusk, when squirrel activity is most intense,
and seasonally during peak periods of breeding activity (mid-May
through July and December through January), when vocalizations are
freqent and males and females are associating with each other via mating
chases. Also, the young are very active after leaving nests, so that period
would likewise be an advantageous time to conduct surveys. However, fox
squirrel daily activity patterns tend to encompass secondary habitats (e.g.,
mangroves, cypress forest, etc.) more frequently during the summer rainy
season, particularly in southern Florida. Surveys during that period
should therefore take that fact into account.

Because fox squirrels are reluctant to enter live traps, capture operations for mark-and-release work require some degree of preparation. Bait-
ing and wiring traps open for several weeks prior to capture operations to
habituate squirrels to the traps might increase ultimate trapping success,
but that strategy is not always successful.

Number 104 and Number 203 Tomahawk™ double-door traps are
adequate and appropriately sized for capturing fox squirrels, and peanuts

in the shell are an effective bait, although bird seed, bananas, shelled corn, and pecans placed on peanut butter also work. Peanut butter and bananas, however, attract fire ants (*Solenopsis invicta*) and hence should not be used where fire ants occur.

Placement of traps can affect trapping success, with effective options being (1) on the ground next to large mast trees (oaks in fall or early winter, pines at other times), (2) wired vertically to tree trunks, (3) wired horizontally on tree limbs, or (4) wired horizontally on L-shaped platforms attached to trunks. Traps should be checked at least twice a day and covered with Spanish moss or some other shading material during hot weather.

The American Society of Mammalogists' (1998) guidelines for the capture, handling, and care of mammals in general might also be consulted prior to embarking on any fox squirrel capture operations.

Management

Fundamental Management Considerations

- Of primary importance to fox squirrels in Florida is the long-term availability of abundant food resources (tree mast). Because mast production among tree species is seasonally asynchronous and year-to-year production is highly variable (especially among oak species), a diverse assemblage of mast-producing tree species is necessary. Moreover, mature trees are more consistent mast producers and produce more mast than do younger trees; the survival and welfare of older trees are thus important.

- Of secondary importance to fox squirrels in Florida, particularly in pine, pine-oak, and savanna-like habitats, is an open understory.

Proactive Management

Periodic prescribed burning should be the management strategy of choice to produce the habitat characteristics needed to promote fox squirrel welfare. Burning promotes mast production yet accommodates seed germination, regeneration, and growth of desirable mast-producing trees and also maintains an open understory. Burns at intervals of 1–2 years would yield best results in that respect but should be executed under climatic conditions and using techniques (e.g., back fires) that would preclude crown fires. Where burning is not feasible, mowing, roller chopping (but outside a tree's drip line), and/or other mechanical means can be employed to produce conditions that at least approach those that burning would produce.

Accommodative Management

Fox squirrels are highly tolerant of human presence, occurring in parks, on golf courses, and in association with other recreational facilities and also in low to mid-density suburban housing. The common denominator in those cases is that mast-producing trees were retained in the course of such facilities being developed, and an open understory is maintained. Livestock grazing is likewise not incompatible with fox squirrel welfare and can be beneficial and thereby useful in supplementing or augmenting proactive burning regimes. Grazing could, in fact, be employed as the principal strategy where burning is not feasible. It is not known, however, at what grazing levels and frequencies fox squirrels would most benefit.

Relevant Literature

American Society of Mammalogists. 1998. Guidelines for the capture, handling, and care of mammals as approved by the American Society of Mammalogists. *Journal of Mammalogy* 79:1416–31.

Arenz, C. L. 1997. Handling fox squirrels: Ketamine-hydrochloride versus a simple restraint. *Wildlife Society Bulletin* 25:107–9.

Baumgartner, L. L. 1940. Trapping, handling, and marking fox squirrels. *Journal of Wildlife Management* 4:444–50.

Benson, B. N. 1980. Dominance relationships, mating behavior and scent marking in fox squirrels (*Sciurus niger*). *Mammalia* 44:143–60.

Brown, B. W., and G. O. Batzli. 1984. Habitat selection by fox and gray squirrels: A multivariate analysis. *Journal of Wildlife Management* 48:616–21.

Edwards, J. W., and D. C. Guynn, Jr. 1995. Nest characteristics of sympatric populations of fox and gray squirrels. *Journal of Wildlife Management* 59:103–10.

Edwards, J. W., D. G. Heckel, and D. C. Guynn, Jr. 1998. Niche overlap in sympatric populations of fox and gray squirrels. *Journal of Wildlife Management* 62:354–63.

Huggins, J. G., and K. L. Gee. 1995. Efficiency and selectivity of cage trap sets for gray and fox squirrels. *Wildlife Society Bulletin* 23:204–7.

Humphrey, S. R., and P. G. R. Jodice. 1992. Big Cypress fox squirrel. Pp. 224–33 in *Rare and Endangered Biota of Florida,* vol. 1: *Mammals,* ed. S. R. Humphrey. University Press of Florida

Jodice, P. G. R. 1993. Movement patterns of translocated Big Cypress fox squirrels (*Sciurus niger avicennia*). *Florida Scientist* 56:1–6.

Jodice, P. G. R., and S. R. Humphrey. 1992. Activity and diet of an urban population of Big Cypress fox squirrels. *Journal of Wildlife Management* 56:685–92.

Jodice, P. G. R., and S. R. Humphrey. 1993. Activity and diet of an urban population of Big Cypress fox squirrels: A reply. *Journal of Wildlife Management* 57:930–33.

Kantola, A. T. 1992. Sherman's fox squirrel. Pp. 234–41 in *Rare and Endangered Biota of Florida*, vol. 1: *Mammals*, ed. S. R. Humphrey. University Press of Florida.

Kantola, A. T., and S. R. Humphrey. 1990. Habitat use by Sherman's fox squirrel (*Sciurus niger shermani*) in Florida. *Journal of Mammalogy* 71:411–19.

Loeb, S. C., and M. R. Lennartz. 1989. The fox squirrel (*Sciurus niger*) in southeastern pine-hardwood forests. Pp. 142–48 in *Proceedings of the Pine-hardwood Mixtures Symposium: Management and Ecology of the Type*, ed. T. A. Waldrop. Southeastern Forest Experiment Station General Technical Report SE-58.

Maehr, D. S. 1993. Activity and diet of an urban population of Big Cypress fox squirrels: A comment. *Journal of Wildlife Management* 57:929–30.

Moore, J. C. 1954. Fox squirrel receptionists. *Everglades Natural History* 2(3):152–60.

Moore, J. C. 1956. Variation in the fox squirrel in Florida. *American Midland Naturalist* 55:41–65.

Moore, J. C. 1957. The natural history of the fox squirrel *Sciurus niger shermani*. *Bulletin of the American Museum of Natural History* 113:1–71.

Turner, D. A., and J. Laerm. 1993. Systematic relationships of populations of the fox squirrel (*Sciurus niger*) in the southeastern United States. Pp. 21–36 in *Proceedings of the 2nd Symposium on Southeastern Fox Squirrels*, ed. N. D. Moncrief et al. Virginia Museum of Natural History Special Publication no. 1.

Weigl, P. D., M. A. Steele, L. J. Sherman, J. C. Ha, and T. S. Sharpe. 1989. *The Ecology of the Fox Squirrel in North Carolina: Implications for Survival in the Southeast*. Tall Timbers Research Station Publication no. 24. 93 pp.

Williams, K. S., and S. R. Humphrey. 1979. Distribution and status of the endangered Big Cypress fox squirrel (*Sciurus niger avicennia*) in Florida. *Florida Scientist* 42:201–5.

Wooding, J .B. 1990. *Status, Life History, and Management of Fox Squirrels in Florida*. Florida Game and Fresh Water Fish Commission Study 7555 Final Report. 13 pp.

Wooding, J. B. 1994. *Population Dynamics, Movement Ecology, and Management of Fox Squirrels in Florida*. Florida Game and Fresh Water Fish Commission Study 7558 Final Report. 31 pp.

7

Beach Mice

Status

Eight of 16 recognized subspecies of the old-field mouse (*Peromyscus polionotus;* Order Rodentia; Family Cricetidae) are collectively called beach mice and occur among coastal dune systems along Florida and Alabama coasts. Five of these eight subspecies occur along the coast of the Gulf of Mexico and the other three along the Atlantic Coast. The remaining eight *P. polionotus* subspecies occupy inland habitats throughout much of the Southeast, including the northern half of the Florida Peninsula. The cotton mouse (*P. gossypinus*) is the only other *Peromyscus* congener native to Florida.

Among the Gulf Coast subspecies, the Alabama beach mouse (*P. p. ammobates*) is restricted to the Fort Morgan Peninsula, between Mobile Bay and Perdido Bay, in Baldwin County, Alabama, and the Perdido Key beach mouse (*P. p. tryssyllepsis*) occurs only on Perdido Key, which is shared by Baldwin County, Alabama, and Escambia County, Florida. The other three Gulf Coast subspecies—the Santa Rosa beach mouse (*P. p. leucocephalus*), Choctawhatchee beach mouse (*P. p. allophrys*), and St. Andrew beach mouse (*P. p. peninsularis*)—are altogether confined to Florida, collectively distributed from Pensacola Bay in Escambia County eastward to Cape San Blas in Gulf County. The three Atlantic Coast subspecies—the Anastasia Island beach mouse (*P. p. phasma*), pallid beach mouse (*P. p. decoloratus*), and southeastern beach mouse (*P. p. niveiventris*)—are likewise confined to Florida, collectively distributed from Ponte Vedra Beach in St. Johns County southward to Hollywood Beach in Broward County.

Each of the beach mouse subspecies has undergone localized extirpations in recent decades due to beachfront development, which not only directly usurps habitat but also indirectly displaces beach mice. Dune systems adjacent to development sites have been invaded by house mice (*Mus musculus*), which can competitively exclude beach mice, and free-roaming house cats (*Felis catus*), which forage nocturnally, as do beach mice, and are highly efficient predators of small mammals. Typically, then, once beachfront development occurs, beach mice disappear not only from the affected site itself but also for considerable distances from it.

The collective distributions of the Alabama, Perdido Key, and Choctawhatchee beach mice may have been affected most in that respect. Those subspecies occupied a cumulative ≈100 linear miles (160 km) of coastline along the Gulf Coast as late as the early 1950s but are now patchily distributed along <22 linear miles (35 km), a reduction of ≈80 percent. Also, available habitat within the range of the southeastern beach mouse along the Atlantic Coast is estimated to have declined in extent by ≈50 percent in recent decades. As a result of that procession, most of the subspecies now have very limited distributions and occur in low numbers, and as such are formally designated endangered and/or threatened species by the jurisdictional governmental agencies involved (table 2).

The Alabama, Perdido Key, Choctawhatchee, and Anastasia Island beach mice, as federally designated endangered species, and the southeastern beach mouse as a threatened species are federally protected under the Endangered Species Act of 1973 (16 U.S.C. 1531). In addition to the "taking" prohibitions inherent in the Endangered Species Act, pursuant to Section 7 therein "critical habitat" has been designated for the Alabama, Perdido Key, and Choctawhatchee beach mice, within which no federal agency may fund, authorize, or participate in any activity that would result in the destruction or adverse modification of beach mouse habitat. Designated critical habitat for the Alabama beach mouse is subdivided into three stretches of coastline along the Fort Morgan Peninsula in Baldwin County, Alabama, and totals 10.6 linear miles (17.2 km). Designated critical habitat for the Perdido Key beach mouse encompasses three stretches of coastline on Perdido Key (Baldwin County, Alabama/Escambia County, Florida) and totals 9.8 linear miles (15.8 km), and critical habitat for the Choctawhatchee beach mouse totals 12.6 linear miles (20.2 km), subdivided into four units in Walton and Bay counties.

Table 2. Status of the eight subspecies of beach mice

Subspecies	Federal status	State status	Estimated population[a]	Historic range (counties)[b]
Gulf subspecies				
Alabama	Endangered	Not listed	<900	Baldwin (Ala.)
Perdido Key	Endangered	Endangered	<100	Baldwin(Ala.)/ Escambia
Santa Rosa	Not listed	Not listed	≈9,000	Escambia/Santa Rosa/Okaloosa
Choctawhatchee	Endangered	Endangered	<500	Okaloosa/ Walton/Bay
St. Andrew	Not listed	Endangered	≈500	Bay/Gulf
Atlantic subspecies				
Anastasia Island	Endangered	Endangered	≈5,000	St. Johns
Pallid	Not listed[c]	Endangered	0	Flagler/Volusia
Southeastern	Threatened	Threatened	?	Volusia/Brevard/ Indian River/ St. Lucie/Martin/ Palm Beach/ Broward

a. Total population numbers are dynamic over time, cyclically ebbing and flowing seasonally, and can be profoundly affected at any given time by catastrophic events such as hurricanes. Accordingly, the estimates here reflect approximate midpoints.

b. None of the subspecies occurs continuously through its respective range.

c. Considered extinct by the U.S. Fish and Wildlife Service.

Distinguishing Characteristics

Beach mice, collectively, have somewhat larger ears and are considerably paler in color than the inland subspecies of *P. polionotus*. The tail is haired and relatively short (<65 percent of head/body length) in comparison to that of other similar-sized mice. Total length (head + body + tail) ranges from ≈4.5 in (11.4 cm) to ≈5.5 in (14.0 cm). The underparts, feet, and legs are white, as are the cheeks and lower face (fig. 18). Size and coloration vary somewhat among the subspecies, and the Atlantic Coast subspecies are collectively somewhat larger than the Gulf Coast forms (table 3). Females are slightly larger than males in all the subspecies.

The most common other small rodent encountered in beach mouse habitat is the cotton mouse (*Peromyscus gossypinus*), but that species can

Fig. 18. St. Andrew beach mouse (Jeffrey A Gore).

be distinguished from beach mice by its larger size, being >6 in (15 cm) in total length; by being much darker in upper parts coloration (dark gray-brown) and having less extensive white on the underparts; and by smaller ears and proportionately longer tails (>65 percent of the head/body length). House mice may also be encountered in beach mouse habitat, particularly near human habitations, and are similar in size to beach mice, but they have scaly rather than haired tails and lack white underparts. Beach mouse, cotton mouse, and house mouse juveniles, however, are much more similar in appearance than are adults, particularly in that each is grayish in overall color, and are therefore more difficult to differentiate.

Habitat

Beach mice occur primarily in mature, sparsely vegetated primary and secondary barrier dune systems (fig. 19). Sea oats (*Uniola paniculata*) either dominate such systems or are co-dominant with dune panic grass (*Panicum amarum*) and/or bluestem (*Schizachrium maritimum*). Other vegetation present may include beach morning glory (*Ipomoea stoloni-*

Table 3. Comparative characteristics of beach mice

Subspecies	Mean total length	Coloration[a]
Gulf subspecies		
Alabama	5.0 in (12.7 cm)	Pale gray
Perdido Key	4.8 in (12.5 cm)	Grayish fawn
Santa Rosa	5.1 in (13.1 cm)	Drab brown
Choctawhatchee	5.2 in (13.3 cm)	Orange-brown to yellow-brown
St. Andrew	5.0 in (12.7 cm)	Pale buff
Atlantic subspecies		
Anastasia Island	5.4 in (13.9 cm)	Pinkish buff
Pallid	5.3 in (13.6 cm)	Pale pinkish buff
Southeastern	5.3 in (13.9 cm)	Tawny buff

a. Descriptive of the upper parts only—all the subspecies have white underparts.

Fig. 19. Gulf Coast beach mouse primary/secondary dune habitat (Jeffrey A. Gore).

fera), pennywort (*Hydrocotyle bonariensis*), pink-flowered railroad vine (*Ipomoea pes-caprae*), sea rocket (*Cakile* spp.), sea lavender (*Tournefortia* [= *Argusia*] *gnaphalodes*), and/or beach cordgrass (*Spartina patens*). Vegetation in the interdunal areas between primary and secondary dune systems often consists of sedges (*Cyperus* spp.), rushes (*Juncus* spp.), and/or salt-grass (*Distichilis spicata*).

Adjacent inland vegetation typically includes scrubby oaks (*Quercus virginiana*), dwarfed magnolia (*Magnolia grandiflora*), saw-palmetto (*Serenoa repens*), sand pine (*Pinus clausa*), prickly pear cactus (*Opuntia humifusa*), beach tea (*Croton punctatus*), and false rosemary (*Ceratiola ericoides*). Such inland zones are sometimes called "scrub dunes" and can also be occupied by beach mice—southeastern beach mice have been found up to ≈0.6 miles (1 km) inland—but at much lower numbers and densities than in the optimal conditions of primary and secondary dune systems.

Life History and Behavior

Little life history or behavioral research has been conducted on beach mice, none at all on most of the subspecies. Much of the information provided here, then, not only reflects a sparse beach mouse life history/behavior database but also incorporates known characteristics of inland subspecies of *P. polionotus*, and as such should not necessarily be assumed to apply to all the subspecies under all circumstances.

Beach mice are nocturnal foragers and feed primarily on seeds of sea oats and/or dune panic grass, and to a lesser degree on seeds of other vegetation. Small invertebrates are also taken, especially during spring and early summer when seeds of sea oats and panic grass are relatively scarce. Foraging activity is particularly high on moonless or cloudy nights.

Beach mice burrow into the sides of dunes for shelter, refuge, food storage, and nesting purposes, but sometimes also use burrows of ghost crabs (*Ocypode albicans*) for the same purposes. Burrow entrances are most often situated at the base of clumpy vegetation, and burrows typically descend obliquely to depths of 2–3 feet (0.6–0.9 m), then continue horizontally to a nest chamber terminus. A secondary "escape tunnel" rises steeply from the nest chamber to within ≈1 in (2.5 cm) of the surface. Multiple (≥20) burrows are excavated and used by individual breeding pairs throughout their home range.

Breeding occurs throughout the year but peaks in November through early January and ebbs in May through early June. The gestation period is 24–28 days, and litter size is 1–8, most often 3 or 4. Sexual maturity is reached at age 6–7 weeks, and littering interval is ≥26 days.

Beach mice are monogamous and remain in their home ranges, once they are established, throughout life. Home range size averages ≈2 acres (0.8 ha) in optimal primary/secondary dune habitat but may be >10 acres (4.3 ha) in marginal adjacent scrub dune habitats. Population numbers fluctuate seasonally, with peaks in winter and spring, and home range size and movements may vary accordingly. Average life span is ≈180 days, but marked individuals exceeding a year in age have been recorded.

Survey and Monitoring Techniques

Beach mouse tracks are virtually indistinguishable from those of cotton mice or house mice, so mere observation of apparent beach mouse tracks in a given area would only indicate their potential presence. Systematic live trapping would therefore be necessary to determine their presence or absence. To attain the most definitive results in that respect, and also to minimize the potential for trap mortality, the following protocol should be followed:

- Survey areas should be subdivided into four sampling zones: frontal dunes, secondary dunes, scrub dunes, and any dry flats inland from dune systems.
- One trapline should transect each sampling zone and be situated parallel to the frontal dunes.
- Trap stations should be spaced at intervals of 30–45 feet (10–15 m) along traplines. Two traps per station would yield the best results.
- Effective baits are long-cooking rolled oats, a mixture of peanut butter and long-cooking rolled oats, or raw, shelled sunflower seeds. Peanut butter, however, attracts fire ants and therefore should not be used where fire ants are common.
- Traps should be baited and set in the late afternoon, checked and tripped in the early morning (beginning at dawn), and remain closed throughout the day. Trapping sessions should encompass at least three consecutive nights, but only so long as trapping remains unsuc-

cessful. Trapping should be discontinued once captures of beach mice are made.

- Balls of cotton batting or other similar material should be placed in each trap for insulation purposes when nighttime temperatures are anticipated to be <65°F (36°C). Trapping should be suspended on nights when nighttime temperatures are anticipated to be <50°F (28°C).

- Should beach mouse presence not be confirmed during the initial trapping session, additional trapping sessions should be scheduled on a seasonal (spring, summer, fall, winter) basis until such time as presence is confirmed, or through two consecutive years of trapping without success.

More intensive capture-mark-recapture efforts would be necessary to determine population numbers and/or densities accurately. Brownie et al. (1978), Otis et al. (1978), and White et al. (1982) can be consulted relative to that methodology, and Rave and Holler (1992) apply it specifically to beach mice. Also, the American Society of Mammalogists (1998) has issued comprehensive and detailed guidelines relative to the capture, handling, and care of all mammals.

Management

Fundamental Management Considerations

- Once a primary/secondary dune plant community reaches successional maturity, it constitutes ideal beach mouse habitat.

- Predatory house cats and competing house mice constitute a significant limiting factor where beach mice occur near human habitation.

- Inland scrub dune zones must be at a relatively early successional stage in order to support beach mouse populations. Scrub dune vegetation eventually develops into a closed-canopy oak forest configuration, unsuitable for beach mouse occupancy, in the absence of periodic successional retardation.

Proactive Management

1. Habitat Security

The major strategy for primary and secondary dune plant communities at or near successional maturity, and inland scrub dune zones at earlier stages, should focus on ensuring habitat security rather than on physically manipulating habitat characteristics. Most important in that respect would be precluding, eliminating, or at least minimizing the invasion of beach mouse habitat by house cats and house mice. Regulatory or law enforcement actions (e.g., enactment and/or stringent enforcement of leash laws or ordinances, deed restrictions prohibiting cats in adjacent housing projects, etc.) may be necessary to exclude house cats. Maintaining good beach hygiene by situating trash receptacles and other public facilities well outside beach mouse habitat, and effective pest control measures in housing areas adjacent to beach mouse habitat, would serve to curtail the house mouse invasion problem.

2. Habitat Enhancement and Rehabilitation

Manipulating the plant communities of primary and secondary dune systems should be necessary only where those communities have been degraded or disturbed and are thus at some successional stage short of maturity. Management strategies for those areas, then, should initially include expediting the plant community succession process. Mechanical restoration of dune contours, if needed, and/or planting of sea oats, along with associated vegetation (e.g., dune panic grass and/or bluestem), would most effectively expedite that successional progression. Conversely, strategies for scrub dune zones should focus on initially rehabilitating those at mature stages, then subsequently retarding succession periodically to sustain early successional characteristics. Historically, natural wildfires performed that function, but fire suppression policies over recent decades have allowed many scrub dune zones to progress toward a mature, closed-canopy stage. Initiating periodic prescribed burns (at intervals approximating historical frequencies or whenever oaks begin dominating), then, would be required to sustain the vegetative characteristics of scrub dune zones necessary for beach mouse occupancy.

3. Population Expansion

Rehabilitated or otherwise unoccupied habitat immediately adjacent to occupied habitat would likely be repopulated through natural dispersal processes as the habitat approaches maturity (or, in the case of scrub dunes, once succession has been retarded). But to reestablish populations in rehabilitated disjunct areas, translocation and release operations would be necessary. Holler and Mason (1987) and Holler et al. (1989) provide effective methodologies for this.

Accommodative Management

Beach mouse welfare is not necessarily incompatible with human recreation, particularly swimming, surf fishing, and other activities restricted to beach zones rather than dune zones. However, beach access through dunes should not compromise dune habitat quality. Raised boardwalks through the fragile dune systems to beaches would be effective. Any recreational opportunities provided within dune zones should be nondestructive in terms of beach vegetation. Vehicular traffic would be especially destructive.

Relevant Literature

American Society of Mammalogists. 1998. Guidelines for the capture, handling, and care of mammals as approved by the American Society of Mammalogists. *Journal of Mammalogy* 79:1416–31.

Blair, W. F. 1951. Population structure, social behavior, and environmental relations in a natural population of the beach mouse *Peromyscus polionotus leucocephalus*. *University of Michigan Contributions to Laboratory Vertebrate Biology* 48:1–47.

Bowen, W. W. 1968. Variation and evolution of Gulf coast populations of beach mice, *Peromyscus polionotus*. *Bulletin of the Florida State Museum of Biological Sciences* 12(1):1–91.

Briese, L. A., and M. H. Smith. 1973. Competition between *Mus musculus* and *Peromyscus polionotus*. *Journal of Mammalogy* 54:968–69.

Brownie, C., D. R. Anderson, K. P. Burnham, and D. S. Robson. 1978. *Statistical Inference from Band Recovery Data: A Handbook*. U.S. Fish and Wildlife Service. 212 pp.

Cox, J. H., H. F. Percival, and S. V. Colwell. 1994. *Impact of Vehicular Traffic on Beach Habitat and Wildlife at Cape San Blas, Florida*. U.S. Biological Survey Technical Report 50. 50 pp.

Extine, D. D., and I. J. Stout. 1987. Dispersion and habitat occupancy of the beach mouse *Peromyscus polionotus niveiventris*. *Journal of Mammalogy* 68:297–304.

Frank, P. A. 1992. Conservation and ecology of the Anastasia Island beach mouse. *Endangered Species Update* 9(12):9.

Frank, P. A. 1993. Anastasia Island beach mouse "at home" at Fort Matanzas National Monument. *Park Science* 13(1):30–31.

Frank, P. A. 1997. Delicate balance: Anastasia Island beach mouse. *Florida Wildlife* 51(1):15.

Frank, P. A., and S. R. Humphrey. 1996. *Populations, Habitat Requirements, and Management of the Endemic Anastasia Island Beach Mouse, Emphasizing the Potential Threat of Exotic House Mice.* Florida Game and Fresh Water Fish Commission Nongame Wildlife Program Project NG88-006 Final Report. 46 pp.

Gore, J. A., and T. L. Schaefer. 1993. Distribution and conservation of the Santa Rosa beach mouse. *Proceedings of the Annual Conference of the Southeastern Association of Fish and Wildlife Agencies* 47:378–85.

Holler, N. R. 1992. Choctawhatchee beach mouse. Pp. 76–86 in *Rare and Endangered Biota of Florida,* vol. 1: *Mammals,* ed. S. R. Humphrey. University Press of Florida.

Holler, N. R. 1992. Perdido Key beach mouse. Pp. 102–9 in *Rare and Endangered Biota of Florida,* vol. 1: *Mammals,* ed. S. R. Humphrey. University Press of Florida.

Holler, N. R., and D. W. Mason. 1987. Reestablishment of Perdido Key and Choctawhatchee beach mice into areas of unoccupied critical habitat. *Journal of the Alabama Academy of Science* 58:66.

Holler, N. R., and E. H. Rave. 1991. Status of endangered beach mouse populations in Alabama. *Journal of the Alabama Academy of Science* 62(1):18–27.

Holler, N. R., D. W. Mason, R. M. Dawson, T. Simons, and M. C. Wooten. 1989. Reestablishment of the Perdido Key beach mouse (*P.p. tryssyllepsis*) on Gulf Islands National Seashore. *Conservation Biology* 3:397–404.

Humphrey, S. R. 1992. Anastasia Island beach mouse. Pp. 94–101 in *Rare and Endangered Biota of Florida,* vol. 1: *Mammals,* ed. S. R. Humphrey.

Humphrey, S. R. 1992. Pallid beach mouse. Pp. 19–23 in *Rare and Endangered Biota of Florida,* vol. 1: *Mammals,* ed. S. R. Humphrey.

Humphrey, S. R., and D. B. Barbour. 1979. *Status and Habitat of Eight Kinds of Endangered and Threatened Rodents in Florida.* Florida State Museum Office of Ecological Services Special Scientific Report no. 2. 93 pp.

Humphrey, S. R., and D. B. Barbour. 1981. Status and habitat of three subspecies of *Peromyscus polionotus* in Florida. *Journal of Mammalogy* 62:840–44.

Humphrey, S. R., W. H. Kern, Jr., and M. S. Ludlow. 1987. *Status Survey of Seven Florida Mammals.* Florida Cooperative Fish and Wildlife Research Unit Technical Report no. 25. 39 pp.

Ivey, R. D. 1949. Life history notes on three mice from the Florida east coast. *Journal of Mammalogy* 30:157–62.

James, F. C. 1992. St. Andrew beach mouse. Pp. 87–93 in *Rare and Endangered Biota of Florida,* vol. 1: *Mammals,* ed. S. R. Humphrey.

James, F. C. 1995. *Endemism in a Beach Population of the Old-field Mouse,*

Peromyscus polionotus peninsularis. Florida Game and Fresh Water Fish Commission Nongame Wildlife Program Project GFC-86-047 Final Report. 23 pp.

Johnson, A. F., and M. G. Barbour. 1990. Dunes and maritime forests. Pp. 429–80 in *Ecosystems of Florida,* ed. R. L. Myers and J. J. Ewel. Orlando: University of Central Florida Press.

Kaufman, D. W., and G. A. Kaufman. 1987. Reproduction by *Peromyscus polionotus:* Number, size, and survival of offspring. *Journal of Mammalogy* 68:275–80.

Oddy, D. M., M. A. Hensley, J. A. Provancha, and R. B. Smith. 1999. Long-distance dispersal of a southeastern beach mouse (*Peromyscus poionotus niveiventris*). *Florida Field Naturalist* 27:124–25.

Otis, D. K., K. P. Burnham, G. C. White, and D. R. Anderson. 1978. Statistical inference from capture data on closed animal populations. *Wildlife Monographs* 62:1–135.

Rave, E. H., and N. R. Holler. 1992. Population dynamics of beach mice (*Peromyscus polionotus ammobates*) in southern Alabama. *Journal of Mammalogy* 73:347–55.

Robson, M. S. 1989. *Southeastern Beach Mouse Survey.* Florida Game and Fresh Water Fish Commission Nongame Wildlife Program Report. 11 pp.

Stout, I. J. 1992. Southeastern beach mouse. Pp. 242–49 in *Rare and Endangered Biota of Florida,* vol. 1: *Mammals,* ed. S. R. Humphrey. University Press of Florida.

Swilling, W. R., Jr., M. C. Wooten, N. R. Holler, and W. J. Lynn. 1998. Population dynamics of Alabama beach mice (*Peromyscus polionotus ammobates*) following Hurricane Opal. *American Midland Naturalist* 140:287–98.

U.S. Fish and Wildlife Service 1987. *Choctawhatchee Beach Mouse, Perdido Key Beach Mouse and Alabama Beach Mouse Recovery Plan.* U.S. Fish and Wildlife Service. 45 pp.

U.S. Fish and Wildlife Service. 1993. *Recovery Plan for the Anastasia Island Beach Mouse and the Southeastern Beach Mouse.* U.S. Fish and Wildlife Service. 19 pp.

U.S. Fish and Wildlife Service. 1999. Southeastern beach mouse. Pp. 4/97–116 in *South Florida Multi-Species Recovery Plan,* U.S. Fish and Wildlife Service.

Vaughan, R. 1992. Beach mouse bingo (part one): Playing games with extinction. *Wild Earth* 2(2):20–23.

Vaughan, R. 1993. Beach mouse bingo (part two): Litigating with extinction. *Wild Earth* 3(1):41–45.

White, G. C., D. R. Anderson, K. P. Burnham, and D. L. Otis. 1982. *Capture-Recapture and Removal Methods for Sampling Closed Populations.* Los Alamos (New Mexico) National Laboratory. 235 pp.

Wood, D. A., and N. R. Holler. 1990. Of men and mice. *Florida Wildlife* 44(4):37–39.

8

Southeastern American Kestrel

Status

The American kestrel (*Falco sparverius;* Order Falconiformes; Family Falconidae) ranges over most of North America and is taxonomically subdivided into 17 subspecies. Two of the subspecies—the southeastern American kestrel (*F. s. paulus*) and eastern American kestrel (*F. s. sparverius*)—occur in Florida, *F. s paulus* as a nonmigratory, year-round resident in the state, and *F. s. sparverius* as an overwintering (September to May) migrant. Thirty-nine *Falco* species (considered the "true" falcons) occur worldwide, among which only *F. s. paulus* breeds in Florida. Two other *Falco* representatives, the peregrine falcon (*F. peregrinus*) and merlin (*F. columbarius*), are migratory overwintering residents.

The range of the southeastern American kestrel extends from Louisiana eastward through the Southeast into southeastern South Carolina. Its Florida range originally encompassed essentially the entire state, including the Keys, but the subspecies is now apparently absent south of Lake Okeechobee as well as from several of the counties along the Atlantic Coast. Numbers are highest along the Central Ridge from Highlands County northward.

Although statewide population numbers or trends have not been quantitatively assessed, anecdotal data and various other sources suggest that population levels and distribution have declined dramatically over the past several decades and are continuing to decline, due primarily to loss of nesting habitat. Declines in foraging habitat quality, however, have also been a factor. One estimate in that context is that as lands were converted to citrus operations from the early 1940s to the early 1980s, populations in north-central Florida declined in numbers by ≈82 percent. Due to those apparent declines, the southeastern American kestrel was listed as a threatened species by the Florida Game and Fresh Water Fish Commission in 1975.

Distinguishing Characteristics

The American kestrel is the smallest American species within the *Falco* assemblage, sometimes referred to as the "sparrow hawk" due to its diminutive size, and *F. s. paulus* is the smallest of the *F. sparverius* subspecies occurring in North America (subspecies in the Caribbean and South America are smaller). Male/female total body lengths are ≈9/12 in (22/31 cm), wingspans are ≈20/24 in (50/60 cm), and body weights are ≈3.2/3.6 ounces (91/103 g). Tail length is ≈4/6 in (10.8/15.2 cm), which is proportionally shorter than that of other falcons.

The most colorful North American falcon, the American kestrel is also strongly sexually dimorphic in color patterns. The upper wing coverts in males are slate blue, usually with black spots, while in females the upper coverts are rufous with black barring. The tail feathers in both males and females are dorsally rufous, but in males these are unbarred and have a wide subterminal black band and white or gray-brown tip. The tail feathers of females have black barring and the tip is whitish to buffy. Both sexes have vertical black stripes in front of and behind each eye, and both have blue-gray crown patches, rufous backs, and spotted, buffy underparts. However, females are browner in overall appearance and more strikingly marked. Immatures resemble adults but have streaked rather than spotted undersides.

Differentiating between representatives of *F. s. paulus* and overwintering eastern American kestrels is difficult in the field, but *paulus* kestrels are ≈25 percent smaller than their *sparverius* counterparts (*paulus* females, however, are only slightly smaller than *sparverius* males). *Paulus* males, however, can often, though not necessarily always, be differentiated from *sparverius* males by their reduced markings, especially the spotting on the breast and flanks, and by having more buff coloration on the breast and abdomen.

The vocal repertoire is limited, with a *killy* call the most common vocalization, uttered in 3–6 short bursts when disturbed or excited as well as during courtship aerial displays. American kestrels are sometimes called "killy hawks" because of that common call. "Whine" and "chitter" calls are also uttered during courtship, the former in association with courtship feeding, copulation, and food begging and the latter with other bodily contact.

Habitat

Southeastern American kestrels are relative generalists in terms of habitat landscapes suitable for nesting and foraging, and as such occur in pine (*Pinus* spp.) flatwoods, mixed pine-hardwood forests, pine scrub, dry prairies, sandhills, and even suburban and agricultural areas. However, only landscape matrices which have as components snags or other nesting substrates and fields or other relatively open areas (≤25 percent tree canopy cover) are habitable for these birds. Snags or similar substrates (e.g., nest boxes, utility poles) are required for breeding, and nearby fields or open areas are required for foraging.

Life History and Behavior

American kestrels are secondary cavity nesters, typically usurping cavities originally excavated by woodpeckers. While the red-cockaded woodpecker (*Picoides borealis*) excavates its cavities in living trees, all other woodpeckers excavate their cavities in dead or dying trees, so snags— most often pine snags—are the most typical kestrel nesting substrate. Snags ≥11.5 in (32 cm) in diameter are selectively preferred in that respect. Kestrel nests are not uncommon, however, in utility poles, building niches, and artificial nest boxes.

Nesting territories vary widely in size, depending on habitat quality (i.e., nest site availability and foraging habitat available near nest sites). Measured territories in Florida have ranged from ≈125 acres (50 ha) to ≈800 acres (325 ha).

Breeding activity begins in late January, with males initiating the pair formation process via aerial displays, courtship feeding, and nest site selection. Egg laying occurs from mid-March through early June, clutch size is 3–5 eggs, incubation lasts 29–31 days, and the young fledge at age 4–5 weeks. Egg coloration is variably white to yellowish to reddish brown, mottled with gray or brown. Both sexes incubate, but the female more so than the male.

The young are fed by the parents for several weeks after fledging and disperse at age ≈24 days. Sexual maturity is reached at age one year.

Double-brooding in a given season occurs if weather conditions are favorable and a sufficient prey base is available. In such instances, however, second clutches are usually smaller and hatching success is lower. Mortality is ≈60 percent in the first year of life, ≈45 percent annually thereafter. Mean life expectancy is ≈1.4 years.

The diet consists of insects, arachnids, small rodents, lizards and other small reptiles, and occasionally small birds. Lizards are particularly important nutritionally during breeding, perhaps to the extent that the availability of lizards influences nest site selection. Prey is captured with the feet and killed with the beak.

Hunting occurs over open areas dominated by short grasses and weedy forbs, often pastures, berms, mowed hayfields, and golf courses and other parklike areas. The most common hunting technique is perch hunting, but flight hunting and hover hunting are also common. Perch sites are typically trees, utility poles or lines, or fence posts, 18–30 feet (6–10 m) above ground and with an unobstructed view of large areas of foraging habitat. Hover hunting is usually from heights of 30–90 feet (15–30 m), with hovers usually not exceeding a minute in duration.

Survey and Monitoring Techniques

Roadside transects are effective in determining the presence or absence of southeastern American kestrels, supplemented with foot transects in areas with limited roads. Surveys should be scheduled for the period April–August (when wintering eastern American kestrels are not present) and conducted on calm, clear days beginning at sunrise and extending through midmorning. Kestrels are most conspicuous early in the breeding season (April–May), so surveys during that time frame would yield the best results. Surveys should be conducted 6–8 times in a given year, spaced 4–7 days apart. Direction of travel should reverse from one survey to the next, and survey personnel should remain constant through a survey period to avoid bias in either respect. Binoculars and/or spotting scopes are a necessity. While surveying, particular attention should be focused on fencerows and utility poles and lines, but kestrels are also commonly observed hovering or perched in trees (especially snags).

Foot transects are usually necessary to detect nest sites. Areas selected for surveying in that regard should be where pairs of kestrels or courtship behavior by individual kestrels were observed during presence/absence surveys. Confirmation of suspected nest cavities requires observation of entry or exit by kestrels.

Deploying balchatri traps is the technique most commonly used to capture kestrels for leg banding, marking, or other purposes, but bow nets have also been used with some success. The appropriate U.S. Fish and Wildlife Service aluminum band size for American kestrels is 3B. Color-coded banding or marking operations should be coordinated with the USFWS to preclude compromising similar operations elsewhere.

Management

Proactive Management

The most critical limiting factor in terms of kestrel welfare is the availability of nesting substrates. Thus the priority focus of proactive management strategies should be to accommodate that need. Snags suitable for nesting can be created by girdling or herbiciding living trees $\geq$11.5 in (32 cm) in diameter, but using that methodology, results benefiting kestrels (i.e., increasing population numbers or densities in a given area) would not be realized for several years. In most cases, the decomposition process of dead trees must be well established before cavity-nesting birds will excavate cavities in them.

Deploying artificial nest boxes is more effective and efficient and should be considered as a supplemental strategy to creating natural nesting substrates, especially where snags and other natural sites are either absent or scarce as the management option of choice. Nest boxes of appropriate dimensions for kestrels can be constructed with relatively few materials. A single 8-foot-long 1 × 10 in board suffices, and completed boxes should have floor dimensions approximating 8 × 8 in and a depth of 12–18 in. The entrance (with a diameter of 3 in) should be drilled 9–12 in above the floor. A perch should be installed ≈3 in below the entrance; 3–5 drain holes (≈1/4 in) should be drilled through the floor; and 2–3 ventilation holes (3/8 in) should be drilled through each side. Needham (1995) and Stys (1993) provide graphic guidance in those respects, as does a pamphlet titled *American Kestrel* available at Busch Gardens in Tampa, and *The Complete Book of Birdhouse Construction for Woodworkers*

(Campbell 1984) is a good resource for birdhouse construction in general. Nest boxes suitable for kestrel nesting can also be purchased from a wide variety of commercial manufacturers.

Nest boxes can be attached to the sides of barns or other buildings or to poles or lone trees (preferably dead). Deployment should be ≥50 feet (15 m) from dense habitat or a forest edge, in or very near meadows, fields, or other open, grassy areas and within 50–100 feet (17–35 m) of perch substrates (utility lines, fencerows, snags, etc.). For best results, boxes should face in a southerly or easterly direction and should be deployed at a height of 12–30 feet (4–10 m). Care should be taken to position boxes such that flight access is not obstructed.

New boxes should be in place by mid-December and arrayed at densities of ≤1 per 25 acres (10 ha). American kestrels do not use nest material, but some of the other species that commonly use nest boxes do, so boxes should be manually cleaned by December each year.

Accommodative Management

The most significant land use conflicts likely to be encountered relative to kestrel welfare are large suburban development projects usurping expanses of kestrel habitat. The Florida Fish and Wildlife Conservation Commission's *Ecology and Habitat Protection Needs of the Southeastern American Kestrel* (Falco sparverius paulus) *on Large-Scale Development Sites in Florida* (Stys 1993) addresses the conflict and provides detailed guidance.

Relevant Literature

Anonymous. n.d. *American Kestrel* (Falco sparverius). Pamphlet, Busch Gardens Conservation Education Department.

Berger, D. D., and H. C. Mueller. 1959. The balchatri: A trap for the birds of prey. *Bird-Banding* 30:18–26.

Bloom, P. H. 1987. Capturing and handling raptors. Pp. 99–123 in *Raptor Management Techniques Manual,* ed. B. G. Pendleton et al.

Bohall-Wood, P. G., and M. W. Collopy. 1987. Foraging behavior of southeastern American kestrels in relation to habitat use. *Raptor Research Report* 6:58–65.

Bortolotti, G. R. 1994. Effect of nest-box size on nest-site preference and reproduction in American kestrels. *Journal of Raptor Research* 28:127–33.

Bryan, J. R. 1988. Radio controlled bow-net for American kestrels. *North American Bird Bander* 13:30–31.

Campbell, S. D. 1984. *The Complete Book of Birdhouse Construction for Wood-workers*. Dover Publications. 46 pp.

Collopy, M. W. 1996. Southeastern American kestrel. Pp. 211–18 in *Rare and Endangered Biota of Florida*, vol. 5: *Birds*, ed. J. A. Rodgers, Jr., et al. University Press of Florida.

Collopy, M. W., and J. R. Koplin. 1983. Diet, capture success, and mode of hunting by female American kestrels in winter. *Condor* 85:369–71.

Dawson, R. D., and G. R. Bortolotti. 1997. Misdirected incubation in American kestrels: A case of competition for nest sites? *Wilson Bulletin* 109:732–34.

Erickson, M. G., and D. M. Hoppe. 1979. An octagonal balchatri trap for small raptors. *Raptor Research* 13:36–38.

Foran, S., M. W. Collopy, M. L. Hoffman, and P. G. Bohall. 1984. Florida's little falcon. *Florida Wildlife* 38(2):14–18.

Fuller, M. R., and J. A. Mosher. 1981. Methods of detecting and counting raptors: A review. Pp. 235–46 in *Estimating Numbers of Terrestrial Birds*, ed. C. J. Ralph and J. M. Scott. Cooper Ornithological Society Studies of Avian Biology no. 6.

Fuller, M. R., and J. A. Mosher. 1987. Raptor survey techniques. Pp. 37–65 in *Raptor Management Techniques Manual*, ed. B. G. Pendleton et al.

Hamerstrom, F., F. N. Hamerstrom, and J. Hart. 1973. Nest boxes: An effective management tool for kestrels. *Journal of Wildlife Management* 37:400–3.

Hoffman, M. L., and M. W. Collopy. 1987. Distribution and nesting ecology of the American kestrel (*Falco sparverius paulus*) near Archer, Florida. Pp. 47–57 in *The Ancestral Kestrel*, ed. D. M. Bird and R. Bowman. Raptor Research Foundation Raptor Research Report no. 6.

Hoffman, M. L., and M. W. Collopy. 1988. Historical status of the American kestrel (*Falco sparverius paulus*) in Florida. *Wilson Bulletin* 100:91–107.

Kast, T. L., and P. E. Allen. 1998. Nest box network pays off. *Birdscope* 12(1):4–5.

Layne, J. N. 1980. Trends in numbers of American kestrels on roadside counts in southcentral Florida from 1968 to 1976. *Florida Field Naturalist* 8:1–36.

Layne, J. N. 1982. Analysis of Florida-related banding data for the American kestrel. *North American Bird Bander* 7:94–99.

McFarlane, R. W. 1973. Florida's sparrow hawks. *Florida Naturalist* 46:20–22.

Miller, H. M., and W. R. Marion. 1995. *Natural and Created Snags and Cavity-nesting Birds in North Florida Pine Forests*. Florida Game and Fresh Water Fish Commission Nongame Wildlife Program Project GFC-84-020 Final Report. 63 pp.

Miller, K. E., and J. A. Smallwood. 1997. Natal dispersal and philopatry of southeastern American kestrels in Florida. *Wilson Bulletin* 109:226–32.

Needham, B. 1995. *Beastly Abodes: Homes for Birds, Bats, Butterflies and Other Backyard Wildlife*. Sterling Publications. 144 pp.

Pendleton, B. G., et al., eds. 1987. *Raptor Management Techniques Manual*. National Wildlife Federation Scientific and Technical Series no. 10.

Plice, L., and T. G. Balgooyen. 1999. A remotely operated trap for American kestrels using nest boxes. *Journal of Field Ornithology* 70:158–62.

Rohrbaugh, R. W., Jr., and R. H. Yahner. 1997. Effects of macrohabitat and microhabitat on nest-box use and nesting success of American kestrels. *Wilson Bulletin* 109:410–23.

Rudolph, S. G. 1982. Foraging strategies of American kestrels during breeding. *Ecology* 63:1268–76.

Savant, S. M. 1998. Natural history of the American kestrel. *Proceedings of the International Wildlife Rehabilitation Council Conference* 20:204–11.

Shalaway, S. 1995. Monitoring and maintaining nest boxes. *WildBird* 9(5):48–53.

Smallwood, J. A. 1990. American kestrel and merlin. Pp. 29–37 in *Proceedings of the Southeastern Raptor Management Symposium and Workshop,* ed. B. G. Pendleton. National Wildlife Federation Scientific and Technical Series no. 14.

Smallwood, J. A., and M. W. Collopy. 1991. The responses of southeastern American kestrels to increased availability of nesting sites in two habitats. *Journal of Raptor Research* 25:160.

Smallwood, J. A., and M. W. Collopy. 1993. Management of the threatened southeastern American kestrel in Florida: Population responses to a regional nest-box program. *Journal of Raptor Research* 27:81.

Smallwood, J. A., and C. Natale. 1998. The effect of patagial tags on breeding success in American kestrels, *Falco sparverius*. *North American Bird Bander* 23:73–78.

Smallwood, P. D., and J. A. Smallwood. 1998. Seasonal shifts in sex ratios of fledgling American kestrels (*Falco sparverius paulus*): The early bird hypothesis. *Evolutionary Ecology* 12:839–53.

Steenhof, K., G. P. Carpenter, and J. D. Bednarz. 1994. Use of mist nets and a live great horned owl to capture breeding American kestrels. *Journal of Raptor Research* 28:194–96.

Stys, B. 1993. *Ecology and Habitat Protection Needs of the Southeastern American Kestrel* (Falso sparverius paulus) *on Large-Scale Development Sites in Florida*. Florida Game and Fresh Water Fish Commission Nongame Wildlife Technical Report no. 13. 35 pp.

Toland, B. R., and W. H. Elder. 1987. Influence of nest-box placement and density on abundance and productivity of American kestrels in central Missouri. *Wilson Bulletin* 99:712–17.

Willoughby, E. J., and T. J. Cade. 1964. Breeding behavior of the American kestrel. *Living Bird* 3:75–96.

Wood, P. B., and M. W. Collopy. 1986. Abundance and habitat selection of two American kestrel subspecies in north-central Florida. *Auk* 103:557–63.

Wood, P. B., and M. W. Collopy. 1986. The American kestrel. *Florida Naturalist* 59:3–5.

Wood, P. B., and M. W. Collopy. 1987. Foraging behavior of southeastern American kestrels in relation to habitat use. Pp. 58–65 in *The Ancestral Kestrel,* ed. D. M. Bird and R. Bowman. Raptor Research Foundation Raptor Research Report no. 6.

Young, L. S., and M. N. Kochert. 1987. Marking techniques. Pp. 125–56 in *Raptor Management Techniques Manual,* ed. B. G. Pendleton et al.

9

∾ ∾

Sandhill Crane

Status

Fifteen species of cranes (Order Gruiformes; Family Gruidae) occur worldwide, two of which are native to North America: the sandhill crane (*Grus canadensis*) and whooping crane (*G. americana*). Both are historically native to Florida, but the whooping crane disappeared in the early 20th century. In 1993, however, Florida Fish and Wildlife Conservation Commission personnel initiated long-term annual releases of 20–40 young, captive-produced whoopers in the state (204 had been released through spring 2000), aimed at ultimately reestablishing the whooping cranes on a viable, self-sustaining, nonmigratory basis. Nesting within the introduced population, numbering 65 survivors at the time, first occurred in spring 1999 with the laying of a single two-egg clutch, although those eggs were lost to a predator. Successful production of young did occur, however, in spring 2000. That nesting effort represents the first known successful breeding of whooping cranes in the wild anywhere in the United States in at least 60 years and the first east of the Mississippi River since the 19th century. More recent breeding had been confined to the Northwest Territories in Canada. It is not clear whether Florida's original whoopers were resident breeders or overwintering migrants.

Six subspecies of the sandhill crane are recognized, two of which occur in Florida: the Florida sandhill crane (*G. c. pratensis*), a nonmigratory year-round resident, and the greater sandhill crane (*G. c. tabida*), a migratory winter resident that nests in the Great Lakes region. The range of the Florida sandhill extends from the Okefenokee Swamp in Georgia southward through most of the Florida Peninsula (fig. 20). Taylor County represents the northwestern limit of its contiguous range, but a disjunct population occurs along the Apalachicola River in Liberty, Gulf, and Franklin counties.

The total population is estimated to number ≈4,000 birds, and that level is believed either to have remained relatively stable or to have increased slightly over the past 2–3 decades. The most substantial subpopulations occur in association with the Kissimmee Prairie (Osceola County); DeSoto Prairie (DeSoto County); Paynes Prairie (Alachua County); Levy Lake Prairie, Putnam Hall Prairie, and Orange Grove Prairie (Putnam County); Emerald Marsh and the Lake Yale marsh (Lake County); and in northern Polk County and throughout Charlotte County.

The Florida wintering range of the greater sandhill crane roughly corresponds with that of the Florida sandhill crane, except that greater sandhills are rarely seen south of Lake Okeechobee. Wintering birds begin arriving in Florida in October, with arrivals continuing through early November. Greater sandhills congregate in larger feeding and roosting flocks than do Florida sandhills and are generally warier of humans, at

Fig. 20. Range of the Florida sandhill crane in Florida.

least upon first arriving. They depart the state from February through early March.

The Florida Game and Fresh Water Fish Commission included the Florida sandhill crane on its initial endangered species list, issued in 1972, but reclassified the species to threatened in 1974.

Distinguishing Characteristics

Florida sandhill cranes are slightly smaller than greater sandhill cranes and somewhat darker in color, especially in the occipital and hind neck areas, but for all practical purposes the two subspecies are virtually indistinguishable in the field. Height when standing is ≈4.0 feet (1.2 m), wingspan is ≈6.0 feet (2.0 m), and weight is ≈9.0 lb (4.1 kg) for females to ≈10.4 lb (4.7 kg) for males (fig. 21). Except for slightly larger body sizes, males are indistinguishable from females in external appearance.

The body plumage is mouse to slate gray and the flight feathers are dark gray with lighter shafts. However, sandhill cranes stain their feathers with soil, particularly the primary and secondary wing coverts, the back, and the upper breast, resulting in a variation in overall coloration among individual cranes, depending on the soil type being used. The most typical result in that respect is drab clay to cinnamon-rufous. The occiput and hind neck are a light gray. The cheeks are yet a paler gray, blending to white on the chin and upper throat. The bill is dark gray, fading to olive-gray in the mid-mandibular area, and the legs and feet are very dark olive to nearly black. The crown, forehead, and lores are unfeathered and reddish in color. Eye color is variable, from orangish to scarlet. The hind toe is vestigial and elevated.

The downy young are brownish, darker on the rump and midback, with pale buffy or tawny underparts (fig. 22). The bill is pinkish (darker toward the tip), the eyes a dark umber, and the feet and legs yellowish. Adultlike appearance is achieved at age 10–14 months.

The vocal repertoire of sandhill cranes features several highly distinctive calls, variously described as bugling, rattling, trumpeting, and croaking. The most typical is a ≈15 note-per-second series of 7–20 broken notes that can be heard from considerable distances, on calm days up to ≈3 miles (5 km) and even farther when downwind. Male and female "unison calls" are sexually diagnostic and uttered only by paired cranes and are thereby the best way of differentiating between sexes in the field. The female voice

Fig. 21. *Left*: Adult
sandhill crane
(Stephen A. Nesbitt).

Fig. 22. *Below*:
Recently hatched
Florida sandhill crane
(Stephen A. Nesbitt).

is higher pitched than the male's, and the individual notes in the male call are 2–3 times longer in duration than in the female's (≈ 0.10–0.15 sec vs. 0.05 sec, respectively).

Sandhill cranes vocalize frequently when in flight. They fly with the neck and legs extended and with snapping wing upstrokes and slower downstrokes. Florida sandhill cranes fly in loose linear flocks; greater sandhills, especially in migration, typically fly in much tighter U-shaped or V-shaped flocks.

Great blue herons (*Ardea herodius*) are comparable in size to and sometimes mistaken for sandhill cranes, but herons fly with the neck curled backward and with evenly paced upstrokes and downstrokes. In general appearance, great blue herons differ in having streaked necks, a gray-blue body, and yellow bill and legs and in lacking a red crown. Another large wading bird native to Florida that has been confused with sandhill cranes, especially in flight, is the wood stork (*Mycteria americana*). Wood storks, however, are white in body color, with a black tail and black primary and secondary wing feathers. The wood stork also has an unfeathered, scaly, dark gray head and neck and a heavy, decurved bill. In flight, the heavy, decurved bill and the contrast of white body color and black tail and wing feathers are particularly conspicuous.

The recently introduced whooping cranes (*G. americana*) are not only similar in size and configuration to sandhills but also have similar flight patterns. Whoopers are therefore even more likely to be mistaken for sandhills, especially the young, which are brownish in both species. The distinctive white body plumage with contrasting black primary wing feathers of whooping cranes, however, begins appearing at age ≈60 days, corresponding to the age at which sandhills begin attaining their gray plumage.

Habitat

Sandhill cranes nest in shallow, emergent palustrine wetlands, particularly those dominated by pickerelweed (*Pontedaria cordata*) and maidencane (*Panicum hemitomon*). They feed in a variety of open, upland habitats, mostly prairies but also human-manipulated habitats such as agricultural lands (sod farms, ranchlands), golf courses, airports, and suburban subdivisions. In natural and some seminatural habitats (e.g., improved pastures), they tend to concentrate in transition zones between wetlands and pastures/prairies and between pastures/prairies and forested habitats.

High winter rainfall creates suitable nesting sites and thereby increases productivity in a given year, whereas high rainfall in spring can render an area unsuitable for nesting and/or decrease productivity through nest flooding. Because of that correlative relationship between rainfall and nesting, some otherwise suitable nesting areas are used only in years of ample winter rainfall.

Life History and Behavior

Sandhill cranes exemplify K-selected species, being long-lived and perennially monogamous, having a low annual reproductive potential, and exhibiting extended parental care. Pairing behavior begins during the second year, but individuals may go through several mates before a reproductively successful pair bond is formed. Physiological sexual maturity is reached at the age of three years, but successful reproduction usually does not occur until age five. The annual breeding cycle commences in January, with egg laying usually peaking from late February through March (earlier in the south than the north). The egg-laying period, however, can extend into June if climatic and habitat conditions remain favorable. After the loss of a mate, the survivor typically secures another mate, sometimes within days.

Home ranges of individual pairs overlap to a large degree with those of adjacent pairs and average ≈1,100 acres (450 ha). The core nesting territories within home ranges vary in size from ≈300 acres (120 ha) to ≈625 acres (250 ha) and are aggressively defended from other cranes, although the remainder of the home range is not. Home ranges are commonly occupied year-round but only if sufficient upland foraging habitat is available nearby. Otherwise, home ranges are occupied only during the breeding/nesting/brood-rearing period.

Nests are typically ≥3 feet (1 m) in diameter and constructed from whatever vegetation is available at the site, with the egg cups lined with finer material than that of the foundation. Nests are normally situated ≈6–7 in (13–14 cm) above standing water ≈12–13 in (32–34 cm) in depth, but occasionally they are constructed on dry ground or floating mats of vegetation. Accessory nests or platforms are often constructed near the primary nest, which are used for brooding hatchlings at night and by hatchlings as day rest sites. Such accessory nests are rarely more than 150 feet (45 m) from the primary nest. (See fig. 23.)

Should initial clutches or chicks be lost to predation or other factors, renesting is undertaken in 18–20 days and can occur up to three times in a given breeding season. Low or declining water levels in nesting marshes delay nest initiation or precipitate nest abandonment. Nest flooding and predation, primarily by raccoons (*Procyon lotor*) and fish crows (*Corvus ossifragus*), are the principal causes of nest failure.

Clutch size is 1–3 eggs, usually 2, both sexes incubate, and the young hatch, usually a day apart, at 29–31 days after laying. The eggs are pale brownish buff with brown and pale gray markings. Brood size averages 1.32 and the hatchlings are precocial and nidifugous, capable of leaving the nest within 24 hours of hatching. Flight capability is attained at age 65–70 days, and dispersal from the family unit occurs at age ≈10 months. First-year juveniles assemble into nonbreeder flocks, typically numbering 2–5, which persist for up to a year. Survival of young to independence is ≈56 percent, with predation by bobcats (*Felis rufus*) and collision with or entanglement in fences, utility lines, and the like being the primary causes of mortality. Florida's expanding coyote (*Canis latrans*) population, however, may ultimately constitute another significant mortality factor.

At any given time, birds <1 year of age constitute ≈11 percent of the total population, juveniles and subadults amount to ≈36 percent of the total, and unpaired adults constitute ≈30 percent of the adult population. The annual survival rate of adults is unknown. Potential life span is more than 30 years, although the average life expectancy of birds having survived to independence is ≈7 years.

The primary natural mortality factor among adults is disease, particularly disseminated visceral coccidiosis, mycotoxicosis (from eating peanuts), and cholangiocarcinomas. Occasional predation by bobcats and bald eagles (*Haliaeetus leucocephalus*) also occurs. The primary nonnatural mortality factors among adults are colliding with or becoming entangled in fences and utility lines and road kills by vehicles. Free-roaming domestic dogs and cats also pose a threat to cranes to some degree. Adults tend to avoid areas frequented by dogs and cats, and some dog/cat nest predation has been observed.

Sandhill cranes are omnivorous, with common plant foods being tubers, rootlets, seeds, acorns, bloodroot (*Lachnanthes caroliniana*), blue-

Fig. 23. Florida sandhill crane nest (Stephen A. Nesbitt).

berries (*Vaccinium* spp.), dew berries (*Rubus* spp.), and some agricultural crops, especially corn and peanuts. Common animal foods are grasshoppers, dragonflies, crayfish, snakes, and frogs, but taking amphiumas (*Amphiuma means*), young common moorhens (*Gallinula chloropus*), and cotton rats (*Sigmodon hispidus*) has also been observed.

A typical 24-hour activity cycle consists of night roosting, a morning feeding period, a midday resting period, and an afternoon preroosting feeding period. Areas with standing water ≈6–7 in (18–20 cm) in depth are used as roost and resting sites.

Sandhill cranes communicate socially through a number of vocalizations, behavioral displays, and postures to convey social status, reproductive stage, alarm, aggressiveness, and submissiveness. Two alert behaviors, seven agonistic behaviors, and eight courtship behaviors have been described. Aggressive displays are most often observed during the breeding season and range from subtle "alert postures" (head up, crown expanded) and "directed walks" to full attack accompanied by "bill sparring," "jump-rakes," and "bill-stabs." During jump-rakes, the middle toe nails, which have sharp, curved edges, are used to rake and cut. "Guard calls" and/or "unison calls" are commonly uttered in association with aggressive behavior. Dancing is common and serves several functions, occurring in all social classes and in a variety of contexts. Dancing consists of bowing, leaping, stiff wing-flapping, and tossing sticks and vegetation over the head.

Survey and Monitoring Techniques

Florida sandhill cranes roost communally from early July through October. Local populations can thus be inventoried effectively during that time by counting individuals either as they arrive at roosts near dusk or as they depart shortly after dawn. Counting nests and determining annual production is most effectively accomplished via aerial transects over nesting areas. Aerial surveys are also effective in inventorying greater sandhill cranes either during migration or on wintering grounds.

The most common techniques for capturing adult sandhill cranes for leg banding and marking work are the use of bait treated with oral tranquilizers and by night-lighting, described in detail in Bishop (1991) and Drewien and Clegg (1992), respectively. Unfledged young can be captured by hand when led by their parents into open areas but will hide and are extremely difficult to locate if pursued in cover. The appropriate U.S. Fish and Wildlife Service leg band size for Florida sandhill cranes is 8. Any color-coded banding or marking operations should be coordinated with the USFWS to preclude compromising similar operations elsewhere.

Management

Fundamental Management Considerations

- Unlike most other wading birds, sandhill cranes use and are dependent on wetlands and uplands roughly equally over a given year.
- Sandhill cranes are sensitive to disturbance during the nesting season, especially during the incubation and brood-rearing periods and while on communal roosts during the non-nesting season. Flushing incubating cranes renders the nest more vulnerable to predation and exposes eggs or nestlings to the elements, and frequent disturbance during brood rearing impedes the ability of adults to provide sufficient care for the young. They are likewise vulnerable to disturbance or

harassment, and even predation, by domestic dogs and cats during the time of nesting and brood rearing, particularly preflight young.

• Cranes prefer to walk, rather than fly, between wetlands and adjacent upland foraging areas as well as while foraging. When a fence or other obstruction impedes their passage, they normally attempt to find a way around or through the impediment rather than fly over it, especially when accompanied by flightless young. Entanglement in fences, then, is not uncommon, especially among young birds, and often results in death.

• Rangewide, colliding with utility lines is a significant sandhill crane mortality factor.

• Cranes can be a nuisance and even dangerous (especially to small children) and destructive where they have become habituated to human contact. Common in such instances are cranes attacking their reflections in mirrors and windows; approaching people aggressively in the expectation of being fed (especially cranes that have been hand-fed) and destroying porch and window screens to reach food; and damaging golf courses and lawns in the course of foraging for mole crickets (*Gryllotalpa* spp.) and other subterranean invertebrates.

Proactive Management

1. Nesting Habitat Quality

The strategy for nesting wetlands should be to promote open, emergent palustrine wetlands dominated by pickerelweed and/or maidencane but interspersed with areas of open shallow water. Wetlands functioning under natural processes may need only non-manipulative accommodation, but artificially manipulating water depths annually, if feasible, may be necessary either to rehabilitate wetlands dominated by cattails or woody vegetation or to sustain ideal conditions in wetlands vulnerable to such invasions. In such cases minimum depths should be ≈12 in (30 cm) and maximum depths ≈24 in (60 cm). A dynamic flushing of targeted wetlands at intervals of 2–5 years is also necessary to sustain their health over time. Deep inundation for ≥1 month followed by complete drying and then burning would yield best results. However, any such manipulative management applications should be scheduled to avoid the nesting period as well as the postnesting period, at least until the young are able to fly (age ≈90 days).

2. Foraging Habitat Quality

Applied upland management should focus on areas proximal to breeding sites, with a strategic objective of promoting open, grassy areas with vegetation ≤18 in (50 cm) in height. Burning, mowing, and/or grazing at appropriate intervals would be effective in that respect.

3. Wetland/Upland Access

Ground access to and from wetland nesting sites and upland foraging habitat should be maintained in an unobstructed state (see discussion under Accommodative Management for situations where fencing is required to address other management exigencies).

4. Disturbance Control

The immediate vicinities of nest sites should be maintained as disturbance-free buffers through the nesting and brood-rearing periods. A radius of ≈400 feet (125 m) around nests would accommodate known "flushing zones" and postnesting movement patterns and would thus be effective. Similar no-disturbance buffers should be observed around traditional communal roosts. Precautions should also be taken to minimize contact with domestic animals during the nesting and brood-rearing periods.

5. Nuisance Crane Resolutions

To minimize damage to lawns, golf courses, and the like, effective insecticides are available that would eradicate mole crickets and other invertebrate foods, thereby eliminating that particular problem. To obviate cranes posing a risk to humans and their habitations, people wishing to feed cranes should do so via planting natural food plants or putting out grain when cranes are not present and at sites considerable distances from human habitations. Otherwise, cranes quickly come to associate people and their dwellings with food and behave accordingly. Altering the behavior of cranes that have already become a problem in this regard, at least in the short term, is difficult if not impossible. Using pyrotechnics, noise-making devices, and other scare tactics to disperse nuisance cranes is effective only for short periods, usually just a few days. Cranes quickly acclimate and become inured to such strategies, especially the Florida sandhill crane (scare tactics are more effective with the more skittish greater sandhill crane). Relocating nuisance cranes also has limited utility. Juveniles may adopt relocation sites, but adults have a strong homing instinct and will not do so. Only through long-term food deprivation can nuisance cranes be slowly "weaned" from associating humans with food resources.

Accommodative Management

1. Agricultural Operations

The primary conflict between sandhill crane welfare and most agricultural operations is fencing, typically to contain domestic livestock, impeding crane movements between wetland nesting areas and upland feeding habitat. Crane movements can, however, be accommodated in such instances without compromising the primary fencing objectives. To achieve this, barbed wire fences should be limited to three strands, with ≥12 in (31 cm) between strands and with the lower strand 16–18 in (40–46 cm) above ground. Welded wire fences should have framed "walk-throughs" 18 × 24 in (46 x 60 cm) in size and at ≈0.3-mile (0.5 km) intervals. Either scenario would allow relatively safe crane passage yet restrain most livestock. Vegetation should be cleared on a regular basis from the vicinity of walk-throughs.

2. Construction and Development Projects

Construction and development projects near wetlands used by sandhill cranes for nesting should be tailored to protect the natural hydrology of areas surrounding those wetlands. In most instances, avoiding the construction of roads adjacent to wetlands or the creation of other impermeable substrates that would retard or otherwise alter water inflow or outflow would be effective. Relegating construction of facilities that would result in perpetual human presence or habitation to distances ≥400 feet (125 m) from nest sites would accommodate known sandhill crane disturbance thresholds.

3. Utility Line Mortality Control

Crane mortality due to colliding with utility lines can be minimized by (1) routing planned lines to avoid crane high-use areas and/or situating lines along forest edges (where cranes would be flying higher than in open habitats), and (2) affixing conspicuous markers to existing lines to make them more visible to flying cranes. Brown and Drewien (1995) and Morkill and Anderson (1991) can be consulted as regards materials effective for this.

Relevant Literature

Bennett, A. J. 1989. Movements and home ranges of Florida sandhill cranes. *Journal of Wildlife Management* 53:830–36.

Bennett, A. J. 1989. Population size and distribution of Florida sandhill cranes in the Okefenokee Swamp, Georgia. *Journal of Field Ornithology* 60:60–67.

Bennett, A. J. 1992. Habitat use by Florida sandhill cranes in the Okefenokee Swamp, Georgia. Pp. 121–29 in *Proceedings of the 1988 North American Crane Workshop*, ed. D. A. Wood. Florida Game and Fresh Water Fish Commission.

Bennett, A. J., and L. A. Bennett. 1990. Productivity of Florida sandhill cranes in the Okefenokee Swamp, Georgia. *Journal of Field Ornithology* 61:224–31.

Bennett, A. J., and L. A. Bennett. 1990. Survival rates and mortality factors of Florida sandhill cranes in Georgia. *North American Bird Bander* 15:85–88.

Bennett, L. A., and A. J. Bennett. 1992. Territorial behavior of sandhill cranes in the Okefenokee Swamp. Pp. 177–84 in *Proceedings of the 1988 North American Crane Workshop*, ed. D. A. Wood. Florida Game and Fresh Water Fish Commission.

Bishop, M. A. 1991. Capturing cranes with alpha-chlorolose (an oral tranquilizer). Pp. 247–53 in *Proceedings of the International Crane Workshop*, ed. J. Harris. International Crane Foundation, Baraboo, Wisc.

Bishop, M. A., and M. W. Collopy. 1987. Productivity of Florida sandhill cranes on three sites in central Florida. Pp. 257–63 in *Proceedings of the 1985 Crane Workshop*, ed. J. C. Lewis. Platte River Whooping Crane Habitat Maintenance Trust.

Bishop, M. A., K. M. Portier, and M. W. Collopy. 1991. Sampling methods for aerial censuses of nesting Florida sandhill cranes in central Florida. Pp. 235–39 in *Proceedings of the International Crane Workshop*, ed. J. Harris. International Crane Foundation, Baraboo, Wisc.

Brown, W. M., and R. C. Drewien. 1995. Evaluation of two power line markers to reduce crane and waterfowl collision mortality. *Wildlife Society Bulletin* 23:217–27.

Depkin, F. C., L. A. Brandt, and F. J Mazzotti. 1994. Nest sites of Florida sandhill cranes in southwestern Florida. *Florida Field Naturalist* 22:39–47.

Drewien, R. C., and K. R. Clegg. 1992. Capturing whooping cranes and sandhill cranes by night-lighting. *Proceedings of the North American Crane Workshop* 6:43–49.

Drewien, R. C., W. M. Brown, and W. L. Kendall. 1995. Recruitment in Rocky Mountain greater sandhill cranes and comparison with other crane populations. *Journal of Wildlife Management* 59:339–56.

Dwyer, N. C., and G. W. Tanner. 1992. Nesting success in Florida sandhill cranes. *Wilson Bulletin* 104:22–31.

Folk, M. J., J. A. Schmidt, and S. A. Nesbitt. 1999. A trough-blind for capturing cranes. *Journal of Field Ornithology* 70:251–56.

Forrester, D. J., F. H. White, and C. F. Simpson. 1976. Parasites and diseases of sandhill cranes in Florida. Pp. 284–90 in *Proceedings of the International Crane Workshop*, ed. J. C. Lewis. Oklahoma State University.

Holt, E. G. 1930. Nesting of the sandhill crane in Florida. *Wilson Bulletin* 152:162–83.

Kilham, L. 1980. Dusting by sandhill cranes in Florida. *Florida Field Naturalist* 8:19–20.

Kushlan, J. A. 1982. The sandhill crane in the Everglades. *Florida Field Naturalist* 4:74–76.

Layne, J. N. 1981. Nesting, development of the young, and parental behavior of a pair of Florida sandhill cranes. *Florida Field Naturalist* 9:51–75.

Layne, J. N. 1982. Status of sibling aggression in Florida sandhill cranes. *Journal of Field Ornithology* 53:272–74.

Layne, J. N. 1983. Productivity of sandhill cranes in south central Florida. *Journal of Wildlife Management* 47:178–83.

Lewis, J. C. 1979. Field identification of juvenile sandhill cranes. *Journal of Wildlife Management* 43:211–14.

Lovvorn, J. R., and C. M. Kirkpatrick. 1981. Roosting behavior and habitat of migrant greater sandhill cranes. *Journal of Wildlife Management* 45:842–57.

Melvin, S. M. 1977. Greater sandhill cranes wintering in Florida and Georgia. *Florida Field Naturalist* 5:8–11.

Morkill, A. E., and S. H. Anderson. 1991. Effectiveness of marking powerlines to reduce sandhill crane collisions. *Wildlife Society Bulletin* 19:442–49.

Morrow, A. J. 1987. Spiked corn and sandhill research. *Florida Wildlife* 41(2):30–33.

Nesbitt, S. A. 1975. Feather staining in Florida sandhill cranes. *Florida Field Naturalist* 3:28–30.

Nesbitt, S. A. 1975. Spring migration of sandhill cranes from Florida. *Wilson Bulletin* 87:424–26.

Nesbitt, S. A. 1976. Capturing sandhill cranes with oral tranquilizers. Pp. 296–98 in *Proceedings of the International Crane Workshop*, ed. J. C. Lewis. Oklahoma State University.

Nesbitt, S. A. 1976. Use of radio telemetry on Florida sandhill cranes. Pp. 299–303 in *Proceedings of the International Crane Workshop*, ed. J. C. Lewis. Oklahoma State University.

Nesbitt, S. A. 1978. The current status and future of the greater sandhill crane in Florida. Pp. 24–26 in *Proceedings of the Greater Sandhill Crane Symposium*, comp. R. E. Feldt. Indiana Department of Natural Resources.

Nesbitt, S. A. 1985. Effects of an oral tranquilizer on survival of sandhill cranes. *Wildlife Society Bulletin* 12:387–88.

Nesbitt, S. A. 1988. Nesting, renesting, and manipulating nesting of Florida sandhill cranes. *Journal of Wildlife Management* 52:758–63.

Nesbitt, S. A. 1989. The significance of mate loss in Florida sandhill cranes. *Wilson Bulletin* 101:648–51.

Nesbitt, S. A. 1992. First reproductive success and individual productivity in sandhill cranes. *Journal of Wildlife Management* 56:573–77.

Nesbitt, S. A. 1996. Florida sandhill crane. Pp. 219–29 in *Rare and Endangered Biota of Florida,* vol. 5: *Birds,* ed. J. A. Rodgers, Jr., et al. University Press of Florida.

Nesbitt, S. A., and G. W. Archibald. 1981. The agonistic repertoire of sandhill cranes. *Wilson Bulletin* 93:99–103.

Nesbitt, S. A., and R. A. Bradley. 1997. Vocalizations of sandhill cranes. *Proceedings of the North American Crane Workshop* 7:29–35.

Nesbitt, S. A., and T. C. Tacha. 1997. Monogamy and productivity in sandhill cranes. *Proceedings of the North American Crane Workshop* 7:10–13.

Nesbitt, S. A., and A. S. Wenner. 1987. Pair formation and mate fidelity in sandhill cranes. Pp. 117–22 in *Proceedings of the 1985 Crane Workshop,* ed. J. C. Lewis. Platte River Whooping Crane Habitat Maintenance Trust.

Nesbitt, S. A., and K. S. Williams. 1990. Home range and habitat use of Florida sandhill cranes. *Journal of Wildlife Management* 54:92–96.

Nesbitt, S. A., and L. E. Williams, Jr. 1973. A trial translocation of sandhill cranes. *Proceedings of the Annual Conference of the Southeastern Association of Game and Fish Commissions* 27:332–35.

Nesbitt, S. A., and L. E. Williams, Jr. 1979. Summer range and migration routes of Florida wintering greater sandhill cranes. *Wilson Bulletin* 91:137–41.

Pearlstine, L. G., L. A. Brandt, W. M. Kitchens, and F. J. Mazzotti. 1995. Impacts of citrus development on habitats of southwest Florida. *Conservation Biology* 9:1020–32.

Stys, B. 1997. *Ecology of the Florida Sandhill Crane.* Nongame Wildlife Technical Report no. 15, Florida Game and Fresh Water Fish Commission. 20 pp.

Tacha, T. C., S. A. Nesbitt, and P. A. Vohs. 1992. *Sandhill Crane.* Birds of North America no. 31, American Ornithologists' Union. 24 pp.

Toland, B. 1999. Nesting success and productivity of Florida sandhill cranes on natural and developed sites in southeast Florida. *Florida Field Naturalist* 27:10–13.

Walkinshaw, L. H. 1949. *The Sandhill Cranes.* Cranbrook Institute of Science Bulletin no. 29. 202 pp.

Walkinshaw, L. H. 1960. Migration of the sandhill crane east of the Mississippi River. *Wilson Bulletin* 72:358–84.

Walkinshaw, L. H. 1976. The sandhill crane on and near the Kissimmee Prairie, Florida. Pp. 1–18 in *Proceedings of the International Crane Workshop,* ed. J. C. Lewis. Oklahoma State University.

Walkinshaw, L. H. 1982. Greater sandhill cranes wintering in central Florida. *Florida Field Naturalist* 10:1–8.

Walkinshaw, L. H. 1982. Nesting of the Florida sandhill crane in central Florida. Pp. 52–63 in *Proceedings of the 1981 Crane Workshop,* ed. J. C. Lewis. National Audubon Society.

Walkinshaw, L. H. 1985. Nest attentiveness by Florida sandhill cranes. *Florida Field Naturalist* 13:67–68.

Wenner, A. S., and S. A. Nesbitt. 1984. The fate of translocated sandhill cranes after 10 years. *Florida Field Naturalist* 12:19–20.

Wenner, A. S., and S. A. Nesbitt. 1987. Wintering of greater sandhill cranes in Florida. Pp. 196–200 in *Proceedings of the 1985 Crane Workshop,* ed. J. C. Lewis. Platte River Whooping Crane Habitat Maintenance Trust.

Williams, L. E., Jr. 1970. Spring departure of sandhill cranes from northern Florida. *Auk* 87:156–57.

Williams, L. E., Jr. 1972. Secrets of the sandhills. *Florida Wildlife* 26(3):10–13.

Williams, L. E., Jr. 1981. Capturing and marking sandhill cranes. Pp. 175–79 in *Crane Research around the World,* ed. J. C. Lewis and H. Masatomi. International Crane Foundation.

Williams, L. E., Jr., and R. W. Phillips. 1972. North Florida sandhill crane populations. *Auk* 89:541–48.

Williams, L. E., Jr., and R. W. Phillips. 1973. Capturing sandhill cranes with alpha-chlorolose. *Journal of Wildlife Management* 37:94–97.

Yosef, R. 1994. Sex-related differences in distraction-displays by Florida sandhill cranes. *Condor* 96:222–24.

10

Crested Caracara

Status

The crested caracara (*Caracara plancus*) is among nine species of caracaras (Order Falconiformes; Family Falconidae; Subfamily Caracarinae), all of which are neotropical in distribution. *Carcara plancus* is monogeneric, is the most widespread of the nine species, and is the only one that occurs in North America. The others are altogether confined to Central America southward into South America.

The crested caracara also occurs throughout most of South America, inclusive of the Falkland Islands. Thus roughly the southern half of its total range overlaps the ranges of the other eight species of caracaras. However, *C. plancus* is taxonomically subdivided into four subspecies— *C. p. audubonii, C. p. pallidus, C. p. plancus,* and *C. p. cheriway*—and only *C. p. audubonii* occurs in North America. Its range extends from the Republic of Panama northward through Central America and Mexico to extreme southern Arizona, southern and southeastern Texas, extreme southwestern Louisiana, and, disjunctly, peninsular Florida and Cuba. A number of crested caracara sightings have come from well outside the species' accepted range, some from as far north as Oregon, Ontario, and several New England states, but those records are believed to be of escaped captives.

The most commonly accepted vernacular for *C. p. audubonii* is Audubon's crested caracara, but in some regions it is also called the Mexican eagle, Mexican buzzard, black-capped eagle, or caracara eagle. It is the national bird of Mexico.

The historic range of *C. p. audubonii* in Florida apparently underwent a contraction from the 1930s to the mid-1970s as suitable habitat was being lost, fragmented, and degraded due to agricultural enterprises, primarily conversion of native habitats to citrus groves, sugarcane farms, tree plantations, and residential development. It is unknown, however, whether population numbers experienced a corresponding decline.

The species' current range in Florida is roughly the southern half of the peninsula (south of the Orlando area). Breeding, however, is concentrated in the south-central prairie region, the Kissimmee River floodplain, and the immediate vicinity of Lake Okeechobee. DeSoto, Glades, Hendry, Highlands, Okeechobee, and Osceola counties, collectively, encompass most current caracara breeding areas. The current Florida population has been estimated to number at least 400–500 individuals (≈150 mated pairs plus 100–200 immatures and other nonbreeders), but that estimate is essentially based on road surveys. Systematic, comprehensive rangewide surveys have not been conducted, and total population numbers could in fact be considerably higher.

The crested caracara was listed as a threatened species by the Florida Game and Fresh Water Fish Commission in 1974, and in 1987 the U.S. Fish and Wildlife Service likewise federally listed the "Florida population" as threatened (the federal designation does not apply to the populations elsewhere). The primary threat to long-term caracara welfare in Florida is the continuing loss of native habitats to intensive farming enterprises and suburban development.

Distinguishing Characteristics

Crested caracaras are strikingly distinctive in appearance, boldly color patterned and having unusually long legs and necks. In adults (fig. 24), the crown (including a crest on the back of the head), upper abdomen, rump, wings, and thighs are blackish, the back is heavily black-and-white barred, and the tail is white with narrow dark crossbars and a wide terminal dark band. The sides of the head and the throat, upper breast, lower abdomen, and undertail coverts are white or cream, and the lower breast is buffy with dark barring. The head is slightly flattened, and the face is unfeathered and reddish orange during times of calm or routine activity (e.g., preening) but blanches progressively to bright yellow during times of excitement or threat. The eyes are orange-brown, the bill is massive and bluish gray, the legs are unfeathered and yellow, and the feet are likewise yellow. In flight, prominent white patches near the outer wing tips are conspicuously visible. Total length is ≈22 in (56 cm), including a ≈10 in (25 cm) tail, wingspan is ≈48 in (124 cm), and weight is ≈2.2 lb (1,050 g).

Fig. 24. Adult crested caracara (Stephen A. Nesbitt).

Females are slightly larger than males, but the sexes are essentially indistinguishable in the field.

Juveniles have the same basic color patterns as adults, but the areas of darker coloration are brownish or tawny rather than blackish, the lighter areas are tan or buffy rather than white or cream, the back and breast have diffuse brown streaks rather than barring, and the facial skin, legs, and feet are gray rather than yellow (although the facial skin is pinkish when the bird is calm). Adult plumage is reached on the fourth molt, at age ≈4 years.

Crested caracaras are strong fliers, with a cruising speed of ≈20 mph (32 km/hr) and a maximum speed of ≈40 mph (64 km/hr). Flight patterns when foraging include frequent dips, turns, and zigzags, and straight-line flights are characterized by deep, rapid wing strokes, interspersed with occasional glides. Caracaras seldom soar.

Although silent most of the time, crested caracaras have a fairly complex vocal repertoire, particularly during the breeding season. The most common call is a croaky rattle, from which the name *caracara* is derived, uttered with the head erect or as the head is being thrown back. Most such vocalizing is in association with aggressive territorial encounters with conspecifics or when intruders approach a nest site or food. Other calls include a raspy juvenile *swee swee* food-begging call, a soft, short, croaky chuckle uttered by adults in association with feeding young, and soft *wuck* notes uttered by adults in association with courtship. Nonvocal bill-clacking is occasionally sounded when an intruder is approaching the nest.

Habitat

Florida's crested caracaras primarily inhabit dry prairies and grasslands with low ground cover vegetation, either devoid of or with very sparse shrubby vegetation, interspersed with ephemeral wetlands and sloughs and with scattered cabbage palms (*Sabal palmetto*) and/or small cabbage palm–live oak (*Quercus virginiana*) hammocks (fig. 25). Lightly wooded areas are also used to some extent but only so long as expanses of grassland are associated with such areas. Accordingly, the historic core of the crested caracara's range in the state corresponded closely with the DeSoto, Okeechobee, and Osceola plains physiographic regions.

Currently, however, because those areas have been greatly altered in recent decades, the bulk (>90 percent) of the population now occurs on private cattle ranches, where improved pastures mirror natural condi-

Fig. 25. Crested caracara habitat (Joan Morrison).

tions, and in areas where remnants of the historic natural prairie remain, particularly the Kissimmee Prairie, DeSoto Prairie, and St. Johns Prairie.

The most common native ground cover plants in caracara habitat are wiregrass (*Aristida* spp.), broomsedge (*Andropogon virginicus*), love grass (*Eragrostis* spp.), torpedo grass (*Panicum repens*), and southern cutgrass (*Leersia hexandra*). Non-native ground cover plants are common in disturbed habitats that mirror natural areas (e.g., some improved pastures) and are occupied by caracaras, primarily bahia (*Paspalum* spp.), pangolagrass (*Digitaria decumbens*), Bermuda grass (*Cynodon dactylon*), and carpet grass (*Axonopus affinis*).

Life History and Behavior

Florida's crested caracaras are nonmigratory (other populations are migratory), monogamous, and maintain year-round home ranges ≈1,500 to ≈6,300 acres (600–2,500 ha) in size, averaging ≈3,200 acres (1,300 ha). They are aggressively territorial as regards their nest sites and areas extending for considerable distances from nest sites, not only toward conspecifics but toward other raptors as well. Minimum tolerable distances between adjacent nest sites in that respect appear to be ≈0.3–0.6 miles (0.5–1.0 km). Population densities of up to one pair per ≈1,335 acres (540 ha) have been recorded.

Nesting occurs from September to early April, although most eggs are laid from late December through February. Nests are well concealed and nearly always (>90 percent) situated in cabbage palms (occasionally live oaks, very rarely other species). They are constructed of vines, weed stalks, and sticks. Caracaras are the only Falconids that construct nests from gathered nesting material. Nests measure ≈2.2 feet (0.7 m) in diameter and ≈1.1 feet (0.5 m) in depth, with shallow nest bowls. Both sexes participate in nest construction, and new nests are usually constructed each year, typically near the previous year's nest site and sometimes on top of the previous year's structure.

Clutch size is 1–3 eggs, usually two, incubation lasts 28–32 days (both sexes incubate), and hatching success is ≈75 percent. Egg coloration is cinnamon brown with brownish blotches. If initial clutches are lost, second clutches are often produced, and double-brooding in a given year occasionally occurs. The young fledge at age 7–8 weeks, most in March–April, but families remain together 3–6 months postfledging. Nesting success (fledging ≥1 young) is ≈64 percent.

Dispersal and movement patterns of juveniles are not well known, but young birds do wander widely and tend to form aggregations in defined congregation areas, at least during portions of their postfledging/prenesting periods. The inexperienced juveniles are particularly susceptible to being struck by vehicles while feeding on road-killed carcasses, with such mortality perhaps amounting to ≥50 percent of total juvenile mortality. Breeding age is attained at age three years. The maximum recorded longevity in the wild is 22 years, but captives have lived 30+ years.

Crested caracaras have a highly variable diet and are highly opportunistic in that respect, either scavenging or taking live prey with equanimity. Any carrion is suitable for scavenging, and feeding at carcasses is often observed in association with turkey vultures (*Cathartes aura*) and/or black vultures (*Coragyps atratus*). Caracaras, however, are dominant in those feeding aggregations. Live prey taken encompasses a wide variety of both terrestrial and aquatic species—essentially any animal, including invertebrates, that can be caught and killed. Birds as large as cattle egrets (*Bubulcus ibis*) and mammals as large as cottontail rabbits (*Sylvilagus floridanus*) are taken.

Most foraging is relegated to early morning and late afternoon hours, and prey is taken by first alighting nearby and then approaching by walking. Occasionally, both pair members cooperatively bring down larger prey or kleptoparasitize vultures or wading birds. They also commonly pursue and harass vultures in flight, inducing them to disgorge, and they pirate food from other caracaras, other raptors, and crows (*Corvus* spp.)

Crested caracaras are adept at walking and running and spend much time foraging on the ground, either chasing prey or scratching and digging in search of or to dislodge prey. They commonly wade into shallow water after fish and other aquatic or semiaquatic animals and also are commonly seen walking in plowed fields or behind tractors, preying on displaced insects, and are attracted by fires to prey on animals being either killed or displaced. Patrolling roads in search of carrion is likewise common, as is perching on roadside fence posts, utility poles, spoil banks, etc., to scout for prey. Unlike most other raptors, caracaras carry food items in their beaks rather than their talons while in flight.

Survey and Monitoring Techniques

Driving road transects through potential caracara habitat (open grassland and savanna-like areas) with periodic stops to scan in the distance should reveal the presence or absence of caracaras in large areas. Factors to accommodate in designing such transects are that (1) crested caracaras maintain large home ranges and thus may not be predictably encountered on any single transect or in any particular area at any specific time; (2) caracaras commonly associate with vultures, so concentrations of vultures should be scanned for caracara presence; and (3) movements during the breeding season are centered around and more restricted to the vicinity of the nest site, hence detecting presence during that time would be more likely near nests but less likely at significant distances from nests. Binoculars or spotting scopes would be necessary equipment in any surveying effort.

Locating nests is difficult except when adults are seen carrying nesting material or food to a given site or other adult behavior indicates that a nest may be present. Nests are well concealed within tree canopy foliage and usually cannot be seen from either the ground or the air.

Capturing caracaras for leg banding, marking, or other purposes is exceedingly difficult. Methods and devices commonly used to capture vultures or other raptors (e.g., balchatri traps, cage traps, ground snares, pole nooses) are ineffective in capturing caracaras. They are extremely wary of traps as well as other unusual objects suddenly appearing in their home ranges, even if situated near or in association with carcass baits. Adults are particularly trap shy, whereas juveniles can occasionally be captured via traditional devices.

One technique has been developed, however, that takes advantage of the caracara's aggressive territorial behavior and is effective to a large degree. Tethering a captive live caracara inside a Q-net, which is similar to a large bow net, induces resident wild caracaras to approach and attempt to repel the "intruder," at which time the trap can be triggered. Morrison and McGehee (1996) provide considerable detail about this technique. The appropriate U.S. Fish and Wildlife Service aluminum leg band size for caracaras is 7A.

Management

Fundamental Management Considerations

- Crested caracaras require prairie or savanna-like habitats with low ground cover vegetation and sparse to absent shrubby vegetation, interspersed with ephemeral wetlands or sloughs and with scattered cabbage palms and/or small cabbage palm–live oak hammocks.

- Crested caracaras are sensitive to disturbance in the vicinity of their nests during the breeding season, especially during the early phases (nest construction, incubation, and brooding). Flushing from nests will occur upon the approach of humans to within ≈300 feet (92 m), and adults tend to leave the nest unattended for as long as humans remain within that distance. Otherwise, however, caracaras are tolerant of low levels of human-related activities, including the occasional presence of people, livestock, and vehicles.

- Crested caracaras cannot coexist with even small-scale suburban development, but ongoing agricultural operations where they currently occur are not necessarily incompatible with caracara welfare. Adverse impacts can occur in that respect, however, due to disturbance during the breeding season or intensified activities.

Proactive Management

1. Habitat Maintenance and Rehabilitation

Prescribed burning at intervals of 2–3 years would sustain prairie/savanna habitat characteristics in existing habitats. Manual manipulation (e.g., roller chopping, tree removal, etc.) may be necessary as preburn treatments to rehabilitate overgrown or otherwise degraded habitats. Burns should be executed under climatic conditions and via techniques (e.g., back-burning) that minimize the potential for developing crown fires, which would threaten cabbage palms or cabbage palm–live oak hammocks. Also, planting cabbage palms in scattered locations on large expanses of treeless grasslands may increase habitat carrying capacity on a regionwide scale.

2. Breeding Season Privacy and Security

A minimum-activity buffer extending ≥300 feet (92 m) outward from active nests should be observed during the breeding season (from the time adults begin nest construction until the young fledge).

Accommodative Management

1. Agricultural Operations

Observing a no-entry zone of 300 feet (92 m) around nests during the breeding season should preclude adverse impacts on the resident caracaras during that critical period. Construction of new buildings or otherwise intensifying activities that would tend to alter the landscape within ≈700 feet (215 m) should be avoided at any time of the year. Removal of cabbage palms or cabbage palm–live oak hammocks within that distance from nests should also be avoided.

Relevant Literature

Abrahamson, W. G., and D. C. Hartnett. 1990. Pine flatwoods and dry prairies. Pp. 103–49 in *Ecosystems of Florida*, ed. R. L Myers and J. W. Ewel. University of Central Florida Press.

Bloom, P. H. 1987. Capturing and handling raptors. Pp. 99–123 in *Raptor Management Techniques Manual,* ed. B. G. Pendleton et al.

Ellis, D. H., D. G. Smith, W. H. Whaley, and C. H. Ellis. 1988. Crested caracara. *National Wildlife Federation Scientific and Technical Series* 11:119–26.

Fuller, M. R., and J. A. Mosher. 1987. Raptor survey techniques. Pp. 37–65 in *Raptor Management Techniques Manual,* ed. B. G. Pendleton et al.

Funderberg, J. F., and G. Heinzman. 1967. Status of the caracara in Florida. *Florida Naturalist* 40:150–51.

Layne, J. N. 1982. The caracara in Florida. *ENFO* 3:10–12.

Layne, J. N. 1985. Audubon's caracara. *Florida Wildlife* 39(1):40–42.

Layne, J. N. 1995. Audubon's crested caracara in Florida. Pp. 82–83 in *Our Living Resources,* ed. E. T. La Roe et al. U.S. Biological Survey.

Layne, J. N. 1996. Crested caracara. Pp. 197–210 in *Rare and Endangered Biota of Florida*, vol. 5: *Birds*, ed. J. A. Rodgers, Jr., et al. University Press of Florida.

Morrison, J. L. 1996. *Crested Caracara.* Birds of North America no. 249, American Ornithologists' Union. 28 pp.

Morrison, J. L. 1999. Breeding biology and productivity of the crested caracara in Florida. *Condor* 101:505–17.

Morrison, J. L., and R. C. Banks. 1999. Methods for gender determination of crested caracaras. *Wilson Bulletin* 111:330–39.

Morrison, J. L., and M. Maltbie. 1999. Methods for gender determination of crested caracaras. *Journal of Raptor Research* 33:128–33.

Morrison, J. L., and S. M. McGehee. 1996. Capture methods for crested caracaras. *Journal of Field Ornithology* 67:630–36.

Pendleton, B. G., et al., eds. 1987. *Raptor Management Techniques Manual*. National Wildlife Federation Scientific and Technical Series no. 10.

Sanderson, J. 1996. Keeping watch on the crested caracara. *Florida Naturalist* 69:17–18.

Smith, G. 1971. The caracara. *Florida Wildlife* 24(9):4–5.

Sprunt, A., Jr. 1954. Audubon's caracara. *Florida Naturalist* 27:99–101, 119.

U.S. Fish and Wildlife Service. 1989. *Recovery Plan for the Florida Population of Audubon's Crested Caracara*. U.S. Fish and Wildlife Service. 24 pp.

U.S. Fish and Wildlife Service. 1999. Audubon's crested caracara. Pp. 4/219–36 in *South Florida Multi-Species Recovery Plan*. U.S. Fish and Wildlife Service.

Yosef, R., and D. Yosef. 1992. Hunting behavior of Audubon's crested caracara. *Journal of Raptor Research* 26:100–1.

Young, L. S., and M. N. Kochert. 1987. Marking techniques. Pp. 125–26 in *Raptor Management Techniques Manual,* ed. B. G. Pendleton et al.

11

Florida Burrowing Owl

Status

The Florida burrowing owl (*Athene cunicularia floridana*) is among 18 subspecies of burrowing owls (Order Strigiformes; Family Strigidae) native to North America, but it occurs altogether disjunctly from the other 17. It is the only subspecies that breeds east of the Mississippi River; the others, collectively, occur from south-central Canada southward to central Mexico and, during winter, farther southward to northern South America.

The statewide range of the Florida burrowing owl encompasses much of the peninsula (fig. 26), from central Suwannee County southward to Collier County on the west coast, and on the east coast southward to southern Dade County and through the Keys, with disjunct populations in the panhandle (Okaloosa County) and in northeast Florida (Duval County). The entirety of its range extends farther southward through the Bahama Islands.

Systematic statewide surveys of burrowing owl populations have not been conducted, but based on what is known about population distribution and demographics, the Florida breeding population is estimated to number 3,000–10,000 pairs. Some local or regional subpopulations occur in substantial numbers and are densely concentrated, particularly on the Cape Coral peninsula (Lee County) and in certain areas of Monroe, Sumter, Lake, Marion, Broward, and Palm Beach counties. Population collapses have occurred in some areas for no apparent reason, especially in parts of Hillsborough and Osceola counties, suggesting that local populations become established but then collapse and/or relocate. The dynamics of that process are not well understood. Some colony sites have been abandoned in a given year only to be reoccupied as soon as the following year, whereas others have remained abandoned indefinitely.

The Florida Game and Fresh Water Fish Commission designated the Florida burrowing owl a "species of special concern" in 1979.

Distinguishing Characteristics

Adult Florida burrowing owls (fig. 27) measure ≈7.8 in (20 cm) in length, wingspan is ≈20 in (51 cm), and weight is ≈1.8 ounces (150 g). The dorsal plumage is dark brown with scattered white bars and spots, the ventral plumage light beige with brown bars (mostly along the flanks). The mid-abdomen, throat, and upper breast are white but with a dark brown band separating the breast and throat. The face is tan and white, and the head is rounded without ear tufts. The iris is typically a striking yellow, but chocolate, olive, and straw-colored irises occur in some populations. The bill is yellow to greenish yellow. The legs are sparsely feathered and appear disproportionately long. Fledged young ≤10 weeks of age have a nearly solid dark brown breast and buffy abdomen.

Fig. 26. Range of the burrowing owl in Florida.

Fig. 27. Adult burrowing owl (Stephen A. Nesbitt).

Males are slightly larger and overall slightly lighter in color than females, but the sexes are difficult to differentiate in the field, especially in
fresh plumage. The color difference is most pronounced during the breeding season, possibly because males spend nearly all their time outside their
burrows and are thereby subjected to sun bleaching, whereas females
spend most of their time during the breeding season within burrows.

The vocal repertoire is extensive, particularly during the breeding season. The most commonly heard song is the male's two-note *coo-coooo*.
Other calls include a defensive/alarm hiss resembling a rattlesnake rattle
and uttered by adults when cornered outside their burrows; a female
copulatory call consisting of a series of down-slurred notes; a female rattle
uttered to summon the male; male and female copulatory warbles; a raspy
female call uttered to summon nestlings from burrows (for feeding); a
likewise female *eep* call to alert nestlings to an approaching threat (nestlings also utter *rasp* and *eep* calls to solicit food); and various clucks,
chatters and screams uttered by both sexes when mobbing predators. A
cack call is sometimes uttered in flight. The primary nonvocal sound is a

series of loud bill snaps when threatened, often in conjunction with defense vocalizations. Bill snapping can result in a bleeding tongue if prolonged, such as when being handled.

Habitat

Florida burrowing owls inhabit open, well-drained areas with low, sparse ground cover. Dry prairies subsequent to natural fires and margins of depressional marshes during dry periods constitute the primary natural habitats. Historically, then, and perhaps currently to some extent, because of the ephemeral nature of such habitats, the burrowing owl was probably distributionally nomadic in Florida, at least regionally.

Currently, however, certain artificially maintained sites having expanses of mowed areas, particularly golf courses, school campuses, athletic fields, airports, cemeteries, and industrial/residential complexes, as well as heavily grazed pastures, mirror ideal natural conditions and thereby support populations. In fact, such artificial habitats currently represent the most important habitats for burrowing owls in Florida in terms of total population numbers and overall distribution.

Life History and Behavior

As its common name implies, the Florida burrowing owl primarily nests and otherwise resides in underground burrows but occasionally also in PVC pipes, in culverts, in niches under sidewalks and under roofs, and even on the ground. Those that occupy burrows most often excavate their own but will adopt burrows of gopher tortoises (*Gopherus polyphemus*) and other burrowing animals (the western subspecies nearly always usurp burrows of burrowing mammals). The belted kingfisher (*Ceryle alcyon*) is the only other burrowing bird that breeds in Florida, but the kingfisher excavates its burrows into vertical banks.

Owl-excavated burrows extend ≈10 feet (3 m) in length and consist of an entrance mound of debris and a twisting tunnel terminating in a nest chamber ≈12 in (0.4 m) underground. Tunnels measure ≈5 in (13 cm) in width and ≈3.5 in (9 cm) in height, and the circular nest chamber is 12–18 in (305–460 cm) in diameter. Burrows can be excavated in ≤2 days. Substrates of bare ground or where the sod has been disturbed are most often selected for burrow excavation, therefore nesting can often be induced at some preferred location by mechanically removing a plug of sod.

Florida burrowing owls are nonmigratory (the western subspecies are partially migratory) and display a high degree of long-term burrow and site fidelity. They are territorial, essentially monogamous, and both males and females can breed at age one year. Nesting is concentrated from early February through late May but has been recorded as early as early October and as late as early July. Prior to egg laying, burrows are lined with grass, palm fronds, and other material, including animal feces, which apparently has an antipredator effect—burrows lined with dung are significantly less prone to predation than those which are not. Subsequent to egg laying, the burrow entrance is often adorned with highly visible objects, such as tinfoil, shells, paper, or plastic, especially when animal feces is not readily available.

Clutch size is 2–6 eggs (most often 3 or 4), egg color is white, incubation lasts 28–30 days (only the female incubates), fledging occurs at age ≈40 days, and mean brood size at fledging is ≈3. Annual reproductive success (nests fledging ≥1 young) is ≈77 percent. Double-brooding in a given year occurs but is rare (<1 percent). The survival rate to age one year is ≈19 percent, but the annual survival rate thereafter is ≈59 percent (females) to ≈68 percent (males). Longevity is unknown, but a banded western burrowing owl lived >8.5 years.

The burrowing owl is unique among North American owls in being active both during the daytime and at night. Most foraging occurs at dusk or at night, and during the day they are frequently observed perched on fence posts or at their burrow entrances. The primary foods are mole crickets (*Gryllotalpa* spp.), June beetles (*Phyllophanaga* spp.), and in southern Florida, the exotic brown anole (*Anolis sagrei*), marine toad (*Bufo marinus*), and Cuban treefrog (*Osteopilus septentrionalis*). Supplemental foods include various amphibians, small rodents, insects and arachnids, and crayfish (*Cambarus* spp.). Burrowing owls hunt on the ground by walking, hopping, or running after prey and aerially by hovering and by capturing insects in flight.

Florida burrowing owls are semicolonial and as such are aggressively territorial only in the vicinities of their burrows. Threshold distances in that respect are variable and not well known. Both males and females attack intruders, typically with outstretched talons. Burrowing owls are commonly harassed by songbirds (as is typical with other owl species), and a variety of other species prey on adults, young, and/or eggs, including great horned owls (*Bubo virginianus*), Cooper's hawks (*Accipiter cooperii*), crows (*Corvus* spp.), red-tailed hawks (*Buteo jamaicensis*), falcons (*Falco* spp.), opossums (*Didelphis virginiana*), weasels (*Mustela* spp.), skunks (*Mephitis* spp.), and domestic dogs and cats.

An additional mortality factor, significant especially where owls and humans coexist, is being struck by vehicles. Road kills can amount to up to ≈25 percent of the total annual mortality in populations occupying suburban habitats. Drowning in burrows during severe spring thunderstorms can also be a regionally significant mortality factor, for both nestlings and adults.

Survey and Monitoring Techniques

Burrowing owls are conspicuously visible where they occur, especially during the breeding season. Documenting their presence or absence or determining relative or gross abundance can therefore usually be effectively accomplished via road surveys and/or widely spaced walking transects. Also, males readily respond to broadcasts of their recorded primary song, thus that technique can also be employed, particularly when more precise population counts are needed.

The accuracy of survey data, however, can be affected to some degree by both the time of year and time of day surveys are conducted. While burrowing owls can be active at any hour of the day or night year-round, they are relatively more nocturnal during the winter months (perhaps as an adaptive avoidance of the winter presence of large numbers of diurnal avian predators, notably Cooper's hawks and falcons), more diurnal during the breeding season, and more crepuscular at the other times of year. For the most effective results, then, survey strategies should accommodate those seasonal activity patterns.

Should determining the status of individual burrows be an objective, burrows can be classified as active not only when owls are observed in attendance but also if they are decorated with shredded paper, tinfoil, or other debris.

Burrowing owls can be captured for banding, marking, or other purposes using noose carpets (monofilament nooses attached to hardware cloth deployed at burrow entrances) and/or appropriately sized Sherman, Tomahawk, or Havahart mammal live traps. The noose carpet methodology is described in detail in Bloom (1987), and live trapping techniques are described in Plumpton and Lutz (1992). Other effective capture techniques include balchatri traps, the specialized owl trap of Botelho and Arrowood (1995), and the noose rod methodology of Winchell and Turman (1992). The appropriate U.S. Fish and Wildlife Service aluminum leg band size for burrowing owls is 4.

Management

Fundamental Management Considerations

- The most elemental characteristic of burrowing owl nesting habitat is low, grass/forb ground cover.
- Burrowing owls typically excavate their burrows where the sod has been disturbed but require nearby perch sites.
- Burrowing owls can coexist proximally to human habitation and other human-related activities, but encroachment into or disturbance within the immediate vicinity of burrows can cause burrow abandonment. They are also vulnerable to being struck by vehicles in suburban areas, especially near street lamps at night while feeding on insects attracted to the light.

Proactive Management

1. Habitat Maintenance

Frequent mowing, prescribed burning, and/or livestock grazing will sustain the low ground cover required by burrowing owls, both where they already occur and as a means to rehabilitate or create habitat.

2. Habitat Enhancement

Where low perches such as fence posts are limited, constructing T-perches ≈3–4 feet (1.0–1.3 m) in height near burrow entrances, or scattered through rehabilitated (but as yet unoccupied) areas, would enhance habitat quality. Also, removing plugs of sod (in conjunction with emplacing T-perches nearby, if needed) can be effective as a means to induce nesting, as can the more intensive management strategy of installing artificial burrows. This methodology is described in detail in Collins and Landry (1977) and Henny and Blus (1981).

Accommodative Management

1. Construction Projects

Any construction of buildings or other intrusive facilities where burrowing owls occur should be restricted to ≥50 feet (17 m) from active burrows. To minimize disturbance and harassment, human entry into owl nesting areas should be deterred (through sign posting and dissemination of educational materials) or prohibited. Also, commencing new construction well in advance of the breeding season near historical, but at the time inactive, burrows would preclude owls reoccupying them during construction activities.

2. Street-related Mortality

Imposing lowered speed limits and/or emplacing speed bumps in nesting areas, especially where there are street lights, would lessen the potential for road kills.

Relevant Literature

Banuelos, G. H. T. 1993. An alternative trapping method for burrowing owls. *Journal of Raptor Research* 27:85–86.

Barrantine, C. D., and K. D. Ewing. 1988. A capture technique for burrowing owls. *North American Bird Bander* 13:107.

Bloom, P. H. 1987. Capturing and handling raptors. Pp. 99–123 in *Raptor Management Techniques Manual*, ed. B. G. Pendlton et al. National Wildlife Federation Scientific and Technical Series no. 10.

Botelho, E. S., and P. C. Arrowood. 1995. A novel, simple, safe and effective trap for burrowing owls and other fossorial animals. *Journal of Field Ornithology* 66:380–84.

Collins, C. T., and R. E. Landry. 1977. Artificial nest burrows for burrowing owls. *North American Bird Bander* 2:151–54.

Courser, W. D. 1979. Continued breeding range expansion of the burrowing owl in Florida. *American Birds* 33:143–44.

Ferguson, H. L., and P. D. Jorgensen. 1981. An efficient trapping technique for burrowing owls. *North American Bird Bander* 6:149–50.

Haug, E. A., and A. B. Didiuk. 1993. Use of recorded calls to detect burrowing owls. *Journal of Field Ornithology* 64:188–94.

Haug, E. A., B. A. Millsap, and M. S. Martel. 1993. *Burrowing Owl*. Birds of North America no. 61, American Ornithologists' Union. 19 pp.

Hennemann, W. W. III. 1980. Notes on the food habits of the burrowing owl in Duval County, Florida. *Florida Field Naturalist* 8:24–25.

Holmes, B. 1998. City planning for owls. *National Wildlife* 36(6):46–53.

James, P. C., and G. A. Fox. 1987. Effects of some insecticides on productivity of burrowing owls. *Blue Jay* 45:65–71.

Lewis, J. C. 1973. Food habits of Florida burrowing owls. *Florida Field Naturalist* 1:28–30.

Lutz, R. S., and D. L. Plumpton. 1999. Philopatry and nest site reuse by burrowing owls: Implications for productivity. *Journal of Raptor Research* 33:149–53.

Martin, D. J. 1973. Selected aspects of burrowing owl ecology and behavior. *Condor* 75:446–56.

Mealey, B. 1997. Reproductive ecology of the burrowing owls, *Speotyto cunicularia floridana,* in Dade and Broward counties, Florida. *Journal of Raptor Research* 9:74–79.

Millsap, B. A. 1996. Florida burrowing owl. Pp. 579–87 in *Rare and Endangered Biota of Florida,* vol. 5: *Birds,* ed. J. A. Rodgers, Jr., et al. University Press of Florida.

Millsap, B. A., and C. Bear. 2000. Density and reproduction of burrowing owls along an urban development gradient. *Journal of Wildlife Management* 64:33–41.

Neill, W. T. 1954. Notes on the Florida burrowing owl, and some new records for the species. *Florida Naturalist* 27:67–70.

Norris, D. 1976. Florida burrowing owl. *Florida Wildlife* 30(1):6–8.

Pendleton, B. G. 1989. Burrowing owls capture the hearts of Cape Coral residents. *Eyas* 12(2):5–6.

Plumpton, D. L., and R. S. Lutz. 1992. Multiple-capture techniques for burrowing owls. *Wildlife Society Bulletin* 20:426–28.

Plumpton, D. L., and R. S. Lutz. 1993. Influence of vehicular traffic on time budgets of nesting burrowing owls. *Journal of Wildlife Management* 57:612–16.

Rhodes, S. N. 1892. The breeding habits of the Florida burrowing owl. *Auk* 9:1–8.

Rowe, M. P. 1987. Burrowing owls in Florida's urban underground. *Bird Watcher's Digest* Sept.–Oct.:17–19.

Trulio, L. A. 1995. Passive relocation: A method to preserve burrowing owls on disturbed sites. *Journal of Field Ornithology* 66:99–106.

Wesemann, T., and M. P. Rowe. 1987. Factors influencing the distribution and abundance of burrowing owls in Cape Coral, Florida. Pp. 129–37 in *Proceedings of the National Symposium on Urban Wildlife,* ed. L. W. Adams and D. L. Leedy. National Institute of Urban Wildlife.

Winchell, C. S. 1999. An efficient technique to capture complete broods of burrowing owls. *Wildlife Society Bulletin* 27:193–96.

Winchell, C. S., and J. W. Turman. 1992. A new trapping technique for burrowing owls: The noose rod. *Journal of Field Ornithology* 63:66–70.

Yosef, R., and M. Deyrup. 1994. Pellet analysis of burrowing owls in southcentral Florida. *Florida Field Naturalist* 22:78–80.

Young, L. S., and M. N. Kochert. 1987. Marking techniques. Pp. 125–56 in *Raptor Management Techniques Manual,* ed. B. G. Pendleton et al. National Wildlife Federation Scientific and Technical Series no. 10.

Zarn, M. 1974. *Burrowing Owl.* U.S. Bureau of Land Management Habitat Management Series on Unique or Endangered Species Report no. 11. 25 pp.

12

❧ ❧

Bats

Status

Eighteen species of bats (Order Chiroptera) representing three families—Vespertilionidae (twilight bats), Molossidae (free-tailed bats), and Phyllostomatidae (leaf-nosed bats)—are native to Florida, occurring in varying degrees of abundance (table 4). None of the 18 is altogether restricted to Florida, and only four—the gray bat, southeastern bat, Seminole bat, and Rafinesque's (= eastern) big-eared bat—are largely restricted to the southeastern United States. One subspecies, however, the Florida mastiff bat, a subspecies of the Wagner's mastiff bat, does occur only in Florida.

The migratory hoary bat does not breed in Florida, and it is doubtful that the Indiana bat, little brown bat, northern long-eared bat, or silver-haired bat do, at least on a sustained basis. The limited areas in northern Florida in which the latter four species have been recorded represent the extreme southern peripheries of their respective total ranges. Whether the Jamaican fruit bat or Pallas' free-tailed bat breed in Florida is unknown. Each of those species was confirmed to occur in the Keys in 1995, and it is unclear whether that apparent recent colonization is transient in nature or will ultimately prove to be permanent.

The Indiana bat was included on the first federal list of endangered species, issued by the U.S. Fish and Wildlife Service in 1967, and the gray bat was federally listed as endangered in 1976. The Florida Game and Fresh Water Fish Commission listed the Indiana bat as a threatened species in 1974 but reclassified it to endangered in 1975, at which time the gray bat was also state-listed as endangered. The Florida mastiff bat was state-listed as endangered in 1993.

Table 4. Status of Florida's 18 native bat species

Species	Florida range	Relative abundance
Twilight bats		
Gray bat (*Myotis grisescens*)	Jackson/Gadsden counties	Very rare[d]
Indiana bat (*Myotis sodalis*)	Jackson County[a]	Very rare[d]
Little brown bat (*Myotis lucifugus*)	Northern tier of counties	Rare[e]
Southeastern bat (*Myotis austroriparius*)	Panhandle/northern peninsula	Abundant
Northern (= Keen's) long-eared bat (*Myotis septentrionalis* [= *keeni*])	Panhandle	Very rare[e]
Hoary bat (*Lasiurus cinereus*)	Panhandle/northern peninsula[b]	Uncommon
Red bat (*Lasiurus borealis*)	Panhandle/northern peninsula	Common
Seminole bat (*Lasiurus seminolus*)	Statewide except the Keys	Common
Northern yellow bat (*Lasiurus intermedius*)	Statewide except the Keys	Abundant
Silver-haired bat (*Lasionycteris noctivagans*)	Panhandle and the Keys	Very rare
Eastern pipistrelle (*Pipistrellus subflavus*)	Statewide except south Florida	Common
Rafinesque's (= eastern) big-eared bat (*Corynorhinus rafinesquii*)	Panhandle/northern peninsula	Rare
Big brown bat (*Eptisicus fuscus*)	Statewide except south Florida	Uncommon
Evening bat (*Nycticeius humeralis*)	Statewide except the Keys	Common
Free-tailed bats		
Brazilian free-tailed bat (*Tadarida brasiliensis*)	Statewide	Common
Florida free-tailed bat (*Eumops glaucinus floridanus*)	South Florida except the Keys	Very rare[f]
Pallas' mastiff bat (*Mollosus mollosus*)	The Keys[c]	Uncommon
Leaf-nosed bats		
Jamaican fruit bat (*Artibeus jamaicensis*)	The Keys[c]	Rare

a. Known only from Florida Caverns State Park.

b. Present in Florida only as migrants in spring and fall.

c. Recently (1995) discovered and may not be permanently established.

d. Designated endangered by the U.S. Fish and Wildlife Service and Florida Fish and Wildlife Conservation Commission.

e. Occurs in Florida only as an occasional transient.

f. Designated endangered by the Florida Fish and Wildlife Conservation Commission.

Distinguishing Characteristics

As their familial common name implies, free-tailed bats have tails that extend beyond the interfemoral membrane. The tails of twilight bats do not. And as their familial common name likewise implies, leaf-nosed bats have noses that are leaflike in appearance. Free-tailed and twilight bats have smooth noses. Differentiating between families is thereby simple, but differentiating between species is often difficult, especially among *Myotis* bats. Species differentiation, though, is substantially important in the present context only with respect to identifying endangered or threatened species, hence only the diagnostic characteristics of those species are here addressed in detail. The more diagnostic characteristics are in italics. *Bats of America* (Barbour and Davis 1969) is a good source for detailed identifying characteristics of all North American bats.

Gray Bat

Pelage

Hairs unicolored (all other similar species have bicolored or tricolored pelage), gray or dusky dorsally, especially after midsummer molt, but often bleaching to chestnut brown or russet between molts, paler ventrally.

Calcar

Unkeeled (some other Florida bats have prominently or slightly keeled calcars).

Tragus

Pointed (non-*Myotis* twilight bats have a rounded tragus).

Muzzle

Haired, color consistent with face (non-*Myotis* twilight bats have an unhaired, black muzzle).

Total Length

3.1–3.7 in (80–96 mm).

Forearm Length

1.6–1.8 in (40–46 mm).

Indiana Bat

Pelage

Bicolored (darker at the base than at the tips), *nonglossy,* chestnut-gray dorsally (but dark umber on the shoulder) and buffy to grayish white ventrally. The little brown bat and northern big-eared bat are closely similar but have glossy, cinnamon-buff to dark brown dorsal pelage.

Calcar

Prominently keeled (the little brown bat and northern big-eared bat have an unkeeled or a slightly keeled calcar).

Tragus

Pointed (non-*Myotis* twilight bats have a rounded tragus).

Ear

<0.6 in (1.6 cm) (some other Florida bats have ears >0.6 in).

Muzzle

Haired, color consistent with face (non-*Myotis* twilight bats have an unhaired, black muzzle).

Total Length

2.7–3.5 in (7.0–9.0 cm).

Forearm Length

1.4–1.6 in (3.5–4.1 cm).

Florida Mastiff Bat

Pelage

Bicolored (lighter at the base than at the tips), glossy, black to cinnamon to brownish gray dorsally, grayish ventrally.

Ears

Conjoined at the base.

Tail

Distal one-half extends beyond the interfemoral membrane (i.e., "free-tailed"). The only other free-tailed Florida bats are the Brazilian free-tailed bat, which is similarly-colored but smaller—total length 3.5–4.3 in (9.0–11.0 cm)—and with ears not conjoined at the base, and the Pallas' mastiff bat, which is similarly smaller and occurs only in the Keys.

Total Length

5.1–6.4 in (13.0–16.5 cm); the Florida mastiff bat is the largest of Florida's bats.

Forearm Length

2.2–2.7 in (5.8–6.9 cm); other free-tailed bats in Florida have forearm lengths <2.1 in (5.3 cm).

Habitat

Florida's bats roost primarily in caves, trees, or buildings, depending on the species, and foraging habitat characteristics likewise vary among species, although most forage near water (table 5). The most common tree roost sites are under loose or shaggy bark, in cavities or hollow areas, in foliage, especially palm tree foliage, and in Spanish moss (*Tillandsia usneoides*). The most common building roost sites are attics, drain pipes, behind shutters, in other dark niches, and under roof tiles. The undersides of bridges and crannies in billboards are also used for roosting.

Life History and Behavior

All Florida bats are nocturnal and, except for the frugivorous Jamaican fruit bat, insectivorous. Roost sites are typically exited at or shortly after dusk. Feeding can be continuous through the night, interspersed with periods of rest, or during the first ≈1–2 hours following roost exit and the final ≈1–2 hours before returning, near dawn, with a rest period of several hours in between. Feeding activity is suppressed during cooler weather.

Primary foods are mosquitos, moths, and other night-flying insects. Prey is detected via echolocation and captured in flight with the mouth, wings, and interfemoral membrane. Individual bats consume approximately their weight in insects nightly.

Most bat species mate during fall or winter, but fertilization in the female is delayed until spring. Birthing occurs in late spring or summer.

Table 5. Primary roosting and foraging habitats of Florida's bats

Species	Roosting habitat	Foraging habitat
Twilight bats		
Gray bat	Caves, bridges, culverts	Wooded streams/pools
Indiana bat	Caves, dead trees (under bark)	Wooded streams
Little brown bat	Caves, hollow trees, buildings, bridges	Near water
Southeastern bat	Caves, buildings, hollow trees, bridges, culverts	Near water
Northern long-eared bat	Caves, buildings, hollow trees, bridges	Wooded areas
Hoary bat	Trees	Wooded areas
Red bat	Trees (in foliage)	Wooded areas
Seminole bat	Trees (in Spanish moss/foliage)	Wooded areas
Northern yellow bat	Trees (in Spanish moss), palms	Open uplands, lake borders
Silver-haired bat	Trees	Wooded areas
Eastern pipistrelle	Caves, trees, culverts	Wooded areas near water
Rafinesque's big-eared bat	Trees, small buildings, caves, bridges	Pine flatwoods, oak hammocks, bottomland hardwoods
Big brown bat	Caves, bridges, buildings	Open uplands
Evening bat	Hollow trees, buildings, bridges	Open uplands
Free-tailed bats		
Brazilian free-tailed bat	Trees, buildings, bridges	Open uplands
Wagner's mastiff bat	Trees, buildings	High altitudes
Pallas' mastiff bat	Buildings, hollow trees	Open uplands
Leaf-nosed bats		
Jamaican fruit bat	Trees	Orchards, wooded areas, residential areas

Litter size is 1–4, depending on the species, although most colonial species produce just one young per year. Newly born bats attach to the mother as she roosts during the day but remain at the roost site at night, during which time the mother periodically returns to nurse. Young bats can fly at age 3–5 weeks, depending on the species. Average life span is 10–12 years, although >30-year life spans have been documented.

Several myths persist about bats that have little or no basis in fact, particularly that they are blind or nearly so, that they attack humans, that they can become entangled in people's hair, that they feed on blood, and that they commonly transmit disease, especially rabies. In fact, though, bats can see quite well, they are not aggressive toward humans, and they do not become entangled in hair. Only three species feed on blood—the common vampire (*Desmodus rotundus*), white-winged vampire (*Diaemus youngi*), and hairy-legged vampire (*Diphylla ecaudata*), all of which are confined to tropical and subtropical Latin America; only *Desmodus rotundus* feeds on the blood of other mammals. And bats are exceptionally resistant to disease. They can contract rabies, as can many mammals. However, rabies is not nearly as common in bats as some believe, occurring in only <0.5 percent of individuals comprising a given population, and in some species the incidence of rabies is virtually zero. For example, the infection rate in the southeastern bat, a common bat in Florida, is 0.05 percent. Moreover, bats infected with rabies rarely become aggressive, as most other rabid mammals do, but rather become paralyzed and die. The threat to human health from rabid bats, therefore, is slight.

Nevertheless, people should never handle wild bats, particularly bats that are on the ground, appear weak or injured, or are otherwise approachable. In the paralyzing stages of the disease, rabid bats are unable to fly and are therefore relatively easy to approach.

Anyone bitten by a bat should wash the wound thoroughly with soap and water as soon as possible and seek medical advice. Also, if the bat can be captured or killed, it should be taken to a public health agency or animal control authority. Rabies can be detected in bats only through laboratory analysis. Capture techniques are described in the Management section of this chapter.

Survey and Monitoring Techniques

Unless altogether impractical, bats using enclosed roosts (mines, caves, etc.) should be inventoried from outside the roosts as they exit in the evening. Most species are highly sensitive to disturbance while roosting, and entering occupied enclosed roosts can result in bats abandoning roosts, females dropping their dependent young, and hibernating bats becoming prematurely active and expending metabolically critical stored fat reserves, ultimately resulting in death. However, under some circumstances (e.g., roosts with multiple exits), entering roosts may be necessary to achieve census objectives. In such instances, the number and duration of visits should be minimized to the extent possible, and only red lights (e.g., headlamps with Kodak Wratten number 29 red filters) should be used.

Advantageous visual observation positions outside roost exits would be those from which exiting bats are backlighted against the sky, and hand counters and night viewing goggles (or other night vision devices) would be valuable tools. Other bat-censusing methodologies include electronic counting devices, photographic methods, and thermal infrared imagery. Fenton et al. (1987) and Kunz (1988) can be consulted as regards the array of bat-censusing techniques (and for other research methodologies). Watson (1971) and Kunz and Brock (1975) specifically address electronic counting devices; Humphrey (1971) and Boogher and Slusher (1978) address photographic methods; and Kirkwood and Cartwright (1991, 1993) and Sabol and Hudson (1995) address thermal infra-red imagery. Regardless of the methodology used, because the first emergents frequently loop and reenter roosts, care should be taken to not double-count those early "scouts."

Standard capture-mark-recapture techniques have also been used to census bat populations, and activity patterns can be monitored using radiotelemetry. Brownie et al. (1978), Otis et al. (1978), and White et al. (1982) can be consulted regarding capture-mark-recapture methodologies, and Carter et al. (1999) address radiotelemetry methodologies specific to bats.

Bats can be captured using a variety of means, but mist netting is the most common and, for most purposes, the most effective technique. For best results, four-shelved black nets should be used, 6 feet (2 m) in height with a mesh size of ≈1.5 in (36 mm). Other techniques effective in capturing bats are by hand (e.g., at roosts), and using bucket traps, bag traps, harp traps, funnel traps, and hoop nets. Greenhall and Paradiso (1968), Fenton et al. (1987), and Kunz (1988) describe bat-capturing techniques and devices in considerable detail, and the American Society of Mammalogists (1998) has issued comprehensive and detailed guidelines relative to the capture, handling, and care of all mammals.

Management

Fundamental Management Considerations

- Roost integrity/security is the most important factor affecting bat welfare in Florida. The most pervasive threat in that respect is indiscriminate entry into occupied caves (and other closed roosts) by humans, which can result in roost abandonment, females dropping dependent young, or hibernating bats becoming prematurely active and expending metabolically critical stored fat reserves.

· Bats (in Florida, particularly the southeastern, big brown, Brazilian free-tailed, and evening bats) can be attracted to artificial roosts, or "bat houses."

· It is not uncommon for bats to colonize attics or wall spaces of buildings inhabited by humans or to wander into living quarters through open windows or accesses to attics or wall spaces. Although such bat presence presents negligible physical threat or health risk, the accumulation of guano (particularly its unpleasant odor) and the noise generated by colonies can constitute a genuine nuisance, as does the presence of a bat within living quarters.

Proactive Management

Bat roosts currently secure from intrusive outside forces such as human entry would require only passive accommodation. Many roosts, however, are subject to such outside forces, so any precaution or measure that would minimize intrusion of outside elements into a given roost, taking into consideration the site-specific circumstances, would benefit the roost's occupants. A common countermeasure taken in that respect has been precluding human entry either by fencing a roost and its immediate vicinity or by gating its entrance. Installing gates, however, has in some instances resulted in bats abandoning roosts due to improper design or deployment; gates can be obstructive to bat exit and entry or can cause temperature changes within the roost. Also, some species are altogether intolerant of gating and others are tolerant only during certain seasons (e.g., during hibernation). Gating cave entrances, then, should be undertaken only when other exclusion methods are impractical and only according to tested methodologies. Tuttle (1977), Tuttle and Stevenson (1977), White and Seginak (1987), Tuttle and Taylor (1994), and/or local bat biologists should be consulted in that regard.

In 1992 the American Society of Mammalogists issued guidelines for the protection of bat roosts (see Sheffield et al. 1992). The human-entry components of those guidelines, in essence, are the recommendations that follow:

1. Exact locations of roosts should not be revealed.

2. Caves or other structures occupied by endangered or threatened spe-

cies should not be entered except as specifically permitted by the U.S. Fish and Wildlife Service and/or state wildlife agencies.

3. Entering hibernacula or nursery caves for monitoring or other necessary purposes at the times they are occupied should be limited to one visit per year (preferably every other year), and for only brief periods. Entry at times when sites are unoccupied should be undertaken only so long as the cave is left unaltered and unpolluted.

4. Persons entering occupied roosts should reduce their potential disruptive impact by (a) minimizing noise and the number of personnel involved, (b) using only lights powered by batteries or cold chemicals (e.g., cyalume), and (c) avoiding approaching roosting bats too closely.

Deploying bat houses is increasing in popularity not only to accommodate bat welfare or simply to enjoy the presence of bats but also as an effective mosquito control strategy. For any purpose, bat houses should be constructed of weather-durable, rough-textured wood (exterior-grade plywood is effective) 0.5 in (1.3 cm) in thickness and constructed to be open-bottomed (but otherwise enclosed), with multiple vertical partitions within, variably spaced ≈0.7–1.0 in (1.9–2.5 cm) apart. The exterior should be caulked and painted to be airtight and watertight.

A small bat house particularly suited for suburban homesites and other smaller properties is the Bat Conservation International (BCI) nursery house, which is ≈31 in (78.7 cm) tall. For best results, such smaller houses should be deployed 12–18 feet (4.0–6.0 m) above ground on the east, southeast, south, or southwest side of a tree or building (for exposure to the morning sun and shade in the afternoon) and near a natural water source or with a nearby and maintained water station provided. Instructional materials for constructing BCI houses as well as other types of small bat houses are available from Bat Conservation International, P.O. Box 162603, Austin, TX 78716–2603.

For insect control purposes in association with parks, college campuses, malls, development communities, and other more expansive properties, larger bat houses would be more appropriate. Several such larger houses are in use in Florida, including those in Gainesville (on the University of Florida Campus, see Conover 1998), Port St. Lucie (on the grounds of the New York Mets' spring training facilities), and Tallahassee (adjacent to Tallahassee Mall parking areas).

The Tallahassee house measures 10 feet × 10 feet (3 m × 3 m), has 46 vertical partitions, and can accommodate ≈5,000 bats. It is elevated 25 feet (7.6 m) above ground on four telephone poles and has a Mediterranean-style tiled roof (fig. 28) and, as a "head start" strategy, is "seeded" with bats captured as nuisances in buildings and homes in the Tallahassee area. The houses in Port St. Lucie and Gainesville are of similar design and are similarly deployed, as is one scheduled for installation in Tampa, but vary in size. Heinrichs (1986), Tuttle (1988a), Kern et al. (1993), Needham (1995), and Tuttle and Hensley (1997) provide considerable detail about the construction, deployment, and effectiveness of various bat houses.

Accommodative Management

Numerous strategies have been and continue to be employed in attempts to evict bats from attics and other spaces where they have become established and constitute a nuisance. However, although some are widely believed to be effective, few indeed are, particularly in the long term. Accordingly, several factors should be considered before embarking on a course to resolve a resident bat problem:

Toxicants

Toxicants cannot altogether eliminate bats from buildings. Moreover, they are illegal to apply in Florida (unless under a permit issued by the Florida Fish and Wildlife Conservation Commission to do so), and, most important, they pose significant health hazards to both humans and non-target animals. The toxicants most commonly used to combat bats are anticoagulants (e.g., chlorophacinone, or Rozol), which (1) are much more toxic than anticoagulants known to cause birth defects in humans; (2) can be absorbed directly through human skin; (3) can travel into human living quarters from treated attics; (4) can increase the potential for bats contracting rabies; and (5) cause sick and dying bats to become grounded, facilitating a higher likelihood of contact with pets, other animals, and people.

Ultrasonic Sound

Ultrasonic devices have been tested as a means to repel bats but with negligible success (some even attract bats), and moreover, some ultrasonic emissions are harmful to humans.

Fig. 28. The bat house near Tallahassee Mall, Tallahassee (Don A. Wood).

Chemical/Aerosol Repellents

Moth balls, when used in quantities sufficient to repel bats, can be hazardous to human health, and in any event soon evaporate, after which the bats return. Burning sulphur candles can repel bats but requires perpetual treatment to be effective in the long term and can be a fire hazard. Spraying aerosol dog or cat repellents on known roosting niches (e.g., under porch roofs) can discourage bats from returning to that particular site for up to several months. However, such aerosols should always be applied when bats are away from the treatment site. Directly spraying roosting bats can result in their accidentally flying into the applicator's face while attempting to escape, and sprayed bats can become sick and grounded, increasing the potential for contact with humans and pets.

Lights/Ventilation

Installing lights and/or improving ventilation in attics can render them unattractive to bats but in most instances is not practical or altogether effective.

Bat Exclusion

Taking measures to prevent bats from returning is the most effective and foolproof way to rid an area of bats and can be accomplished either while they are away foraging or during the time of year, usually winter, when they may be elsewhere (e.g., in hibernation caves). Permanently sealing entry/exit points is the most efficient strategy in dealing with attic/wall space nuisance bats. As a pre-repair measure in that respect, or when such repairs cannot be made in a timely fashion, 0.25 in (0.6 cm) polypropylene bird netting (typically used to protect fruit trees from birds and available in garden centers) or clear sheets of plastic can be used as a one-way exclusion valve until permanent repairs can be made.

Such netting or plastic sheet should be hung during the day, attached to buildings with staples or duct tape several inches above the hole or crack and extending ≥2 feet to either side and below it. The sides of the netting can also be attached, but only ≈¾ of the way to the bottom. The bottom must hang loosely free. Bats will exit by crawling down the netting and flying out at the bottom but will be unable to find their way back in upon their morning return (bats fly directly into their entry points when they return from foraging). It would be preferable to leave the barrier in place through at least three nights before making permanent repairs to ensure that all bats have been excluded. Exclusion measures, however, should never be taken during the time of year flightless young are present (usually mid-April through August). Without parental care, the young will starve, resulting in a significant odor problem.

Bats encountered within human living quarters can be evicted either by facilitating their exit or by physically removing them. If the intruding bat is flying or otherwise active, it can usually be induced to leave by closing all doors leading to other parts of the house, opening all doors and windows leading outside, and turning on all lights in the room. One can prompt the bat to fly if it is not already flying and then either leave or stand in the center of the room while the bat echolocates its way to an open exit. Should that prove unsuccessful, it can be captured with a butterfly or other mesh net, which should be swung from behind to avoid the bat detecting it, or by waiting until the bat lands and then capturing it by hand (wearing leather work gloves) or by placing a coffee can or similar container over it and sliding a piece of cardboard underneath to trap the bat inside. The latter strategy can also be used to capture torpid or otherwise inactive bats.

Intruder bats typically enter living quarters through open windows or doors, down chimneys, through vents, or through spaces past loose-fitting screen doors. Precluding further visits would thus require screening windows, grating chimneys, and/or installing more tightly fitting screen doors. Some intruders, however, enter living quarters from attics or wall spaces, and eliminating these entry points (some bats can enter through holes or cracks as small as $\frac{1}{4}$ in $\times$ 1 in) might require sealing them. Cracks should not be sealed with caulk in the afternoon (bats may contact the uncured caulk that evening), nor should expanding foam be used when bats are present.

Relevant Literature

Adams, F. H. 1996. First bat colonies in the Keys. *Florida Wildlife* 50(1):2–5.

Altringham, J. D. 1996. *Bats: Biology and Behaviour.* Oxford University Press. 262 pp.

American Society of Mammalogists. 1998. Guidelines for the capture, handling, and care of mammals as approved by the American Society of Mammalogists. *Journal of Mammalogy* 79:1416–31.

Bailey, M. M., J. T. Baccus, and R. D. Welch. 1995. Managing visitors to prevent disruption of emergence of bats. *Proceedings of the Annual Conference of the Southeastern Association of Fish and Wildlife Agencies* 49:348–55.

Bain, J. R., and S. R. Humphrey. 1986. Social organization and biased primary sex ratio of the evening bat, *Nycticeius humeralis. Florida Scientist* 49:22–31.

Barbour, R. W., and W. H. Davis. 1969. *Bats of America.* University Press of Kentucky. 286 pp.

Barclay, M. R. B., D. W. Thomas, and M. B. Fenton. 1980. Comparison of methods used for controlling bats in buildings. *Journal of Wildlife Management* 44:502–6.

Belwood, J. J. 1992. Florida mastiff bat. Pp. 216–23 in *Rare and Endangered Biota of Florida,* vol. 1: *Mammals,* ed. S. R. Humphrey. University Press of Florida.

Belwood, J. J. 1992. Southeastern big-eared bat. Pp. 287–93 in *Rare and Endangered Biota of Florida,* vol. 1: *Mammals,* ed. S. R. Humphrey. University Press of Florida.

Best, T. L., and M. K. Hudson. 1996. Movements of gray bats (*Myotis grisescens*) between roost sites and foraging areas. *Journal of the Alabama Academy of Science* 67:6–14.

Best, T. L., B. A. Milam, T. D. Haas, W. S. Cvilikas, and L. R. Saidak. 1997. Variation in diet of the gray bat (*Myotis grisescens*). *Journal of Mammalogy.* 78:569–83.

Brack, V., Jr. 1989. The Indiana bat. Pp. 609–22 in *Audubon Wildlife Report 1988–1989,* ed. W. J. Chandler. Academic Press.

Brigham, R. M., and M. B. Fenton. 1987. The effect of roost sealing as a method to control maternity colonies of big brown bats. *Canadian Journal of Public Health* 78:47–50.

Brittingham, M. C., and L. M. Williams. 2000. Bat boxes as alternative roosts for displaced bat maternity colonies. *Wildlife Society Bulletin* 28:197–207.

Brown, L. N. 1985. First occurrence of the little brown bat, *Myotis lucifugus,* in Florida. *Florida Scientist* 48:200–1.

Brown, L. N. 1986. First record of the silver-haired bat, *Lasionycteris noctivagans,* in Florida. *Florida Scientist* 49:167–68.

Brownie, C., D. R. Anderson, K. P. Burnham, and D. S. Robson. 1978. *Statistical Inference from Band Recovery Data: A Handbook.* U.S. Fish and Wildlife Service. 212 pp.

Carter, T. C., M. A. Menzel, B. R. Chapman, K. V. Miller, and J. R. Lee. 1999. A new method to study bat activity patterns. *Wildlife Society Bulletin* 27:598–602.

Clark, D. R. 1981. *Bats and Environmental Contaminants: A Review.* U.S. Fish and Wildlife Service Special Scientific Report Wildlife no. 235. 27 pp.

Clawson, R. L. 1984. Recovery efforts for the endangered Indiana bat (*Myotis sodalis*) and gray bat (*Myotis grisescens*). Pp. 301–7 in *Proceedings of the Workshop on Management of Nongame Species and Ecological Communities,* ed. W. C. McComb. University of Kentucky Department of Forestry.

Conover, A. 1998. This university goes to bat for thousands of winged residents. *National Wildlife* 36(6):68–70.

Constantine, D. G. 1967. *Activity Patterns of the Mexican Free-tailed Bat.* University of New Mexico Publications in Biology no. 7. 79 pp.

Constantine, D. G. 1979. Bat rabies and bat management. *Bulletin of Vector Ecology* 4:1–9.

Cope, J. B., and S. R. Humphrey. 1977. Spring and summer swarming behavior in the Indiana bat, *Myotis sodalis*. *Journal of Mammalogy* 58:93–95.

Cox, J. A., and R. S. Kautz. 2000. *Habitat Conservation Needs of Rare and Imperiled Wildlife in Florida*. Florida Fish and Wildlife Conservation Commission. 156 pp.

Davis, W. H. 1966. Population dynamics of the bat *Pipistrellus subflavus*. *Journal of Mammalogy* 47:383–96.

Fenton, M. B., P. Racey, and J. M. V. Rayner. 1987. *Recent Advances in the Study of Bats*. Cambridge University Press. 470 pp.

Frank, P. A. 1997. First record of *Artibeus jamaicensis* Leach (1821) from the United States. *Florida Scientist* 60:37–39.

Frank, P. A. 1997. First record of *Molossus molossus tropidorhynchus* Gray (1839) from the United States. *Journal of Mammalogy* 78:103–5.

Franz, R., J. Bauer, and T. Morris. 1994. Review of biologically significant caves and their faunas in Florida and south Georgia. *Brimleyana* 20:1–109.

Gardner, J. E., J. D. Garner, and J. E. Hofman. 1989. A portable mist netting system for capturing bats with emphasis on *Myotis sodalis* (Indiana bat). *Bat Research News* 30:1–8.

Goehring, H. H. 1972. Twenty-year study of *Eptesicus fuscus* in Minnesota. *Journal of Mammalogy* 53:201–7.

Gore, J. A. 1992. Big brown bat. Pp. 343–48 in *Rare and Endangered Biota of Florida*, vol. 1: *Mammals*, ed. S. R. Humphrey. University Press of Florida.

Gore, J. A. 1992. Gray bat. Pp. 63–70 in *Rare and Endangered Biota of Florida*, vol. 1: *Mammals*, ed. S. R. Humphrey. University Press of Florida.

Gore, J. A., and J. A. Hovis. 1992. The southeastern bat: Another cave-roosting bat in trouble. *Bats* 10(2):10–12.

Gore, J. A., and J. A. Hovis. 1998. Status and conservation of southeastern *Myotis* maternity colonies in Florida caves. *Florida Scientist* 61:160–70.

Greenhall, A. M. 1982. *House Bat Management*. U.S. Fish and Wildlife Service Resource Publication no. 143. 33 pp.

Greenhall, A. M., and J. L. Paradiso. 1968. *Bats and Bat Banding*. U.S. Fish and Wildlife Service Resource Publication no. 72.

Hall, J. S. 1962. A life history and taxonomic study of the Indiana bat, *Myotis sodalis*. *Reading Public Museum and Art Gallery Scientific Publication* 12:1–68.

Hardin, J. W., and M. D. Hassell. 1970. Observations on waking periods and movements of *Myotis sodalis* during hibernation. *Journal of Mammalogy* 51:829–31.

Harvey, M. J. 1975. Endangered Chiroptera of the southeastern United States. *Proceedings of the Annual Conference of the Southeastern Association of Game and Fish Commissions* 29:429–33.

Heinrichs, J. 1986. Build your own bat house. *International Wildlife* 16(1):42–43.

Hill, J. E., and J. D. Smith. 1984. *Bats: A Natural History*. University of Texas Press. 243 pp.

Humphrey, S. R. 1971. Photographic estimation of population sizes of the Mexican free-tailed bat, *Tabarida brasiliensis*. *American Midland Naturalist* 86:220–23.

Humphrey, S. R. 1978. Status, winter habitat, and management of the endangered Indiana bat, *Myotis sodalis*. *Florida Scientist* 41:65–76.

Humphrey, S. R. 1992. Indiana bat. Pp. 54–62 in *Rare and Endangered Biota of Florida*, vol. 1: *Mammals*, ed. S. R. Humphrey. University Press of Florida.

Humphrey, S. R., and J. A. Gore. 1992. Southeastern brown bat. Pp. 335–42 in *Rare and Endangered Biota of Florida*, vol. 1: *Mammals*, ed. S. R. Humphrey.

Humphrey, S. R., A. R. Richter, and J. B. Cope. 1977. Summer habitat and ecology of the endangered Indiana bat, *Myotis sodalis*. *Journal of Mammalogy* 58:334–46.

Johnson, S. A., V. Brack, Jr., and R. E. Rolley. 1998. Overwinter weight loss of Indiana bats (*Myotis sodalis*) from hibernacula subject to human visitation. *American Midland Naturalist* 139:255–61.

Jones, C., and R. D. Suttkus. 1975. Notes on the natural history of *Plecotus rafinesquii*. *Occasional Papers of the Louisiana State University Museum of Zoology* 47:1–14.

Kern, W. H., Jr. 1992. Northern yellow bat. Pp. 349–56 in *Rare and Endangered Biota of Florida*, vol. 1: *Mammals*, ed. S. R. Humphrey. University Press of Florida.

Kern, W. H., Jr., and S. R. Humphrey. 1995. *Habitat Use by the Red Bat and Seminole Bat in Northern Florida*. Florida Game and Fresh Water Fish Commission Nongame Wildlife Program Project GFC-86-009 Final Report. 88 pp.

Kern, W. H., Jr., J. J. Belwood, and P. G. Koehler. 1993. *Bats in Buildings*. University of Florida Cooperative Extension Service Fact Sheet ENY-272. 8 pp.

Kirkwood, J., and A. Cartwright. 1991. Behavioral observations in thermal imaging of the big brown bat. *Proceedings of the Society of Photo-Optical Instrumentation Engineers (SPIE)* 1467:369–71.

Kirkwood, J., and A. Cartwright. 1993. Comparison of two systems for viewing bat behavior in the dark. *Proceedings of the Indiana Academy of Science* 102(1–2):133–38.

Kunz, T. H. 1988. *Ecological and Behavioral Methods for the Study of Bats*. Washington, D.C.: Smithsonian Institution. 533 pp.

Kunz, T. H., ed. 1982. *Ecology of Bats*. Plenum Press. 425 pp.

Kunz, T. H., and C. E. Brock. 1975. A comparison of mist nets and ultrasonic detectors for monitoring flight activity of bats. *Journal of Mammalogy* 56:907–11.

LaVal, R. K., and M. L. LaVal. 1979. Notes on reproduction, behavior and abundance of the red bat, *Lasiurus borealis*. *Journal of Mammalogy* 60:209–12.

LaVal, R. K., and M. L. LaVal. 1980. *Ecological Studies and Management of Missouri Bats, with Emphasis on Cave-dwelling Species*. Missouri Department of Conservation Terrestrial Series no. 8. 53 pp.

LaVal, R. K., R. L. Clawson, M. L. LaVal, and W. Caire. 1977. Foraging behavior and nocturnal activity patterns of Missouri bats, with emphasis on the endangered species *Myotis grisescens* and *Myotis sodalis*. *Journal of Mammalogy* 58:592–99.

Lazell, J. D., and K. F. Koopman. 1985. Notes on bats of Florida's lower keys. *Florida Scientist* 48:37–41.

Ludlow, M. E., and J. A. Gore. 2000. Effects of a cave gate on emergence patterns of colonial bats. *Wildlife Society Bulletin* 28:191–96.

Mazzotti, F. J., and L. A. Brandt. n.d. *Bats of South Florida*. University of Florida Cooperative Extension Service Publication SS-WIS-10. 6 pp.

Needham, B. 1995. *Beastly Abodes: Homes for Birds, Bats, Butterflies and Other Backyard Wildlife*. Sterling Publishing. 144 pp.

Neilson, A. L., and M. B. Fenton. 1994. Responses of little brown myotis to exclusion and to bat houses. *Wildlife Society Bulletin* 22:8–14.

O'Farrell, M. J., and W. L. Gannon. 1999. A comparison of acoustic versus capture techniques for the inventory of bats. *Journal of Mammalogy* 80:24–30.

Otis, D. L., K. P. Burnham, G. C. White, and D. R. Anderson. 1978. Statistical inference from capture data on closed populations. *Wildlife Monographs* 62:1–135.

Rice, D. W. 1957. Life history and ecology of *Myotis austroriparius* in Florida. *Journal of Mammalogy* 38:15–32.

Robson, M. 1989. *Status Survey of the Florida Mastiff Bat*. Florida Game and Fresh Water Fish Commission Nongame Wildlife Program. 17 pp.

Robson, M., and S. Cerulean. 1992. Delicate balance: Florida mastiff bat. *Florida Wildlife* 46(6):15.

Sabol, B. M., and M. K. Hudson. 1995. Technique using thermal infrared-imaging for estimating populations of gray bats. *Journal of Mammalogy* 76:1242–48.

Schneider, N. J., J. E. Scatterday, A. L. Lewis, W. L. Jennings, H. D. Venters, and A. V. Hardy. 1957. Rabies in bats in Florida. *American Journal of the Veterinary Medicine Association* 169:1207–13.

Sheffield, S. R., J. H. Shaw, G. A. Heidt, and L. R. McClenaghan. 1992. Guidelines for the protection of bat roosts. *Journal of Mammalogy* 73:707–10.

Shump, K. A., Jr., and A. V. Shump. 1982. *Lasiurus borealis*. Mammalian Species no. 183. American Society of Mammalogists. 6 pp.

Taylor, A. K., F. J. Mazzotti, and C. W. Huegel. n.d. *Bats: Information for the Florida Homeowner*. University of Florida Cooperative Extension Service Publication SS-WIS-32. 6 pp.

Thomas, D. W. 1995. Hibernating bats are sensitive to nontactile human disturbance. *Journal of Mammalogy* 76:940–46.

Thorne, J. 1990. Bats and caves. *Bats* 8(1):10–14.

Tidemann, C. R., and D. P. Woodside. 1978. A collapsible bat-trap and a comparison of results obtained with the trap and with mist nets. *Australian Wildlife Research* 5:355–62.

Trimarchi, C. V. 1980. Bat rabies in the United States. *National Speleological Society Bulletin* 42:64–66.

Tuttle, M. D. 1974. An improved trap for bats. *Journal of Mammalogy* 55:475–77.

Tuttle, M. D. 1976. Population ecology of the gray bat (*Myotis grisescens*): Philopatry, timing and patterns of movement, weight loss during migration, and seasonal adaptive strategies. *Occasional Papers of the University of Kansas Museum of Natural History* 54:1–38.

Tuttle, M. D. 1977. Gating as a means of protecting cave dwelling bats. Pp. 77–82 in *Proceedings of the 1976 National Cave Management Symposium,* ed. T. Aley and D. Rhodes. Speleobooks Publishing.

Tuttle, M. D. 1979. Status, causes of decline, and management of endangered gray bats. *Journal of Wildlife Management* 43:1–17.

Tuttle, M. D. 1984. Harmless, highly beneficial, bats still get a bum rap. *Smithsonian* 14(10):74–81.

Tuttle, M. D. 1988a. *America's Neighborhood Bats.* Austin: University of Texas Press. 96 pp.

Tuttle, M. D. 1988b. *The Importance of Bats.* Bat Conservation International. 8 pp.

Tuttle, M. D., ed. 1987. *Bats, Pesticides and Politics.* Bat Conservation International, 42 pp.

Tuttle, M. D., and D. Hensley. 1997. *The Bat House Builder's Handbook.* Bat Conservation International. 35 pp.

Tuttle, M. D., and S. J. Kern. 1981. Bats and public health. *Milwaukee Public Museum Contributions to Biology and Geology* 48:1–11.

Tuttle, M. D., and D. E. Stevenson. 1977. Variation in the cave environment and its biological implications. Pp. 108–21 in *Proceedings of the 1977 National Cave Management Symposium,* ed. R. Zuber et al. Adobe Press.

Tuttle, M. D., and D. A. R. Taylor. 1994. *Bats and Mines.* Bat Conservation International Resource Publication no. 3. 41 pp.

U.S. Fish and Wildlife Service. 1982. *Gray Bat Recovery Plan.* U.S. Fish and Wildlife Service. 22 pp.

U.S. Fish and Wildlife Service. 1999. *Recovery Plan for the Indiana Bat.* U.S. Fish and Wildlife Service. 53 pp.

Venters, H. D., W. R. Hoffert, J. E. Scatterday, and A. V. Hardy. 1954. Rabies in bats in Florida. *American Journal of Public Health* 44:182–85.

Watkins, L. C. 1971. A technique for monitoring the nocturnal activity of bats, with comments on the activity patterns of the evening bat (*Nycticeius humeralis*). *Transactions of the Kansas Academy of Science* 74:261–68.

Watkins, L. C. 1972. *Nycticeius humeralis.* Mammalian Species no. 23, American Society of Mammalogists. 14 pp.

Watkins, L. C., and K. A. Shump. 1981. Behavior of the evening bat, *Nycticeius humeralis,* at a nursery roost. *American Midland Naturalist* 105:258–68.

Wenner, A. S. 1984. Current status and management of gray bat caves in Jackson County, Florida. *Florida Field Naturalist* 12:1–6.

White, D. H., and J. T. Seginak. 1987. Cave gate designs for use in protecting endangered bats. *Wildlife Society Bulletin* 15:445–49.

White, G. C., D. R. Anderson, K. P. Burnham, and D. L. Otis. 1982. *Capture-Recapture and Removal Methods for Sampling Closed Populations.* Los Alamos National Laboratory. 235 pp.

Williams, L. M., and M. C. Brittingham. 1997. Selection of maternity roosts by big brown bats. *Journal of Wildlife Management* 61:359–68.

Wimsatt, W. A., ed. 1970–77. *Biology of Bats.* Academic Press. 3 vols. 406, 477, 651 pp.

Zinn, T. L., and S. R. Humphrey. 1981. Seasonal food resources and prey selection of the southeastern brown bat (*Myotis austroriparius*) in Florida. *Florida Scientist* 44:81–90.

13

~ ~

Saltmarsh Songbirds

Seaside Sparrows and Marsh Wrens

Status

Seaside Sparrow

Among the many songbirds (Order Passeriformes) native to Florida, only the seaside sparrow (*Ammodramus maritimus;* Family Emberizidae) is altogether restricted to coastal or near-coastal marshes. Its total range extends from coastal Maine on the Atlantic Coast to southern Texas on the Gulf Coast. Nine subspecies are currently recognized as having made up the *A. maritimus* assemblage, but two of those—the Smyrna seaside sparrow (*A. m. pelonota*) and dusky seaside sparrow (*A. m. nigriscens*)— are extinct. Both of the extinct forms were year-round Florida residents, as are the four extant subspecies. Ten subspecies had until recently been recognized, but the Wakulla seaside sparrow (*A. m. junicolus*), once recognized as among three subspecies occurring along the upper Gulf Coast— along with the Louisiana seaside sparrow (*A. m. fisheri*) and Scott's seaside sparrow (*A. m. peninsulae*)—is now considered synonymous with *A. m. peninsulae.*

On Florida's Atlantic Coast, only MacGillivray's seaside sparrow (*A. m. macgillivraii*) and the migratory, overwintering northern seaside sparrow (*A. m. maritimus*) are extant. *A. m. macgillivraii* occurs along the extreme northeast coast from the St. Johns River in Duval County northward through Nassau County, but its total range extends farther northward, to Albemarle Sound in North Carolina.

The two extinct subspecies also once occurred along the Atlantic Coast, the Smyrna seaside sparrow southward from the St. Johns River in Duval County into Volusia County and the dusky only in Brevard County (on Merritt Island and on the mainland along the east side of the St. Johns River). The validity of the Smyrna seaside sparrow as a distinct subspecific taxon, however, is questionable, and it is considered by some to be synonymous with *A. m. macgillivraii*. Whether a subspecies or a population, its range shrank from south to north beginning in the 1920s, due to a gradual northward invasion of mangroves (and, at least speculatively, to mosquito control spraying with DDT); it was last recorded in the early 1970s.

The dusky seaside sparrow had become extinct on Merritt Island by 1978 and functionally extinct on the mainland by the late 1970s, by which time only a few males remained (females had not been observed since 1976) and were declining in number by about one-half each year. Consequently, in 1980, the U.S. Fish and Wildlife Service and the Florida Game and Fresh Water Fish Commission jointly decided to remove all surviving males from the wild for safekeeping should females later be found, and/or to interbreed them with female Scott's seaside sparrows. The long-term objective of the interbreeding initiative was to release a population of mostly dusky intergrades into remaining habitat.

Accordingly, six dusky males were found and captured, maintained at the Game and Fresh Water Fish Commission's research facilities in Gainesville for ≈1 year, then remanded to captive facilities at the Santa Fe Community College Teaching Zoo in Gainesville. Ultimately they were transferred to specially constructed facilities (secluded from public view) on Discovery Island at Walt Disney World, Orlando. The interbreeding effort resulted in a few intergrade offspring but was largely unsuccessful, at least in terms of generating substantial numbers. The last of the six captive males died in the Discovery Island facilities on 16 June 1987.

The extinction of the dusky seaside sparrow on Merritt Island was attributable to impounding the salt marshes there for mosquito control purposes; factors on the mainland involved a combination of marsh drainage (resulting in woody vegetation invasion) for agricultural purposes, wildfires, and disruption of water flow patterns as a result of the construction of canals and the Beeline Expressway.

The Cape Sable seaside sparrow (*A. m. mirabilis*) is the only avian taxon altogether confined to the Everglades ecosystem. Its historic range was essentially extreme southwestern Florida, encompassing western Dade County, mainland Monroe County, including Cape Sable, and extreme southern Collier County. The Cape Sable seaside sparrow and the extinct dusky seaside sparrow were unique among the nine subspecies in not being altogether restricted to salt marshes, also occurring in brackish and freshwater marshes farther inland. In fact, although it once occurred in salt marshes (on Cape Sable), the Cape Sable subspecies now occurs only in such inland marshes. As was also the case with the dusky seaside sparrow, water control projects, aimed at either draining or flooding, have had significant adverse effects on Cape Sable seaside sparrow habitat availability and quality.

Six distinct population concentration areas were once distributed within the subspecies' historic range, but only two are currently occupied, one in southwestern Dade County and the other in northeastern Monroe County–northwestern Dade County. Its current distribution is entirely on public land—Everglades National Park and the Big Cypress National Preserve. The total population is estimated to be ≈3,000 birds, a decline from slightly over 6,000 birds in 1992.

The Louisiana seaside sparrow currently occurs only in Santa Rosa County (on East Bay and on the east side of Escambia Bay), but it also previously occurred on the west side of Escambia Bay in Escambia County.

The currently recognized distribution of the Scott's seaside sparrow, inclusive of that of the previously recognized Wakulla seaside sparrow (which was from Bay County eastward to Taylor County), encompasses a disjunct population on Choctawhatchee Bay in Walton County, intermittent populations from St. Vincent Island in Franklin County eastward to Wakulla County, and from there a fairly continuous population extending southward to Port Richey in Pasco County. This sparrow once also occurred farther southward, to upper Tampa Bay in Pinellas County.

The U.S. Fish and Wildlife Service included both the dusky and Cape Sable seaside sparrows on the first federal list of endangered species, issued in 1967, and the Florida Game and Fresh Water Fish Commission likewise included both on the first State of Florida endangered species list, issued in 1972. The dusky, as an extinct taxon, was removed from the federal list in 1991 and from the state list in 1992. The Louisiana seaside sparrow was state-listed as threatened in 1975, but delisted in 1978, and the Scott's and Wakulla seaside sparrows have been state-listed as "species of special concern" since 1979.

Four other *Ammodramus* congeners occur in Florida, three of which are overwintering migrants: the sharp-tailed sparrow (*A. caudacutus*), LeConte's sparrow (*A. leconteii*), and Henslow's sparrow (*A. henslowii*).

Two subspecies of the other native *Ammodramus* species—the grasshopper sparrow (*A. savannarum*)—occur in Florida: the eastern grasshopper sparrow (*A. s. pratensis*), likewise an overwintering migrant, and the Florida grasshopper sparrow (*A. s. floridanus;* see chapter 5), a nonmigratory year-round resident, as are the resident seaside sparrow subspecies. The sharp-tailed sparrow is the only one of the other native congeners that also occupies salt marshes (the others are grassland/prairie residents) and is phylogenetically the nearest seaside sparrow relative.

Marsh Wren

The marsh wren (*Cistothorus palustris;* Family Troglodytidae) is one of two congeneric *Cistothorus* species native to North America, the other being the closely related and sympatrically occurring sedge wren (*C. platensis*), a common overwintering migrant in Florida. Until fairly recently, the marsh wren was known as the long-billed marsh wren and the sedge wren as the short-billed marsh wren. Two other congenerics occur in South America.

Cistothorus palustris is not restricted to coastal marshes, as the seaside sparrow is, but the only two year-round (= breeding) resident Florida subspecies—Marian's marsh wren (*C. p. marianae*) and Worthington's marsh wren (*C. p. griseus*)—are, and are restricted to and coinhabit coastal salt marshes with seaside sparrows. The distribution of Marian's marsh wrens along the Gulf Coast corresponds with the collective distribution of Louisiana and Scott's seaside sparrows, that is, intermittently from Santa Rosa County eastward (except not where Scott's seaside sparrows occur disjunctly in Walton County) to Wakulla County, then continuously southward to Pasco County. Worthington's marsh wrens occur along the upper Atlantic Coast, sympatrically with MacGillivray's seaside sparrows in Duval and Nassau counties. Both Marian's and Worthington's marsh wrens have been state-listed as species of special concern since 1979.

Florida also hosts significant numbers of overwintering (= nonbreeding) migratory marsh wrens, an amalgamation of four subspecies—*C. p. palustris, C. p. waynei, C. p. dissaeptus,* and *C. p. iliacus*—distributed essentially statewide and occupying both coastal and inland (i.e., freshwater) marshes. Fourteen *C. palustris* subspecies are recognized.

Distinguishing Characteristics

Seaside Sparrow

Adult seaside sparrows measure 5.5–6.0 in (13–15 cm) in total length, the approximate size of house sparrows (*Passer domesticus*). The plumage is weakly patterned, but overall coloration varies somewhat among the subspecies. In general, the upper parts are gray, grayish brown, or grayish olive, the breast is heavily streaked with gray or brown, and the underparts are grayish white. However, seaside sparrows molt only once annually, between mid-August and October, so by late spring or summer of each year the body plumage has faded considerably due to wear.

The chin and throat are white, a dark "mustache" streak extends from the jaw down the throat, and—its most distinctive feature, diagnostic of the species—a prominent yellow supraloral "eyebrow" extends over the eye from the base of the bill, and a likewise yellow line decorates the bend of the wing. Females are slightly smaller than males, but otherwise the sexes are indistinguishable in appearance. Juveniles are similar in appearance to adults but somewhat paler in coloration and with more heavily streaked breast and flanks.

The primary seaside sparrow song consists of a weak introductory note followed by a buzzy trill, resembling that of the red-winged blackbird (*Agelaius phoeniceus*) but much weaker.

Marsh Wren

Adult marsh wrens measure 4–5 in (10–12 cm) in total length, approximately the size of house wrens (*Troglodytes aedon*). The upper parts of Worthington's marsh wrens are grayish brown and the underparts are pale grayish, whereas the upper parts of Marian's marsh wrens are cinnamon brown to dark brown, with grayish brown underparts. The upper back in each has a triangular patch longitudinally streaked with white, and each has a distinctive white superciliary "eyebrow" line. Juveniles are similar in appearance but lack the white streaking on the upper back. Males are considerably larger than females but otherwise the sexes are indistinguishable in appearance. Each subspecies is darker in overall body coloration than any of the northern subspecies that overwinter in Florida.

The primary song is a rapid series of gurgling, reedy notes and rattles. Not particularly melodic, the song has been described as resembling the sound of an old-fashioned sewing machine or the grating of a rusty hinge. The alarm call is a sharp *tsuk,* sometimes doubled.

Habitat

Along the upper Atlantic and Gulf coasts, both seaside sparrows and marsh wrens occur in dense tidal salt marshes dominated by either salt-marsh cordgrass (*Spartina alterniflora*) or needlerush (*Juncus roemerianus*). *Spartina* is the more dominant vegetation in Atlantic Coast marshes, and *Juncus* is more dominant in Gulf Coast marshes, typically interspersed with stands of salt grass (*Distichlis spicata*). Cape Sable seaside sparrows in southwest Florida currently occur in marshes farther inland, primarily freshwater marshes, mostly "muhly prairies" dominated by hair-grass (*Muhlenbergia filipes*) but also in mixed hair-grass and/or *Spartina bakeri* marshes. Historically, however, they primarily occupied the extensive stands of *S. bakeri* marshes, which were once characteristic of the region but have disappeared. Water level control regimes affecting water flow into southwest Florida have dried up most of those areas.

Life History and Behavior

Seaside Sparrow

The Florida seaside sparrow subspecies are nonmigratory (the northern subspecies are migratory), monogamous, and territorial. Except during the breeding season, when singing males are conspicuously exposed, they are rarely seen, spending nearly all their time on the marsh floor.

Home ranges measure 0.25–8.90 acres (0.1–3.6 ha) and are defended via breast-to-breast fighting (but typically only early in the nesting season), visual displays, and intensified singing by males. Territories are defended not only from invading conspecifics but also from invading marsh wrens and sharp-tailed sparrows (seaside sparrows and sharp-tailed sparrows are also aggressive toward each other in captive environments).

The subspecies occurring in northern Florida nest from April through June, the Cape Sable subspecies in southwest Florida from late February through August, peaking April–May. Males sing throughout the breeding season and beyond that into the fall, with an interim lull during the molt (August–September) season. Singing occurs intermittently throughout a given day, peaking shortly after dawn and again near dusk, usually from perches near the tops of vegetation, with occasional flight forays 15–30 feet (5–10 m) above the marsh. When they are threatened by an avian predator or disturbed by strong winds, however, singing is often from hidden locations within vegetation.

Nest sites are most often in "high marsh" areas where tidal fluctuations are slight and flooding is rare, with approximately equal proportions of low vegetation, usually salt grass, and high vegetation, usually needlerush. Nest sites are rarely, if ever, found in extensive, pure stands of either salt grass or needlerush.

Nests are constructed of grass and situated in vegetation ≈8 in to 3 feet (0.1–1.0 m) above ground, occasionally in small shrubs or mangroves but most commonly in salt grass, cordgrass, or needlerush. The nest cup is usually open but occasionally partially domed. Clutch size is 2–4 eggs (average 3.5), and the eggs are grayish to bluish white with reddish brown spots. The female selects the nest site, constructs the nest, incubates, and broods, but the male shares in feeding of the young.

The incidence of nest loss is high, with predation, primarily by rice rats (*Oryzomys palustris*), fish crows (*Corvus ossifragus*), raccoons (*Procyon lotor*), and snakes, and flooding, both tidal and artificial, being the principal nest mortality factors. Females readily renest nearby when nest loss occurs.

The young hatch at ≈12 days after laying and leave the nest at age 9–11 days, although flight capability is not attained until ≈16 days of age. Upon dispersal, juveniles wander for varying distances up to ≈1.5 miles (2.5 km). Breeding age is reached the spring following hatching. Annual adult survival rate may be as high as ≈87 percent among Florida's northern subspecies and 50–60 percent with respect to the Cape Sable subspecies. Longevity in the wild is 8–9 years but on average likely ≤5 years.

The seaside sparrow food base consists of insects, arachnids, mollusks, amphipods, decapods, marine worms, and the seeds of vegetation, primarily *Spartina* (especially in winter). Feeding most often occurs in cordgrass-dominated areas, typically near tidal creeks and mudflats. Feeding behavior involves walking and running on the marsh floor, gleaning some items from vegetation and some from the surface of the substrate, and probing in the mud. Less frequently, feeding occurs above the marsh floor via hopping or climbing through vegetation and gleaning whatever is encountered.

Marsh Wren

As with seaside sparrows, Florida's two year-round resident marsh wren subspecies are nonmigratory and territorial and establish home ranges in tidal creek marshes dominated by cordgrass or needlerush. They also are rarely seen, being even more secretive than seaside sparrows. Although males of both species are conspicuous during the nesting season, male seaside sparrows are conspicuous because of their characteristic of singing from exposed perches, whereas male marsh wrens, which sometimes sing from cover, are primarily conspicuous because of their loud and unmistakable song.

Neither of Florida's resident marsh wren subspecies has been the subject of comprehensive, systematic life history studies. Consequently, the detail imparted here in that respect is based on anecdotal accounts and inferential information specifically applicable to more northerly subspecies.

Although the northern marsh wren subspecies are polygynous, the two resident Florida subspecies are apparently typically monogamous. Home ranges are usually linear in configuration and are among the smallest maintained by any passerine, averaging only ≈900 square feet(100 m²) in size, and tend to be congregated into loose "colonies." In contrast to the proclivity of seaside sparrows to nest in "high marsh" areas having slight tidal fluctuations, marsh wren nesting habitat consists of "low marsh" areas having a much greater amplitude of tidal fluctuations.

Territorial defense is most intense early in the breeding season and is characterized by males chasing intruders and vigorously singing. Territorial singing is most intense in the early morning and late afternoon but continues throughout much of the day and sometimes at night. Females participate in territorial defense only in the immediate vicinity of nests. Males typically begin singing from their roost nests early and sing from them again after returning in the evening.

Early in the nesting process, the male constructs a number of globular-shaped nests throughout the home range, secured near the tops of marsh grasses or rushes ≈3–5 feet (1.0–1.5 m) above the substrate and consisting of intertwined dead and green leaves of rushes and grasses. The female, escorted by the male, inspects each nest and selects one for nesting. She then lines it with grasses and other soft materials, such as feathers or fur, and commences egg deposition. Height/width of nests is ≈7/5 in (18/13 cm), and each has a single side entrance. Egg laying peaks from approximately mid-April through early June and again ≈6 weeks later, extending beyond the time when males have ceased singing for the year.

The adaptive function of males constructing auxiliary "dummy" nests is not well understood. It may serve courtship purposes (males sing from the nests during the prenesting courtship period), but males commonly continue constructing additional nests even after the female has selected one for nesting and is incubating. Alternatively, the multiple nests may serve to decoy nest predators and/or to provide shelter for newly fledged young, especially during winter. Or, at least with respect to the two Florida subspecies, the behavior may reflect the polygynous nature of the northern subspecies of *C. palustris*—it may have to do with attempting to attract additional females.

Clutch size is 3–5 eggs, egg color is brownish with dark spots, hatching occurs 12–13 days after laying, and the young fledge at age 13–15 days. Only the female incubates, during which time she defends the nest site from the male's approach, perhaps because of the egg-destroying nature of marsh wrens. The female likewise broods exclusively, but both sexes share in feeding fledglings.

The primary causes of nest loss are predation, mainly by rice rats and raccoons, egg and/or nest destruction by other marsh wrens (marsh wrens also destroy the eggs and nests of other species), and tidal flooding. Females renest after a nest loss but not in the same nest. Rather, they complete and use nearby dummy nests.

The diet consists mainly of insects and arachnids and, to a lesser degree, small crustaceans, mollusks, and other invertebrates, gleaned from vegetation. Marsh wrens do forage on the marsh floor but not nearly to the extent that seaside sparrows do; mostly they flit through vegetation, hitching up and down stems as they proceed.

Survey and Monitoring Techniques

Walking transects through appropriate habitat during the spring male singing season is the most effective population inventory technique for both seaside sparrows and marsh wrens. Males of both species readily respond to playbacks of recorded territorial songs, so this strategy might be employed in conjunction with foot transects.

Mist netting is the most effective method of capturing both seaside sparrows and marsh wrens for leg banding or other purposes, although marsh wrens can also be trapped (see Picman 1980). The appropriate U.S. Fish and Wildlife Service leg band size for seaside sparrows is 1B and for marsh wrens 0.

Management

Fundamental Management Considerations

· Invasion of salt marshes by woody vegetation currently represents the primary threat to seaside sparrow and marsh wren welfare. Both species can tolerate minimal shrub or tree invasion of occupied habitat but will abandon a site as such invasion becomes substantial.

Proactive Management

1. Habitat Maintenance

Any manipulation of marshes that would retard, eliminate, or prevent woody plant invasion—through burning (fires at intervals of ≈5 years are effective), mechanical means, or more efficiently, water level manipulation—would be prudent in terms of sustaining existing populations of seaside sparrows and/or marsh wrens.

2. Habitat Rehabilitation

Historic marshes altered by flooding or, conversely, by draining for mosquito control or other purposes, can be rehabilitated via breaching dikes or blocking selected ditches, respectively, whereupon habitat maintenance strategies can be initiated. Creating salt marshes wherever possible may also be a viable proactive management strategy.

Accommodative Management

Past dredging and filling of salt marshes and other forms of habitat destruction and degradation have eliminated seaside sparrows and marsh wrens from many sites, but most coastal marshes are now protected by both state and federal laws. Accommodating either species in the course of an impending land use change, then, should rarely be a significant consideration. But when marshes may be adversely affected, precautions should be taken to avoid altering the natural water inflow and outflow patterns.

Relevant Literature

Austin, O. L., Jr. 1968. Seaside sparrow: Eastern Gulf Coast subspecies. Pp. 838–40 in *Life Histories of North American Cardinals, Grosbeaks, Buntings, Towhees, Finches, Sparrows and Allies,* ed. O. L. Austin.

Austin, O. L., Jr. 1968. Smyrna seaside sparrow. Pp. 835–38 in *Life Histories of North American Cardinals, Grosbeaks, Buntings, Towhees, Finches, Sparrows and Allies,* ed. O. L. Austin.

Austin, O. L., Jr., ed. 1968. *Life Histories of North American Cardinals, Grosbeaks, Buntings, Towhees, Finches, Sparrows and Allies.* U.S. National Museum Bulletin 237[2].

Baker, J. L. 1978. Smyrna seaside sparrow. Pp. 115–16 in *Rare and Endangered Biota of Florida,* vol. 2: *Birds,* ed. W. Kale II. University Press of Florida.

Bass, O. L., Jr., and J. A. Kushlan. 1982. *Status of the Cape Sable Sparrow.* Everglades National Park South Florida Research Center Report no. T-672. 41 pp.

Cox, J. A., and R. S. Kautz. 2000. *Habitat Conservation Needs of Rare and Imperiled Wildlife in Florida.* Florida Fish and Wildlife Conservation Commission. 156 pp.

Curnutt, J. L. 1996. Cape Sable seaside sparrow. Pp. 137–43 in *Rare and Endangered Biota of Florida,* vol. 5: *Birds,* ed. J. A. Rodgers, Jr., et al. University Press of Florida.

Curnutt, J. L., A. L. Mayer, T. M. Brooks, L. Manne, O. L. Bass, Jr., D. M. Fleming, M. P. Nott, and S. L. Pimm. 1998. Population dynamics of the endangered Cape Sable seaside sparrow. *Animal Conservation* 1:11–21.

Eleuterius, L. N., and C. K. Eleuterius. 1979. Tide levels and salt marsh zonation. *Bulletin of Marine Science* 29:394–400.

Greenlaw, J. 1992. Seaside sparrow, *Ammodramus maritimus.* Pp. 211–32 in *Migratory Nongame Birds of Management Concern in the Northeast,* ed. K. Schneider and D. Pence. U.S. Fish and Wildlife Service.

Holder, G. L., M. K. Johnson, and J. L. Baker. 1980. Cattle grazing and management of dusky seaside sparrow habitat. *Wildlife Society Bulletin* 8:105–9.

Kale, H. W. II. 1965. *Ecology and Bioenergetics of the Long-billed Marsh Wren, Telmatodytes palustris griseus, in Georgia Salt Marshes.* Nuttall Ornithological Club Publication no. 5. 142 pp.

Kale, H. W. II. 1978. Marian's marsh wren. Pp. 102–3 in *Rare and Endangered Biota of Florida,* vol. 2: *Birds,* ed. W. Kale II. University Press of Florida.

Kale, H. W. II. 1978. Worthington's long-billed marsh wren. Pp. 103–4 in *Rare and Endangered Biota of Florida,* vol. 2: *Birds,* ed. W. Kale II. University Press of Florida.

Kale, H. W. II. 1983. Distribution, habitat, and status of breeding seaside sparrows in Florida. Pp. 41–48 in *The Seaside Sparrow, Its Biology and Management,* ed. T. L. Quay et al.

Kale, H. W. II. 1996. Dusky seaside sparrow. Pp. 7–12 in *Rare and Endangered Biota of Florida,* vol. 5: *Birds,* ed. J. A. Rodgers, Jr., et al. University Press of Florida.

Kale, H. W. II. 1996. Marsh wrens. Pp. 602–7 in *Rare and Endangered Biota of Florida,* vol. 5: *Birds,* ed. J. A. Rodgers, Jr., et al. University Press of Florida.

Kale, H. W. II. 1996. Seaside sparrows. Pp. 608–15 in *Rare and Endangered Biota of Florida,* vol. 5: *Birds,* ed. J. A. Rodgers, Jr., et al. University Press of Florida.

Karr, J. R. 1981. Surveying birds with mist nets. Pp. 62–67 in *Estimating Numbers of Terrestrial Birds,* ed. C. J. Ralph and J. M. Scott. Cooper Ornithological Society Studies in Avian Biology no. 6.

Kaufman, K. 1996. Field identification: Marsh wren. *Birder's World* 10(4):74–75.

Kroodsma, D. E., and J. Verner. 1997. *Marsh Wren.* Birds of North America no. 308, American Ornithologists' Union. 31 pp.

Kushlan, J. A., O. L. Bass, Jr., L. L. Loope, W. B. Robertson, Jr., P. C. Rosedahl, and D. L. Taylor. 1982. *Cape Sable Sparrow Management Plan.* Everglades National Park South Florida Research Center Report no. M-660. 37 pp.

Leonard, M. L., and J. Picman. 1987. Nesting mortality and habitat selection by marsh wrens. *Auk* 104:491–95.

Light, S. S., and J. W. Dineen. 1994. Water control in the Everglades: A historical perspective. Pp. 47–84 in *Everglades: The Ecosystem and Its Restoration,* ed. S. M. Davis and J. C. Ogden. St. Lucie Press.

Lockwood, J. L., K. H. Fenn, J. L. Curnutt, D. Rosenthal, K. L. Balent, and A. L. Mayer. 1997. Life history of the endangered Cape Sable seaside sparrow. *Wilson Bulletin* 109:720–31.

Lodge, T. E. 1994. *The Everglades Handbook: Understanding the Ecosystem.* St. Lucie Press. 228 pp.

Mackay, K. 1998. Bird on the brink. *National Parks* 72(5–6):38.

Marshall, M. 1996. The dusky's demise: The extinction of *Ammodramus maritimus nigrescens. Wild Earth* 6(2):24–25.

McDonald, M. V. 1988. *Status Survey of Two Florida Seaside Sparrows and Taxonomic Review of the Seaside Sparrow Assemblage.* Florida Cooperative Fish and Wildlife Research Unit Technical Report no. 32.

McDonald, M. V. 1989. The function of song in Scott's seaside sparrow (*Ammodramus maritimus peninsulae*). *Animal Behavior* 38:468–85.

McIvor, C. C., J. A. Ley, and R. D. Bjork. 1994. Changes in freshwater inflow from the Everglades to Florida Bay: A review. Pp. 117–46 in *Everglades: The Ecosystem and Its Restoration,* ed. S. M. Davis and J. C. Ogden. St. Lucie Press.

Montague, C. L., and R. G. Wiegert. 1990. Salt marshes. Pp. 481–516 in *Ecosystems of Florida,* R. L. Myers and J. J. Ewel. University of Central Florida Press.

Nicholson, D. J. 1950. Disappearance of Smyrna seaside sparrow from its former haunts. *Florida Naturalist* 23:104.

Nott, N. P., O. L. Bass, Jr., D. M. Fleming, S. E. Killeffer, N. Fraley, L. Manne, J.

L. Curnutt, T. M. Brooks, R. Powell, and S. L. Pimm. 1998. Water levels, rapid vegetational changes, and the endangered Cape Sable seaside sparrow. *Animal Conservation* 1:23–32.

Picman, J. 1977. Intraspecific nest destruction in the long-billed marsh wren. *Canadian Journal of Zoology* 55:1997–2003.

Picman, J. 1980. A new trap for long-billed marsh wrens. *North American Bird Bander* 5:8–10.

Picman, J., and J. C. Belle-Isles. 1987. Intraspecific egg destruction in marsh wrens: A study of mechanisms preventing filial ovicide. *Animal Behavior* 35: 236–46.

Post, W. 1974. Functional analysis of space-related behavior in the seaside sparrow. *Ecology* 55:564–75.

Post, W. 1981. The influence of rice rats *Oryzomys palustris* on the habitat use of the seaside sparrow *Ammospiza maritima. Behavioral Ecology and Sociobiology* 9:35–40.

Post, W., and F. Antonio. 1981. Breeding and rearing of seaside sparrows, *Ammospiza maritima,* in captivity. *International Zoo Yearbook* 21:123–28.

Post, W., and J. S. Greenlaw. 1975. Seaside sparrow displays: Their function in social organization and habitat. *Auk* 92:461–92.

Post, W., and J. S. Greenlaw. 1994. *Seaside Sparrow.* Birds of North America no. 127, American Ornithologists' Union. 27 pp.

Post, W., J. S. Greenlaw, T. L. Merriam, and L. A. Wood. 1983. Comparative ecology of northern and southern populations of the seaside sparrow. Pp. 123–36 in *The Seaside Sparrow, Its Biology and Management,* ed. T. L. Quay et al.

Quay, T. L., J. B. Funderburg, Jr., D. S. Lee, E. F. Potter, and C. S. Robbins, eds. 1983. *The Seaside Sparrow: Its Biology and Management.* Occasional Papers of the North Carolina Biological Survey, North Carolina State Museum of Natural History.

Quinlan, S. E., and R. L. Boyd. 1976. Mist netting success in relation to weather. *North American Bird Bander* 1:168–70.

Read, M. 1996. Musician of the marsh. *Birder's World* 10(4):24–28.

Sprunt, A., Jr. 1968. MacGillivray's seaside sparrow. Pp. 831–35 in *Life Histories of North American Cardinals, Grosbeaks, Buntings, Towhees, Finches, Sparrows and Allies,* ed. O. L. Austin.

Stevenson, H. M., and W. W. Baker. 1978. Louisiana seaside sparrow. P. 47 in *Rare and Endangered Biota of Florida,* vol. 2: *Birds,* ed. W. Kale II. University Press of Florida.

Stevenson, H. M., and W. W. Baker. 1978. Scott's seaside sparrow. Pp. 106–7 in *Rare and Endangered Biota of Florida,* vol. 2: *Birds,* ed. W. Kale II. University Press of Florida.

Stevenson, H. M., and W. W. Baker. 1978. Wakulla seaside sparrow. P. 107 in *Rare and Endangered Biota of Florida,* vol. 2: *Birds,* ed. W. Kale II. University Press of Florida.

Stimson, L. A. 1968. Cape Sable Sparrow. Pp. 859–68 in *Life Histories of North American Cardinals, Grosbeaks, Buntings, Towhees, Finches, Sparrows and Allies,* ed. O. L. Austin.

Stout, J. P. 1984. *The Ecology of Irregularly Flooded Salt Marshes of the Northeastern Gulf of Mexico: A Community Profile.* U.S. Fish and Wildlife Service Biological Report no. 85(7.1). 98 pp.

Sykes, P. W., Jr. 1980. Decline and disappearance of the dusky seaside sparrow from Merritt Island, Florida. *American Birds* 34:728–37.

Trost, C. H. 1968. Dusky seaside sparrow. Pp. 849–59 in *Life Histories of North American Cardinals, Grosbeaks, Buntings, Towhees, Finches, Sparrows and Allies,* ed. O. L. Austin.

U.S. Fish and Wildlife Service. 1979. *Dusky Seaside Sparrow Recovery Plan.* U.S. Fish and Wildlife Service. 15 pp.

U.S. Fish and Wildlife Service. 1983. *Cape Sable Seaside Sparrow Recovery Plan.* U.S. Fish and Wildlife Service. 52 pp.

U.S. Fish and Wildlife Service. 1999. Cape Sable seaside sparrow. Pp. 4/345–70 in *South Florida Multi-Species Recovery Plan,* U.S. Fish and Wildlife Service.

Verner, J. 1965. Breeding biology of the long-billed marsh wren. *Condor* 67:6–30.

Verner, J., and G. H. Engelsen. 1970. Territories, multiple nest building, and polygyny in the long-billed marsh wren. *Auk* 87:557–67.

Walters, M. J. 1992. *A Shadow and a Song: The Struggle to Save an Endangered Species.* Chelsea Green Publishing. 238 pp.

Werner, H. W. 1983. The Cape Sable sparrow: Its biology and management. Pp. 55–75 in *The Seaside Sparrow, Its Biology and Management,* ed. T. L. Quay et al.

Wheeler, H. E. 1931. The status, breeding range, and habits of Marian's marsh wren. *Wilson Bulletin* 43:247–67.

Wiegert, R. G. 1979. Ecological processes characteristic of coastal *Spartina* marshes of the southeastern United States. Pp. 467–90 in *Ecological Processes in Coastal Environments,* ed. R. L. Jeffries and A. J. Davy. Blackwell Publishing.

Wiegert, R. G., and B. J. Freeman. 1990. *Tidal Salt Marshes of the Southeastern Atlantic Coast.* U.S. Fish and Wildlife Service Biological Report 85(7.29). 82 pp.

Zink, R. M., and H. W. Kale. 1995. Conservation genetics of the extinct dusky seaside sparrow (*Ammodramus maritimus negriscens*). *Biological Conservation* 74:69–71.

14

Wood Stork

Status

Nineteen species of storks (Order Ciconiiformes; Family Ciconiidae) occur worldwide but only three in the Western Hemisphere, and only the wood stork (*Mycteria americana*) occurs in the United States. The other two New World species—the maguari stork (*Ciconia maguari*) and the jabiru (*Jabiru mycteria*)—are restricted to South America and Central and South America, respectively. Two *Mycteria* (the "wood storks") congeners occur in Asia, the milky stork (*M. cinerea*) of Malaysia and the painted stork (*M. leucocephala*) of India and southern China, and a third in Africa, the yellow-billed stork (*M. ibis*).

The historic breeding range of the wood stork in the United States extended from eastern Texas eastward through the southern tier of Gulf Coast states, but the majority of nesting has always occurred in peninsular Florida. Currently, however, breeding is restricted to northern (east of the Apalachicola River) and peninsular Florida, extreme southern and southeastern Georgia, and, as a result of relatively recent range expansions, extreme southern South Carolina. Approximately 38 breeding sites are habitually used in Florida, ≈14 in Georgia, and ≈6 in South Carolina. Wood storks wander widely during the non-nesting season, and during that time records from areas well north and west of the breeding range are common. Elsewhere, breeding populations occur in Cuba, Mexico, Central America, and South America.

The total population in the southeastern United States in the 1930s is estimated to have been ≈60,000 storks (≈20,000 breeding pairs and ≈20,000 nonbreeding individuals). However, due to loss of both foraging and breeding habitat, by the early 1960s the breeding population had declined to ≈10,000 pairs and by the mid-1990s to ≈7,050 pairs (≈5,500 in Florida, ≈1,700 in Georgia, and ≈850 in South Carolina).

Historically, the largest breeding concentration was in south Florida, especially the Everglades–Big Cypress system, amounting to 80–88 percent of the total breeding population. However, changes in the Everglades ecosystem—initially drainage projects to facilitate agricultural enterprises and later, particularly since the 1960s, manipulation of water flow into the system—have degraded foraging habitat. Consequently, most historic foraging areas there are permanently drained and dry, are flooded at times of year disadvantageous to storks, or are drained at equally disadvantageous times. A gradual northward shift of the southern Florida breeding population has resulted, and by the mid-1980s only ≈13 percent of the total breeding population was nesting in south Florida.

New breeding colonies have gradually been established in the course of that northward population shift, and in fact that progression was responsible for the current populations in Georgia and South Carolina. A colony established in Georgia in 1976 and one established in South Carolina in 1981 represented the first time wood storks had nested in either of those states in the 20th century, at least to any appreciable degree.

The wood stork was included on the Florida Game and Fresh Water Fish Commission's initial endangered species list, issued in 1972, was reclassified to threatened in 1974, then was returned to the endangered category in 1975. The U.S. Fish and Wildlife Service federally listed it as endangered in 1984.

The primary current threat to wood stork welfare continues to be loss of foraging habitat, but degradation of nesting habitat is also a significant factor.

Distinguishing Characteristics

Adult wood storks (figs. 29 and 30) have wingspans of 60–65 in (150–165 cm) and body lengths of 35–45 in (85–115 cm); they measure 5.0–5.5 feet (1.5–1.7 m) tall when standing. The body plumage is white except for iridescent black primary and secondary wing feathers and tail. Early in the nesting season, pale salmon coloring under the wings and fluffy undertail coverts extending beyond the end of the tail appear.

The legs, head, and neck are dark gray to blackish, unfeathered and scaly, and the eyes are a deep brown. The feet are pinkish, but the toes brighten to a vivid salmon during the breeding season. The bill is black, heavy, and very thick at the base and decurves to a blunt point. Males are

Fig. 29. Adult and nestling wood storks (Stephen A. Nesbitt).

Fig. 30. Adult wood stork (Barry Mansell).

slightly larger than females and have somewhat longer, heavier bills, but otherwise the sexes are indistinguishable in appearance. Immatures, up to age ≈3 years, are similar in appearance to adults, but are slightly grayish in body color and have straw-colored bills, rather than black, and varying amounts of dusky feathering on the head and neck.

Wood storks fly with neck and legs extended (fig. 30), often soaring in groups at considerable heights. The whooping crane (*Grus americana*), which has recently been reestablished in Florida, and the sandhill crane (*G. canadensis*) are of comparable size and also fly with neck and legs extended, but the wood stork's heavy, decurved bill and the striking contrast between its white body color and black primary and secondary wing feathers render it relatively easy to identify in flight, at least at low altitudes. The sandhill crane's body color is a fairly uniform grayish or brownish, and although adult whooping cranes are white in body color and also have black wing feathers, only the primaries are black. Also, both crane species have thin, straight bills.

The only other wading birds in Florida of similar appearance to wood storks are the great blue heron (*Ardea herodius*) and white ibis (*Eudo-*

cimus albus). The great blue heron is comparable in size but has dark plumage and, as with all herons and egrets, flies with the neck recoiled backward. The white ibis also has a decurved bill, but the bill is much thinner and with a more pronounced decurvature. White ibises are also mostly white with black wing feathers, but they are considerably smaller in size and only the primaries are black.

White pelicans (*Pelecanus erythrorhynchos*) are present in Florida in winter and during that time are perhaps more likely to be confused with wood storks than any other species, at least at high altitudes. White pelicans also are white with black primaries and secondaries; they are comparable in size to wood storks; they also soar in groups at considerable heights, especially during migration; and at a distance, the white pelican's bill has the appearance of an extended neck. The legs of white pelicans, however, do not extend beyond the tail, and the tail is white rather than black.

Adult wood storks are silent most of the time, the most common vocalizations being a deep, grating croak, uttered when disturbed, hisses emitted in association with pair bonding, and a low, rasping *fizz* similar to that of turkey vultures (*Cathartes aura*). An important nonvocal sound is loud bill-clappering by males in association with both copulation and defending nest sites from rivals. Hatchlings utter high-pitched squeaks resembling those of newly hatched alligators (*Alligator mississippiensis*) and a croaking *wonk* resembling the croak of bullfrogs (*Rana catesbeiana*). Older nestlings utter a monotonous, braying *nyah-nyah-nyah,* not dissimilar from the braying of a donkey, audible at distances up to several hundred yards.

Habitat

Wood storks nest colonially in freshwater and estuarine forested habitats, in both natural and artificially created freshwater swamps, and on islands. An overstory of cypress (*Taxodium distichum*), black gum (*Nyssa biflora*), southern willow (*Salix carolina*), or pond apple (*Annona glabra*), or some combination thereof, characterizes most of the freshwater nesting swamps. However, some of the artificially created sites (sites impounded by roads, levees, etc.) are dominated by pines (*Pinus* spp.), oaks (*Quercus* spp.), Australian pine (*Casuarina equisetifolia*), Brazilian pepper (*Schinus* rise unsuitable. The longer-distance forays often necessitate overnight roosting at the foraging site.

Daily colony departures occur once thermals have developed, normally about midmorning. Return times vary from early to late afternoon, depending on how far away from the colony suitable foraging habitat was found. Late in the nesting period, when the young are large and feeding forays are less frequent, overnight roosting at foraging sites is not uncommon. Incoming adults returning from foraging usually have ingested enough prey to regurgitate several loads of food over a period of ≥1 hour.

The availability of suitable nearby foraging habitat during the breeding season in a given year significantly affects reproduction that year. Colonies having limited proximal foraging resources average fledging 0.5–1.0 young per active nest, whereas those with unlimited prey availability average fledging 2.0–3.0 young per active nest.

Wood storks disperse widely following the breeding season as water levels rise with the onset of the rainy season, usually sometime in June. They wander extensively, typically in flocks, throughout the nonbreeding season to find foraging habitat, remaining in a given area only so long as suitable food resources are available. Color-marked storks from Florida colonies have been observed during summer in Georgia, South Carolina, and Alabama as well as throughout Florida.

Survey and Monitoring Techniques

Wood stork colonies have been censused both from the ground and via aircraft overflights. The former results in much more accurate data; flights, while much more time efficient, yield less accurate data, primarily because of the array of other white-plumaged wading birds that often nest in association with wood storks. For accurate short-term population data collection, then, ground censusing should be employed to the extent possible, but for longer-term trend data collection, aerial censusing may suffice. However, aerial surveys cause less disturbance than ground surveys, not only to nesting storks but also to other nesting species present, most of which are less tolerant of human intrusion into colonies than are storks. That disturbance factor should therefore also be considered when developing census strategies.

Nestling wood storks have been successfully color-marked for future identification purposes (see Rodgers 1986), and both standard and satel-

terebinthefolius), or—particularly on created islands—prickly pear cactus (*Opuntia stricta*). Use of such artificial sites has increased dramatically over the past few decades. Only ≈10 percent of all nesting pairs nested at artificial sites in 1960, but that percentage has increased to >80 percent currently.

Many artificial sites, especially impoundment islands, are temporary in nature because the pioneering vegetation (e.g., willows) in which wood storks nest eventually disappears due to lack of recruitment, to anaerobic soil conditions caused by permanent flooding, and/or to vegetational succession. Guano deposition also can result in death of nesting vegetation.

Coastal island colonies are characteristically surrounded by broad expanses of open water and, in Florida, are dominated by red mangroves (*Rhizophora mangle*), black mangroves (*Avicennia germinans*), or white mangroves (*Laguncularia racemosa*). The coastal colony sites in Georgia are dominated by black gum, southern willow, cypress, and/or buttonbush (*Cephalanthus occidentalis*).

Colony sites that remain undisturbed and have sufficient feeding habitat available nearby are used annually over many years, with the number of nests present varying from year to year by only 10–20 percent. Somewhat less stable sites are also used annually, but nest numbers in those colonies vary 50–75 percent annually, and even less stable sites average being active only 2–3 years out of every five. Some colonies appear in a given year but are never used again, perhaps as a temporary reaction to unfavorable habitat conditions at the resident birds' traditional colony site.

Wood storks forage in a wide variety of shallow wetlands, and because they rely on a concentrated prey base, the highest quality habitats in that respect are ephemeral bodies of water in a drainage or drying cycle. Accordingly, storks are often seen foraging in seasonal or managed ponds, sloughs, rain-flooded roadside and agricultural ditches, and tidal creeks and depressions. Because of that dependence on drying or draining wetlands, the amount and distribution of rainfall in a given year determines to a large extent where and when storks forage during the year.

Wood storks roost in habitats often structurally similar to nesting habitat but wider in variety, including cypress heads and swamps, marsh pine and hardwood tree islands, mangrove islands, willow thickets, and, less commonly, in stands of trees over dry ground and sites such as open marshes and levees. Some roosts are traditionally used over long periods, others for relatively brief periods, depending on the proximal availability of feeding habitat.

Life History and Behavior

Wood storks attain breeding age at ≈3 years, they are seasonally monogamous, and they nest colonially, often in association with other wading bird species, most commonly great egrets (*Ardea albus*) and/or great blue herons (*Ardea herodia*). Anhingas (*Anhinga anhinga*) also commonly nest in such mixed-species associations. Annual initiation of the breeding cycle varies geographically, ranging from late December to late March in southern Florida to February–April in central and northern Florida and later still in Georgia and South Carolina. The breeding cycle extends 110–150 days, hence colonies can be occupied until June–July in southern Florida and July–August in central and northern Florida.

Prenesting courtship is highly ritualistic and can last for periods from a few hours up to several days. Typically, a male establishes himself at a potential nest site, repelling rival males via bill-clappering and grabbing of the rival's bill. Females approach established males and are initially rejected, but after repeated approaches, during which the male exhibits ritual preening and the female displays via spread wings and gaping bill, the male accepts her. Thereafter, members of mated pairs greet each other with exaggerated up-and-down head movements, bill-clappering, and hisses. Copulation is accompanied by loud bill-clappering by the male.

Cypress, black gum, or southern willow are typically selected as nest trees in the natural freshwater colony sites; southern willow, Brazilian pepper, prickly pear cactus, or Australian pine are typically selected in the artificially created sites; and mangroves are selected in the coastal island sites. Nesting has also occurred on man-made structures.

Nests are up to ≈3 feet (1 m) in diameter and constructed of sticks, vines, leaves, and Spanish moss (*Tillandsia usneoides*), with a liner of finer material. Both sexes participate in nest construction, which consists of an initial period of 2–3 days of intense activity, diminishing to periodic maintenance through incubation and the nestling period. In freshwater colonies, nests are situated at varying heights in trees, on limbs as low as ≈3 feet (1 m) above water to as high as 100 feet (30 m) in the tops of cypress trees.

In coastal colonies, height of nests is largely determined [by] the nesting vegetation but is typically ≈3–15 feet (1.0–5.0 [m]).

Clutch size is 1–6 eggs, usually three, laid at every-othe[r]. Hatching occurs ≈28 days after laying (both sexes incuba[te] occurs at age ≈9 weeks, followed by a post-fledging nest [pe]riod of 15–30 days. If nests are lost early in the cycle, renes[ting] occurs within several weeks. Both adults contribute to [the] feeding of the young (by regurgitating whole fish). The you[ng] times per day, more frequently earlier in the nestling perio[d] likewise more frequently when food resources are abund[ant] limited. For 3–4 weeks after hatching, at least one of the [adults] nest at all times. Fledglings remain in the vicinity of the [colony] weeks postfledging but return to the nest daily to be fed.

The primary mortality factors for eggs and nestlings [are] typically by raccoons (*Procyon lotor*) or crows (*Corvus* sp[p.]) intraspecific aggression, and stress due to exposure or incle[ment]. Little is known about mortality postfledging. The life span [of] in the wild is unknown, the oldest documented age being [≈] they have lived in captivity for >30 years.

Wood storks forage in water 2–15 in (5–40 cm) deep vi[a] rather than sight, wading with bill immersed and partially o[pen] ally stirring the water with their feet to roust prey, and gras[ping] is opportunistically encountered. Such tactile feeding beh[avior] feeding in turbid water and at night but requires a concentra[tion] and because prey becomes concentrated in water bodies [in a] drying or drainage cycle, wood storks must wander widely t[o find] foraging habitat. Prey consists almost entirely of fish 1–10 in[ches] length, the most common species being sunfish (*Lepomis* [spp.) (*Amia calva*), redfin pickerel (*Esox americanus*), lake [chubsucker] (*Erimyzon sucetta*), flagfish (*Jordanella floridae*), sailfin mo[lly] (*latipinna*), marsh killifish (*Fundulus* spp.), yellow bullhea[d (Ictalurus] *natalis*), and mosquito fish (*Gambusia affinis*). Crustaceans, [amphibians,] and small reptiles are occasionally taken.

Under normal conditions during the breeding season, woo[d storks rou]tinely make foraging forays, in groups and almost entirely vi[a flight, up] to 25 miles (40 km) from colony sites. However, foraging fo[rays up to] ≈80 miles (130 km) occur when proximal feeding sites are [depleted].

lite radio transmitters have been successfully used to monitor wood stork movements. In banding operations, the appropriate U.S. Fish and Wildlife Service aluminum leg band size for wood storks is 7A.

Management

Fundamental Management Considerations

- The primary limiting factor as regards wood stork welfare is the availability during the birds' reproductive cycle of sufficient foraging habitat—shallow wetlands undergoing a drying or drainage cycle.

- The most important component of wood stork nesting habitat is standing water in the colony throughout the nesting cycle, ideally at depths of 3–5 feet (1.0–1.5 m). Terrestrial predators, especially raccoons, can otherwise reach nests and decimate the production of young in a given year, not only because of the physical barrier standing water represents but also because standing water in most situations facilitates the presence of alligators (*Alligator mississippiensis*). Alligators have a significant deterrent effect on terrestrial predators.

- Wood storks have a somewhat higher tolerance level for human encroachment into colony areas than do most other wading birds but will still vacate nests when that tolerance level is exceeded, and they will remain gone as long as humans are present, exposing eggs and young to the elements.

- Both adults and fledglings fly at low altitudes in the vicinity of their colonies, therefore towers situated near colonies, especially those requiring guy wires, represent a significant mortality risk to those colonies' resident storks.

Proactive Management

1. Foraging Habitat Maintenance

Where water levels within ≈25 miles (30 km) of colonies can be manipulated, gradual drawdowns coinciding with the nesting season would ensure maximum concentrated prey availability during that critical period. When more than one impoundment is involved, drawdowns should be incremental among them throughout the nesting season to extend the period of high quality foraging habitat availability.

2. Foraging Habitat Enhancement

To supplement either managed existing impoundments or natural feeding areas, artificial ponds can be excavated near colonies, with drawdowns of those ponds scheduled for best provision of foraging resources based on the stage at which the particular hydroperiod affecting the target colony is. Coulter et al. (1987), Coulter (1990), Robinette and Davis (1992), Bryan and Coulter (1995), and Coulter and Bryan (1995b) can be consulted relative to the specifics of pond dimensions that have been successful in attracting wood stork use in Georgia and South Carolina. Browder (1978) describes a supplemental feeding pond excavated in association with the colony situated in the National Audubon Society's Corkscrew Swamp Sanctuary in Collier County. Artificially stocking ponds early each fall with appropriate prey species would further enhance the value of that technique. Batzer et al. (1999) can be consulted as regards maintaining foraging resources in feeding ponds. It is unlikely, however, because of the extent of foraging habitat needed, that artificial ponds could make a significant contribution to nesting success or otherwise sustain a colony throughout a given breeding cycle. That strategy, then, should be regarded only as a measure to supplement existing foraging areas and not as a primary management focus.

3. Nesting Habitat Maintenance

All feasible strategies to sustain standing water in a given colony throughout the reproductive period should be employed. Cypress-dominated colonies that are perpetually flooded will have no cypress regeneration, so at least every few years, cypress colonies where water levels can be controlled should be drained during the non-nesting season to simulate natural drought conditions. However, because the non-nesting season in Florida (August–January) coincides with the high water point in the hydrocycle, draining colony areas at the most advantageous times would be problematic in most years.

4. Nesting Habitat Enhancement

Wood storks will nest on artificial structures, so in existing or previous colonies where the nesting vegetation is lacking or degraded, artificial structures can be deployed. Successful structures used in Georgia have been constructed using 4 × 4 wooden posts, steel rebars, coated screens, and artificial "silk" foliage. Robinette and Davis (1992) provide specifications.

5. Nesting Habitat Security

Occupied colonies should be protected from intrusive human activity. A minimum effective no-entry buffer for nesting storks in that regard would be 250 feet (75 m) for colonies well screened by surrounding vegetation, but 400 feet (120 m) would be needed for those having no vegetative screen.

Accommodative Management

1. Colony Integrity

When land use changes are planned or contemplated that may conflict with wood stork welfare, precautions can be taken to minimize the potential for such adverse impacts. The U.S. Fish and Wildlife Service's *Habitat Management Guidelines for the Wood Stork in the Southeast Region* (Ogden 1990) provides detailed guidance in that respect, calling for significant construction or other land use changes to be relegated to distances exceeding 500 feet (152 m) from colonies well buffered by vegetation or expanses of water and distances >1,000 feet (305 m) from colonies not so buffered.

2. Water Quality Maintenance

The use of chemicals (fertilizers, herbicides, pesticides, etc.) that would adversely impact the wood stork prey base should be avoided if that use would result in their introduction into either nesting or feeding areas.

3. Mortality Avoidance

Construction of towers or power lines should be restricted to distances at which wood stork flight patterns to and from colonies will not be compromised.

4. Foraging Habitat Accommodation

Managing impoundments for other exigencies that require periodic drawdowns, including for waterfowl use, can be compatible with wood stork welfare as long as drawdowns are scheduled to coincide with the wood stork nesting period.

Relevant Literature

Allen, R. P. 1964. Our only stork, the wood ibis. *National Geographic* 125:294–306.

Bancroft, G. T., W. Hoffman, R. J. Sawicki, and J. C. Ogden. 1992. The importance of the water conservation areas in the Everglades to the endangered wood stork (*Mycteria americana*). *Conservation Biology* 6:392–98.

Batzer, D. P., A. S. Shurtleff, and J. R. Robinette. 1999. Managing fish and invertebrate resources in a wood stork feeding pond. *Journal of Freshwater Ecology* 14:159–65.

Browder, J. S. 1978. A modeling study of water, wetlands, and wood storks. Pp. 325–46 in *Wading Birds*, ed. A. Sprunt IV et al. National Audubon Society Research Report no. 7.

Browder, J. S. 1984. Wood stork feeding areas in southwest Florida. *Florida Field Naturalist* 12:81–96.

Bryan, A. L., Jr., and M. C. Coulter. 1995. Wood stork use of the Kathwood foraging ponds: 1986–1993. Pp. 53–56 in *Proceedings of the Wood Stork Symposium*. Georgia Conservancy.

Bryan, A. L., Jr., M. C. Coulter, and C. J. Pennycuick. 1995. Foraging strategies and energetic costs of foraging flights by breeding wood storks. *Condor* 97:133–40.

Clark, E. S. 1978. Factors affecting the initiation and success of nesting in an east-central Florida wood stork colony. *Colonial Waterbirds* 2:178–88.

Coulter, M. C. 1987. Foraging and breeding ecology of wood storks in east-central Georgia. Pp. 21–27 in *Proceedings of the 3rd Southeastern Nongame and Endangered Wildlife Symposium*, ed. R. R. Odom et al. Georgia Department of Natural Resources.

Coulter, M. C. 1990. Creation and management of artificial foraging habitat for wood storks. Pp. 262–67 in *Ecosystem Management: Rare Species and Significant Habitats*, ed. R. S. Mitchell et al. New York State Museum Bulletin no. 471.

Coulter, M. C., and A. L. Bryan, Jr. 1995a. Factors affecting reproductive success of wood storks (*Mycteria americana*) in east-central Georgia. *Auk* 112:237–43.

Coulter, M. C., and A. L. Bryan, Jr. 1995b. The design and management of the Kathwood ponds: Artificial foraging ponds for wood storks in east-central Georgia. Pp. 47–52 in *Proceedings of the Wood Stork Symposium*. Georgia Conservancy.

Coulter, M. C., W. D. McCort, and A. L. Bryan, Jr. 1987. Creation of artificial foraging habitat for wood storks. *Colonial Waterbirds* 15:219–25.

Coulter, M. C., J. A. Rodgers, Jr., J. C. Ogden, and F. C. Depkin. 1999. *Wood Stork*. Birds of North America no. 409, American Ornithologists' Union. 28 pp.

Coulter, M. C., A. L. Bryan, Jr., H. E. Mackey, Jr., J. R. Jensen, and M. E. Hodgson. 1987. Mapping of wood stork foraging habitat with satellite data. *Colonial Waterbirds* 10:178–80.

Cox, J. 1991. Land-cover correlates of wood stork productivity in north and central Florida. *Colonial Waterbirds* 14:121–26.

Davis, S. M., and J. C. Ogden, eds. 1994. *Everglades: The Ecosystem and Its Restoration*. St. Lucie Press.

Ewel, K. C. 1990. Swamps. Pp. 281–323 in *Ecosystems of Florida,* ed. R. L. Myers and J. J. Ewel. University of Central Florida Press.

Fleming, D. M., W. F. Wolff, and D. L. DeAngelis. 1994. Importance of landscape heterogeneity to wood storks in the Florida Everglades. *Environmental Management* 18:743–57.

Frederick, P. C., and M. W. Collopy. 1988. *Reproductive Ecology of Wading Birds in Relation to Water Conditions in the Florida Everglades*. Florida Cooperative Fish and Wildlife Research Unit Technical Report no. 30. 259 pp.

Frederick, P. C., and S. M. McGehee. 1994. Wading bird use of wastewater treatment wetlands in Central Florida, USA. *Colonial Waterbirds* 17:50–59.

Frederick, P. C., and J. C. Ogden. 1997. Philopatry and nomadism: Contrasting long-term movement behavior and population dynamics of white ibises and wood storks. *Colonial Waterbirds* 20:316–23.

Gunn, E. 1997. Wild places: Corkscrew Swamp, Florida. *Wildlife Conservation* 100(6):60–61, 65.

Hodgson, M. E., J. R. Jensen, H. E. Mackey, Jr., and M. C. Coulter. 1988. Monitoring wood stork foraging habitat using remote sensing and geographic information systems. *Photogrammetric Engineering and Remote Sensing* 54:1601–7.

Hoffman, W., G. T. Bancroft, and R. J. Sawicki. 1994. Foraging habitat of wading birds in the Water Conservation Areas of the Everglades. Pp. 585–614 in *Everglades: The Ecosystem and Its Restoration,* ed. S. M. Davis and J. C. Ogden.

Kahl, M. P. 1964. Food ecology of the wood stork (*Mycteria americana*) in Florida. *Ecological Monographs* 34:97–117.

Kahl, M. P., and L. J. Peacock. 1963. The bill-snap reflex: A feeding mechanism in the American wood stork. *Nature* 199:505–6.

Kenney, B. 1998. Ol' flinthead. *Birder's World* 12(3):42–45.

Klinkenberg, J. 1998. Coming back on its own terms. *National Wildlife* 36(3):52–61.

Kushlan, J. A. 1979. Effects of helicopter censuses on wading bird colonies. *Journal of Wildlife Management* 43:756–60.

Kushlan, J. A., and P. Frohring. 1986. The history of the southern Florida wood stork population. *Wilson Bulletin* 98:368–86.

Kushlan, J. A., J. C. Ogden, and A. L. Higer. 1975. *Relation of Water Level and Fish Availability to Wood Stork Reproduction in the Southern Everglades, Florida*. U.S. Geological Survey Open File Report no. 75–43. 56 pp.

Light, S. S., and J. W. Dineen. 1994. Water control in the Everglades: A historical perspective. Pp. 47–84 in *Everglades: The Ecosystem and Its Restoration,* ed. S. M. Davis and J. C. Ogden.

Manry, D. E. 1990. Living on the edge: Wood storks face an uncertain future. *Birder's World* 4(5):10–14.

McIvor, C. C., J. A. Ley, and R. D. Bjork. 1994. Changes in freshwater inflow from the Everglades to Florida Bay: A review. Pp. 117–46 in *Everglades: The Ecosystem and Its Restoration,* ed. S. M. Davis and J. C. Ogden.

Ogden, J. C. 1985. The wood stork. Pp. 458–70 in *Audubon Wildlife Report 1985,* ed. R. L. DiSilvestro. National Audubon Society.

Ogden, J. C. 1990. *Habitat Management Guidelines for the Wood Stork in the Southeast Region.* U.S. Fish and Wildlife Service. 11 pp.

Ogden, J. C. 1991. Nesting by wood storks in natural, altered, and artificial wetlands in central and northern Florida. *Colonial Waterbirds* 14:39–45.

Ogden, J. C. 1994. A comparison of wading bird nesting colony dynamics (1931–1946 and 1974–1989) as an indication of ecosystem conditions in the southern Everglades. Pp. 533–70 in *Everglades: The Ecosystem and Its Restoration,* ed. S. M. Davis and J. C. Ogden.

Ogden, J. C. 1996. Wood stork. Pp. 31–41 in *Rare and Endangered Biota of Florida,* vol. 5: *Birds,* ed. J. A. Rodgers, Jr., et al. University Press of Florida.

Ogden, J. C., and S. A. Nesbitt. 1979. Recent wood stork population trends in the United States. *Wilson Bulletin* 91:512–23.

Ogden, J. C., J. A. Kushlan, and J. T. Tilmant. 1976. Prey selectivity by the wood stork. *Condor* 78:324–30.

Ogden, J. C., D. A. McCrimmon, Jr., G. T. Bancroft, and B. W. Patty. 1987. Breeding populations of the wood stork in the southeastern United States. *Condor* 89:752–59.

Robinette, J. R., and J. P. Davis. 1991. Management for nesting wood storks on Harris Neck National Wildlife Refuge. Pp. 55–56 in *Proceedings of the Coastal Nongame Workshop,* comp. D. P. Jennings.

Rodgers, J. A., Jr. 1986. A field technique for color-dyeing nestling wading birds without capture. *Wildlife Society Bulletin* 14:399–400.

Rodgers, J. A., Jr. 1993. Surveying wood stork colonies in Florida: Evaluation of the accuracy of aerial estimates using fixed-wing aircraft. Pp. 19–29 in *Proceedings of the Wood Stork Symposium.* Georgia Conservancy.

Rodgers, J. A., Jr., and S. T. Schwikert. 1997. Breeding success and chronology of wood storks *Mycteria americana* in northern and central Florida. *Ibis* 139:76–91.

Rodgers, J. A., Jr., and H. T. Smith. 1995. Set-back distances to protect nesting bird colonies from human disturbance in Florida. *Conservation Biology* 9:89–99.

Rodgers, J. A., Jr., S. B. Linda, and S. A. Nesbitt. 1995. Comparing aerial estimates with ground counts of nests in wood stork colonies. *Journal of Wildlife Management* 59:656–66.

Rodgers, J. A., Jr., A. S. Wenner, and S. T Schwikert. 1987. Population dynamics of wood storks in north and central Florida, USA. *Colonial Waterbirds* 10:151–56.

Savage, A., E. F. Stevens, F. W. Koontz, C. Koontz, L. Brisbin, A. L. Bryan, Jr., and J. Robinette. 1999. Satellite tracking of wood storks (*Mycteria americana*) in the southeastern United States. *Endangered Species Update* 16(3):64–66.

Stangel, P. W., J. A. Rodgers, Jr., and A. L. Bryan, Jr. 1990. Genetic variation and population structure of the Florida wood stork. *Auk* 107:614–19.

Streich, J. 1993. Land conservation tools that can be used to protect wood storks. Pp. 69–71 in *Proceedings of the Wood Stork Symposium*. Georgia Conservancy.

Sykes, P. W., and G. S. Hunter. 1978. Bird use of flooded agricultural fields during summer and early fall and some recommendations for management. *Florida Field Naturalist* 6:36–43.

U.S. Fish and Wildlife Service. 1997. *Wood Stork Recovery Plan*. U.S. Fish and Wildlife Service. 40 pp.

U.S. Fish and Wildlife Service. 1999. Wood stork. Pp. 4/393–428 in *South Florida Multi-Species Recovery Plan*, U.S. Fish and Wildlife Service.

Van Den Busche, R. A., S. A. Harmon, R. J. Baker, A. L. Bryan, Jr., J. A. Rodgers, Jr., M. J. Harris, and I. L. Brisbin, Jr. 1999. Low levels of genetic variation in North American populations of the wood stork (*Mycteria americanus*). *Auk* 116:1083–92.

Appendix

Legal Accommodations

This appendix consists of synopses of selected elements of the most salient of the laws and regulations extending accommodation to the species targeted in this book, as individually identified in each synopsis under Targeted Species Applicability.

The transcriptions are not verbatim accounts of the referenced laws and regulations, nor do they necessarily represent all the provisions a given law or regulation may involve. Rather, only those elements that apply specifically to the targeted species are presented. Readers should consult the full text of any of the laws and regulations cited if more precise or complete information is needed. Also, because laws and regulations are subject to periodic amendment and repeal, none referenced here should necessarily be assumed to be in effect in perpetuity.

United States Laws

Endangered Species Act of 1973
16 U.S.C. 1531

Targeted Species Applicability

Alabama beach mouse, Anastasia Island beach mouse, Cape Sable seaside sparrow, Choctawhatchee beach mouse, crested caracara, Florida grasshopper sparrow, Florida scrub-jay, gray bat, Indiana bat, Perdido Key beach mouse, red-cockaded woodpecker, southeastern beach mouse, and wood stork.

Prohibitions

Harassing, harming, pursuing, hunting, shooting, wounding, killing, trapping, capturing, or collecting, or attempting to engage in any such conduct (collectively defined as "taking"), or possessing, selling, delivering, carrying, transporting, or shipping any endangered species, or violating any regulation pertaining to any endangered or threatened species, unless permitted to do so by the Secretary of the Interior. Permits in those respects can be issued only for scientific, propagation, or survival purposes or for actions incidental to, and not the purpose of, the carrying out of otherwise lawful activities,

Associated Regulations

50 CFR 13 (permitting), 50 CFR 17 (lists of endangered and threatened vertebrate and invertebrate species), 50 CFR 23 (lists of endangered and threatened plant species).

Penalties

Up to $50,000 fine and/or one year imprisonment for criminal violations, up to $25,000 fine for civil violations, and forfeiture of all guns, vehicles, equipment, etc., used in the commission of violations.

Special Provisions

Section 7 of the act precludes any federal agency from participating in, funding, or sanctioning any activity that would (1) likely jeopardize the continued existence of any endangered or threatened species, or (2) result in the destruction or adverse modification of its critical habitat. Among the targeted species, critical habitat pursuant to section 7 has been designated only for the Alabama, Perdido Key, and Choctawhatchee beach mice; hence the second preclusion applies only to those three taxa.

Bald and Golden Eagle Protection Act
16 U.S.C. 668–668d

Targeted Species Applicability
Bald eagle.

Prohibitions

Pursuing, shooting, shooting at, poisoning, wounding, killing, capturing, trapping, collecting, molesting, or disturbing (collectively defined as "taking") any bald eagle, alive or dead, or any part, nest, or egg thereof, except as permitted by the Secretary of the Interior. Permits in those respects can be issued only for scientific or exhibition purposes (but only when such is compatible with the preservation of the bald eagle) or when necessary for the protection of wildlife or of agricultural interests (but only pursuant to special regulations prescribed for such).

Associated Regulations

50 CFR 22.

Penalties

Up to $250,000 fine ($500,000 for organizations) and/or two years imprisonment and forfeiture of all guns, vehicles, equipment, etc., used in the commission of violations.

Migratory Bird Treaty Act
16 U.S.C. 701–711

Targeted Species Applicability

All birds.

Prohibitions

Pursuing, hunting, shooting, wounding, killing, trapping, capturing, or collecting (collectively defined as "taking"), or attempting such, or selling, offering to sell, possessing, buying, shipping, or transporting any protected migratory bird, or any part, nest, or eggs thereof, except as permitted by the Secretary of the Interior or as allowed by special regulation.

Associated Regulations

50 CFR 10 (prohibitions and lists of affected bird species), 50 CFR 20 (hunting), and 50 CFR 21 (permitting).

Penalties

Up to $2,000 fine and/or two years imprisonment.

State of Florida Laws

Endangered and Threatened Species Act of 1977
Section 372.072, Florida Statutes

Targeted Species Applicability

Anastasia Island beach mouse, bald eagle, Cape Sable seaside sparrow, Choctawhatchee beach mouse, crested caracara, Florida grasshopper sparrow, Florida mastiff bat, Florida sandhill crane, Florida scrub-jay, gray bat, Indiana bat, pallid beach mouse, Perdido Key beach mouse, red-cockaded woodpecker, southeastern American kestrel, southeastern beach mouse, St. Andrew beach mouse, wood stork.

Prohibitions

None.

Associated Regulations

None.

Special Provisions

Subsection 2 of the act establishes conservation and wise management of endangered and threatened species to be the policy of the State of Florida and identifies provision for research and management to conserve and protect endangered and threatened species to be the intent of the Legislature.

Penalties

None.

Endangered and Threatened Species Protection Act
Section 372.0725, Florida Statutes

Targeted Species Applicability

Anastasia Island beach mouse, bald eagle, Big Cypress fox squirrel, Cape Sable seaside sparrow, Choctawhatchee beach mouse, crested caracara, Florida grasshopper sparrow, Florida mastiff bat, Florida sandhill crane, Florida scrub-jay, gray bat, Indiana bat, pallid beach mouse, Perdido Key beach mouse, red-cockaded woodpecker, southeastern American kestrel, southeastern beach mouse, St. Andrew beach mouse, and wood stork.

Prohibitions

Intentionally killing or wounding, or intentionally destroying the eggs or nests of, any species designated by the Florida Fish and Wildlife Conservation Commission (formerly the Game and Fresh Water Fish Commission) as endangered, threatened, or of special concern.

Associated Regulations

None.

Penalties

Violations involving endangered and threatened species are punishable as third degree felonies, with fines up to $5,000 and/or up to five years imprisonment for first offenses and with additional penalties thereafter. Violations involving species of special concern are punishable as second degree misdemeanors, with fines up to $500 and/or 60 days imprisonment for first offenses and with additional penalties thereafter.

Wildlife Code of the State of Florida
Chapter 39, Florida Administrative Code

Chapter 39–4.001: General Prohibitions

Targeted Species Applicability

All.

Prohibitions

Taking, attempting to take, pursuing, hunting, molesting, capturing, or killing (collectively defined as "taking"), transporting, storing, serving, buying, selling, possessing, or wantonly or willfully wasting any wildlife, or their nests, eggs, young, homes, or dens, except as otherwise specifically allowed under other regulations inherent in chapter 39 of the Florida Administrative Code.

Penalties

Punishable as a second degree misdemeanor, with up to $500 fine and/or 60 days imprisonment for first offenses, additional penalties thereafter.

Chapter 39–25.002: General Provisions for Reptiles

Targeted Species Applicability

Gopher tortoise.

Prohibitions

Taking, attempting to take, pursuing, hunting, molesting, capturing, or killing (collectively defined as "taking"), buying, selling, or possessing (unless acquired before 1 July 1988), any gopher tortoise, or any part thereof, except as permitted by the Florida Fish and Wildlife Conservation Commission, or possessing any tortoise on which paint has been applied.

Penalties

Punishable as a second degree misdemeanor, with up to $500 fine and/or 60 days imprisonment for first offenses, additional penalties thereafter.

Chapter 39–27.011: Killing Endangered Species

Targeted Species Applicability

Anastasia Island beach mouse, Cape Sable seaside sparrow, Choctaw-hatchee beach mouse, Florida grasshopper sparrow, Florida mastiff bat, gray bat, Indiana bat, Perdido Key beach mouse, St. Andrew beach mouse, and wood stork.

Prohibitions

Killing, attempting to kill, or wounding any endangered species.

Penalties

Punishable as a second degree misdemeanor, with up to $500 fine and/or 60 days imprisonment for first offenses, additional penalties thereafter.

Chapter 39–27.003: Endangered Species

Targeted Species Applicability

Anastasia Island beach mouse, Cape Sable seaside sparrow, Choctaw-hatchee beach mouse, Florida grasshopper sparrow, Florida mastiff bat, gray bat, Indiana bat, Perdido Key beach mouse, St. Andrew beach mouse, and wood stork.

Prohibitions

Pursuing, molesting, harming, harassing, capturing, possessing, or selling any endangered species, or parts thereof or their nests or eggs, except under permit from the Florida Fish and Wildlife Conservation Commission. Permits in those respects can be issued only when the permitted activity will clearly enhance the survival potential of the targeted species.

Penalties

Punishable as a second degree misdemeanor, with up to $500 fine and/or 60 days imprisonment for first offenses, additional penalties thereafter.

Chapter 39–27.004: Threatened Species

Targeted Species Applicability

Bald eagle, Big Cypress fox squirrel, crested caracara, Florida sandhill crane, Florida scrub-jay, red-cockaded woodpecker, southeastern American kestrel, and southeastern beach mouse.

Prohibitions

Taking, attempting to take, pursuing, hunting, molesting, capturing, or killing (collectively defined as "taking"), possessing, transporting, molesting, harassing, or selling any threatened species, or their nests or eggs, except under permit from the Florida Fish and Wildlife Conservation Commission. Permits in those respects can be issued only for scientific or conservation purposes and only upon a showing by the permit applicant that the permitted activity will not have a negative impact on the survival potential of the targeted species.

Penalties

Punishable as a second degree misdemeanor, with up to $500 fine and/or 60 days imprisonment for first offenses, additional penalties thereafter.

Chapter 39–27.005: Species of Special Concern

Targeted Species Applicability

Florida burrowing owl, Marian's marsh wren, Sherman's fox squirrel, and Worthington's marsh wren.

Prohibitions

Taking, attempting to take, pursuing, hunting, molesting, capturing, or killing (collectively defined as "taking"), possessing, transporting, or selling any species of special concern, or any part thereof or their nests or eggs, except under permit from the Florida Fish and Wildlife Conservation Commission. Permits in those respects can be issued only upon reasonable conclusion that the permitted activity will not be detrimental to the survival potential of the target species.

Penalties

Punishable as a second degree misdemeanor, with up to $500 fine and/or 60 days imprisonment for first offenses, additional penalties thereafter.

Relevant Literature

Barker, R. 1993. *Saving All the Parts: Reconciling Economics and the Endangered Species Act.* Island Press. 268 pp.

Cobb, C. 1993. Living with the Endangered Species Act. *Forest Farmer* 52(3):22–23.

Czech, B., and P. R. Krausman. 1998. The species concept, species prioritization and the technical integrity of the Endangered Species Act. *Transactions of the North American Wildlife and Natural Resources Conference* 63:514–24.

Czech, B., and P. R. Krausman. 1998. Twelve faulty assumptions underlying the Endangered Species Act. *Endangered Species Update* 15(4):52–58.

Dodd, L. B. 1992. Endangered species protection through local land-use regulations. *Transactions of the North American Wildlife and Natural Resources Conference* 57:665–73.

Frank, A. G. 1997. Reforming the Endangered Species Act: Voluntary conservation agreements, government compensation and incentives for private action. *Columbia Journal of Environmental Law* 22:137–67.

Gidari, A. 1994. The Endangered Species Act: Impact of section 9 on private landowners. *Environmental Law* 24:419–500.

Harvey, H. R. 1996. Florida Game and Fresh Water Fish Commission v. Flotilla, Inc. *Natural Resource Journal* 36:87–101.

Hill, K. 1977. Florida's Wildlife Inspections Unit: A specialized solution to expanding law enforcement responsibilities. *Proceedings of the Annual Conference of the Southeastern Association of Fish and Wildlife Agencies* 31:664–68.

Phillips, M. 1998. The Wild Bird Conservation Act. *Endangered Species Bulletin* 23(4):32–33.

Tasso, J. P. 1997. Habitat conservation plans as recovery vehicles: Jump-starting the Endangered Species Act. *UCLA Journal of Environmental Law Policy* 16:297–318.

Walsingham, R. G. 1996. Private property rights versus the rights of domain. *Proceedings of the Annual Conference of the Southeastern Association of Fish and Wildlife Agencies* 50:665–73.

Wood, D. A. 1991. *Legal Accommodation of Florida's Endangered Species, Threatened Species and Species of Special Concern.* Florida Game and Fresh Water Fish Commission. 19 pp.

Yaffee, S. L. 1982. *Prohibitive Policy: Implementing the Federal Endangered Species Act.* Massachusetts Institute of Technology Press. 239 pp.

Index

Page numbers in italics refer to photos and tables.

Don A. Wood served as the Florida Fish and Wildlife Conservation Commission's Endangered Species Coordinator, Tallahassee, 1977–96, and as editorial coordinator for the Division of Wildlife within that agency, 1996–2000.